Police Supervisory Practice

Photograph courtesy of Berkeley, California, Police Department.

Police
Supervisory
Practice

William J. Osterloh

Professor, Administration of Justice
Ohlone College

JOHN WILEY & SONS, New York   London   Sydney   Toronto

Library of Congress Cataloging in Publication Data

Osterloh, William J.   1916–
  Police supervisory practice.

  Includes bibliographical references and index.
  1. Supervision of police personnel. I. Title.
HV7936.S8085   353.001'02   74-23482
ISBN 0-471-65712-3

Printed in the United States of America

10 9 8 7 6 5 4 3 2 1

To Moo

Preface

Almost one hundred years went by following the establishment of the first American police organization before it was realized that a police officer should be a *trained* police officer. Another quarter of a century elapsed before it became accepted that a police supervisor should be a *trained* police supervisor. This book is devoted to the subject of how to become a proficient supervisor in a police or sheriff's department.

There is an extensive literature on the many aspects of general personnel-administration. Most of it is not immediately applicable to the field of police endeavor. The job of the policeman is different. His working environment is not that of the office or factory; his clientele is not one of impersonal customers who make up the world of consumers; a policeman does not stop being a policeman with the blast of a plant whistle. The police officer is a special kind of individual—specially motivated and specially oriented. His pursuit calls for a special discipline, and it uses special communication. Thus, the police supervisor must be a special kind of supervisor.

This book has for its subject matter two police officers, a patrolman and his supervisor. Both are human beings, representing a complexity of virtues and faults and of strengths and weaknesses. Their relationship is that of two people who have come from a common mold of experience. Yet the two men are different in the roles they play. One is the leader, and one is the led. One is the decision-maker, and the other implements the decision.

If there is a predominant goal of this work, it is to attain complete relevancy. The usual abstract topics that comprise a course in personnel supervision—leadership, communication, morale, motivation, decision-making, and so on—all are included, but are here translated into a very real form. The 12 chapters, presenting an ordered sequence of subjects extending from the supervisor's exercise of leadership to his promotion of professionalism, describe relevant problems, delineate relevant situations, and suggest relevant approaches. This practical perspective is not intended to play down the formally expressed principles of employee supervision. The full-dimensional analysis of supervisory practice presented is designed to validate the standard theory which is usual in this kind of study.

To accompany this realistic approach is a deliberately invoked conversational and relaxed mood. If the environment of our considerations is to be the actual world of police enterprise, then the discourse should somewhat fit into the informal setting of squad room, patrol car, and foot beat. Thus each of the subjects is presented in a factual "this is what it is about," and "this is what might be done about it," style of coverage.

Each topic is pointedly introduced, completely developed, and concisely summarized. Each chapter includes summaries using a set of single sentences which recapitulate the principal points that have been made. They, in turn, are categorized under simple headings. These abbreviated thoughts serve the usual purpose of summation and review for the individual reader. They also may be used to provide specific subjects for group discussion by the class.

The author, who spent many years in the police service, asks the reader not to ascribe to any of his observations a dogmatic or singular point of reference. For example, a student supervisor who prides himself in being the champion of his men, may read into the chapter on the citizen's complaint a too dominant sympathy with the maker of complaints. The chapter on alcoholism and mental disturbance might be poorly received by a supervisor who sees undue emphasis on the potential emotional defects in an officer. Or another reader, knowing well the abuse an officer must take and danger he must face, may take exception to the suggestion that there may be an abrasiveness in a policeman's manner while zealously performing his duty. If provocation is still read into these or any other lines, mixed emotions will be experienced by the writer—regret that offense has been taken where no offense was intended, but satisfaction in knowing that thought has been prompted in a field where fresh thinking can only serve a positive purpose.

San Francisco, California   Willam J. Osterloh

Contents

x   Contents

SECTION I

CHAPTER 1

Relating to the Supervised

No self-respecting police sergeant, team leader or first-line supervisor can properly refer to himself as a boss and stay fashionable. Even though his acceptance by the men might lead his squad or team to label him affectionately "one helluva good boss," if a superior officer functions as a boss, he has much to learn about modern supervisory practice. The boss of yesterday's police force has been replaced by the leader of today's police organization.

More than just the terminology has changed. Effective and efficient supervision is exercised better by a leader than a boss, as police organizations, along with the nation's industries, are becoming increasingly aware. This shift applies greater emphasis on the positive methods of harnessing the energies and dedication of men, rather than relying on negative, coercive procedures.

The Concept of Leadership

Everyone wants a leader. The desire to have someone to follow is built into our animal nature. Bees panic when they lose their queen. The herd of cattle eagerly follows its bell-equipped representative. The need for a leader is built into organisms far lower on the zoological scale than humankind.

Perhaps more obvious than this instinctual reference, there is also a practical psychological basis to the notion of leadership. People generally cannot analyze the complexities that are involved in living. They cannot perceive in simple terms goals that are naturally complex. Abstract ideas cannot move the public to action unless they are endowed with a kind of selfhood. As social animals we are people-oriented rather than abstraction-oriented. For example, complex economic and social forces alone could not have moved a German people. It took an Adolf Hitler to lead them to a second World War. A Russian populace could not have supported the theories of Marxism without a Lenin to personify the abstract principles. People need a leader to dramatize ends which otherwise could have little meaning.

In a police organization, for the individual policeman, the superior officer is an embodiment of the principles on which the organization exists and operates. He is its discipline, its motivation, and its morale. He provides the security which the man wants. While the chief of police is the ultimate symbol that becomes identified with the organization as a whole—with its successes and failures—it is the sergeant or his equivalent who is in the immediate focus of the patrolman. In only the smallest department is the chief close enough to be a full reality for the policeman. But in agencies both large and small, the sergeant becomes the symbol that gives shape to the individual's identity. The dynamic first-line supervisor is the force that makes real what otherwise would remain unrealized in the police officer.

The Building Blocks of Leadership

To have it said that "this man is a leader," the supervisor must possess certain traits that make up the leadership tag. Primarily, he has to be endowed with a quantity of vigor and drive. He may have to take charge when a difficult task has to be accomplished. At times this may even extend to doing the work which is normally that of the patrolman. If someone has to do the job that nobody wants to do, for example, making a notification of death, the supervisor may be the one who should get it done.

Going with this should be the ability to generate enthusiasm in the men. The supervisor can display enough sense of willing involvement to dramatize the excitement that can be found in doing the work. He has to show the same satisfaction in responding to the emergency as a rookie. Enthusiasm is not something that is turned off forever after the first year or two in law enforcement.

There has to be a quantity of physical and emotional well-being that characterizes the supervisor-leader. He has to be able to wind and unwind with ease. He cannot give way to sleepless nights worrying about something that has happened or will happen on the job. He should be able to feel fresh at all times, in a way that the well-adjusted person always feels fresh. He has to be able to withstand the pressures that come from both a physical environment outside himself and a psychic realm within. He has to have the capacity to score that big win Plato described 24 centuries ago: Of all victories, the first and greatest is for a man to conquer himself!

However, one cannot get by with drive and enthusiasm alone—you have to know what you are doing. Decisions must be made based on a fund of working knowledge. While this does not mean the supervisor has to be all-knowing and all-wise, he should anticipate the questions and problems that are apt to come up during the duty tour. He should know where to acquire the knowledge that may not be at his fingertips. The usual selection method of civil service, the one that determines the worth for advancement on how much data an applicant holds in his fund of useful and useless information, may not be entirely valid. Yet a supervisor has to know as much as possible about the job if he is to instill confidence in his subordinates that will win him the leadership credential.

Coupled with knowledge should be a sense of objective. He should have a flexible and orderly mind, not a concrete one—all mixed up and firmly set. The ability to lead is largely synonymous with the ability to instill confidence. Confidence follows from recognizing that the supervisor-leader is able to analyze acutely and plan astutely.

High in the order of importance in leadership qualifications is the need to stay attuned to the wavelength of the followers. No matter how sure he is of the one right way, the leader who ignores the peer attitudes of the followers will not stay in control long. He cannot disregard a group perspective. If he disapproves of it, he may only try to bend and redirect, not completely change it. There is a sense of image and identity that goes with group feeling, and this should not be offended. Thus men should be gently swayed from their positions, rather than being jarred loose through all-out frontal assaults.

Finally, the leader has to be a really nice fellow. While it may be true in the world of contest that "nice guys don't win," this does not imply they must be brutal tyrants in driving their teams to victory. The day is gone when a coach took his men into the dressing room at half-time, and systematically unloosened the bleacher beams with language designed to make an old-time Army sergeant blush. The newer theory of friendliness in leadership is that it softens the subordinate for "the big kill"—it conditions him for shaping and fashioning by the leader. Nice guys do win. They win ball games; and they win other nice guys—and even bad guys—over to their side.

Qualifying for the Leadership Post

There are many ways of becoming physically fit. Most people who set out on a program of body improvement lose their enthusiasm shortly. But a police supervisor who wants to be a leader should undertake a program of psychic conditioning he will cling to persistently, no matter how difficult the process.

Vigor and drive can be cultivated as personality traits. There is the familiar experience of getting up feeling so badly the sufferer wonders how he will be able to get through the day. But when the regular routine gets under way, there is an awareness of an unexpected degree of performance. What can be learned from this experience of the unanticipated is that the mental blocks to vigor and drive can be eliminated. It is as possible to push oneself up from the psychic floor, as to do pushups from the gymnasium mat. The best exercise is to do what one most dislikes doing, and to do it at times one most dislikes doing it.

Similarly, enthusiasm that is generated through effort does not have to be artificial. The police job is naturally intriguing, and the intrigue should last. The administrator should find renewed fascination when he rides in a patrol car after long absence from the line. The enthusiasm does not come from repeating one hundred times, "I want to be enthusiastic." It comes from the deliberate effort at becoming involved and enjoying it. Enthusiasm is self-generating. There is satisfaction in leading. The supervisor can be swept up in this wave automatically while he provides energetic leadership for the team.

Much has been written on the do-it-yourself methods of developing emotional well-being. Knowing oneself leads to being able to fashion oneself. A commonplace inducement to attaining balance is a built-in sense of organization. One has to develop habits that are free of excesses as end products. For example, the supervisor who works midnight watches must develop sleeping patterns that are not forced. Thus, a separate morning and evening shift of slumber may be better than a single one that is less restful. Self-programming is conducive to living a more satisfying life; and a satisfying life does not drain off the energy needed for conversion into leadership.

Little need be said on the way to develop a fund of expert knowledge. What is important is for the supervisor to devote his learning time to worthwhile matters. He should keep up with what is going on in his territory. For example, if there is a college campus in his section, he should learn the statutes governing the administrators' legal powers, and how they are invoked. Or his educational needs may extend merely to getting to know a few of the potential troublemakers in his sector. It is more worthwhile to plan what has to be learned than merely to attempt learning everything haphazardly and without purpose. While not endeavoring to become a walking encyclopedia for his patrolmen's reference use, the supervisor should have a modest fund of working knowledge the men may regularly tap.

A sense of objective can be developed. Stopping, looking, and listening are prerequisites for determining a planned direction in any given instance. Using the built-in drawing board for mentally designed approaches is an exercise directed to sharpening the sense of objective. All undertakings should follow from a clearly defined "why?" Then the "how?" may follow with surprising ease. Deliberately making plans, deliberately making decisions, are the best ways for cultivating a sense of objective that will serve as a Pied Piper pipe for attracting his patrolman followers.

It is easy enough to stay abreast of what the men are thinking. It is not difficult to find what they really want. When adequate channels of communication, both to and from the men, are set up, the flow of signals is continuous and definite. It may sometimes be difficult to accept their perspective. But honest communication is the mortar that binds the bulwark of a team together and this will be discussed in detail later in the chapter.

The supervisor can also work at simply being a nice fellow. The police supervisor who boasts that the only time he sees his neighbors is when he takes them to court does not have to be that way. He can gracefully put himself out to be accepted. In doing so it is not necessary to run around announcing that his office door is always open, that he wants to help. He does not have to spread far and wide a folklore of love for his fellow man. What he can do is smile, respect the subordinate's feelings, listen, and try to make the other person feel his worth by saying the right things to him. Both the policeman and his supervisor can attain a reputation for being a good fellow that stands the test of action.

How the Leader Is Seen by the Led

Having developed the traits of leadership, the supervisor puts them into action. The job of being a leader in today's police agency is not routine and automatic. There are new forces directed from within and projected from without that have added complexity to the task. For example, from outside there is the anarchistic militancy that has been beating senselessly against the morale and emotional stamina of the men. From the inside there is a corresponding defensive stance which sometimes has taken on an unyielding resistance to needed compromise and change.

The supervisor is more than just in the middle of the directed forces—he is in the middle of the middle. He has to perceive clearly that the policeman is threatened not only from the outside. He has to understand that tradition within a police department is not necessarily right, and that new perspectives do not have to be rejected. He has to recognize that peer group attitudes, in the face of unjustified attack from without, can become stereotyped, and even masochistic and paranoid if left unchallenged. So he has the duty of trying to moderate attitudes as his more seasoned perspective dictates.

This communication of attitude cannot be accomplished wholly through words. When the police supervisor is accepted as a leader, his role itself will soften the pressures on his men. Better communication is often one of demeanor rather than words. Accordingly, the supervisor has to realize that to lead is to influence. While talk will be needed in getting the job done, he has to know that talk will fall flat if it represents a mere voice, set apart from the man wearing stripes who is doing the talking. For a supervisor to lead his team he must communicate—but the communication is the supervisor, and the supervisor is the communication, much like McLuhan's "the medium is the message." An important lesson the team leader must learn is that when speech stands by itself it may be a somewhat worthless tool of his craftsmanship.

What a policeman must perceive in his supervisor's person is guts. He must realize that the supervisor will say his patrolman is right when circumstances make him right. But the patrolman must be aware that the supervisor will hold him wrong when the wrong is inexcusable. The need of popularity will not dictate his choice, nor the fear of factions.

The men have to see in their leader one who can carry them through the ticklish moments of the job. They have to feel the comfort of being in the hands of one who can make up his mind what to do, knows what he is doing, and then sees clearly what he has done. There cannot be the unsure, nervous, and double standard response to decision-making. The policeman has to perceive a knowledgeable, reasonable, and confident team leader whose action is going to be correct when the man's well-being demands a correct decision.

The qualities of courage and knowhow possessed by the good supervisor must be supplemented by the personal touch that will move people over to his side. He must be seen as a friendly fellow, a fair supervisor, and one who is genuinely interested in the man who is his subordinate. He must be looked on as one with whom a man can talk—more than that—even bare his soul, should there be a need of emotional catharsis. The supervisor has to be recognized as confidant and counselor. He has to be seen as a good friend to whom one can turn when trouble becomes overwhelming.

When the image of a leader has been affixed in the minds of the men, then communication can begin. The words should be frank, pointed, and devoid of double-talk. They should leave nothing to the imagination as to their significance. They should not be designed defensively, or put together to shield or apologize. Above all, they should be positive. They should not tear down, but construct. Attack should be minimal, and approbation predominant. The listeners must be made aware that the speaker speaks for one purpose—to convey a thought accurately, adequately, and objectively—for this is the language of leadership.

In a police organization, it will be the man in the ranks who fixes either the label of leader or the label of boss to the man on the level above. It is the man who is led who will make or break the man who leads. The leader will have to work at leading—hard, relentlessly, yet sensitively. If he finds leading easy, then perhaps he really isn't leading at all. Perhaps this should be his cue that he is violating the first rule of supervisory practice: that the first-line supervisor should be a leader instead of a boss.

How to Talk with a Policeman

Speech takes its place with many other forms of communication—writing, doing, acting. Speaking is the most common. It also is the easiest. The tongue never has to be hunted for like that elusive ballpoint. It requires neither ink nor thought to do its communicating. The baby's babble is true speech, pure expression that may convey no specific meaning. The philosopher's learned discourse is also true speech, a form that transmits much meaning. However, while babies do not engage in philosophical discussion, adults—and perhaps even philosophers—sometimes engage in talk that approximates baby's babble. Man is a babbling animal, and his ability to talk may not be designed just to fulfill some specific vital need. Expression gives him selfhood, it bestows identity, it makes him a person.

In the realm of police supervision, speech is the usual medium for bridging the gap between team leader and patrolman. Yet it is not the word alone that carries the full impact of meaning. The way the word is uttered—with kindness, with sincerity, with sarcasm—will contribute to determining meaning for the receiver. Accordingly, to make sure that what is communicated is that which is intended to be communicated, the person who talks should remain aware of the dynamics that go into speech, over and above the mere sounds that make up the words he uses.

The Occasions of Talk to the Men

Then there was the little fellow who did not talk during his first five years, and one morning blurted out, "The mush is lousy!" When his amazed parents asked why he had never said anything before, he explained simply, "Everything has been alright up to now."

His simple perspective concerning the limited value of speech may be that of many of his elders, as well. Asked what his on-the-job talk to his men should be, a police supervisor may give the stock answer that it should involve giving orders, describing assignments, and correcting error. In practice too he may limit most of his official speech to the cold items of getting the job done. However, he is missing a dimension of his role if he fails to recognize that much of two-way small talk serves a very practical purpose of filling some important voids in the working environment.

First of all, much of the work talk will simply establish the necessary rapport between supervisor and the supervised. It is a way of getting to know the other fellow, and to guide the one in relating to the other. In addition, attitudes and ideas will be exchanged. There will be a mutual talking through of problems. The people and things on the police scene will be discussed. Even the smallest of small talk will contribute to permitting a more valid self to be presented to the beholder, making it possible for one person to better accept the other.

Then everyone needs a little recognition for what he does. While not necessarily going through one's supervisorial life conferring a never ending chorus of "nice work, Joe" on his subordinates, a word of comment on an arrest made or situation handled, at least indicating simple awareness that it happened, serves this purpose. Making it possible for the man to imply from your attention that he is of value to the organization is the best motivation to further accomplishment. It will ward off that sterile feeling that all his effort is going into an impersonal and anonymous fund of labor. Now what has been achieved remains the product of the craftsman for him to behold in pride.

Also, talk can provide the feeling of security craved by the men. An air of secrecy often pervades a police organization. When two supervisors customarily huddle behind closed doors, and neglect spending at least equal time conferring with their men, they are contributing to this atmosphere of mystery. Rumors spring up. Doubts and distortions come to the surface.

In contrast, free and open discussion removes the dark atmosphere that breeds hidden uncertainties and fears. The light of day gets rid of pessimism that sometimes pervades personnel attitudes. It is not so much what is being communicated up and down the ladder, but communication itself, that causes the air to stay clear of mistrust that breeds when there is no communication.

Then too, talk provides something else: the cooperation so badly needed for good police performance. As commonly used, the word "cooperation" has a flat significance. Of course there is cooperation in a police department, the zealous practitioner will insist. But in contradiction it might be suggested that one of the biggest weaknesses in police performance is the nearly total individual enterprise in the ranks. Every man may be on his own. The information he gathers is looked on as his sacred property. Men of the same team may be working on the same case with tug-of-war conflicting effort.

If a police supervisor promotes talk among his men, it is inevitable that cooperative effort will become an end product of communication. The private property his discussion uncovers will be spread out for common use. If someone has been concealing a lead, it can be made accessible to all having need. The sergeant can spread word on a man's unique key to handling situations, so that all may adopt the profitable technique. But the supervisor may not have to continue acting as an information clearinghouse. Having stimulated the two-way communication, it can be expected that there will be an automatic and free exchange of information. This is necessary for giving full dimensional meaning to that vital notion of cooperation in the police service.

Ground Rules for Good Talk

An old-time police boss stepped to the rear of a classroom where a new young instructor was conducting an academy class. He had presented a case for consideration, and the participants were arguing back and forth in arriving at a conclusion. Dismayed at the liberalism of presentation, the veteran called the creative teacher aside, and told him to change his technique. "You don't ask them—you tell them!" he said.

This old perspective may be the reason for a supervisor's ineffective communication with his men. The patrolman is an object at whom talk is directed. He is not a party of equal status in the exchange. In short, the superior is violating the most prominent rule of good conversation. He is talking to, rather than with, his subordinate. Thus the communication lacks the quality that makes it one's own, and fails to move the recipient in the way that is intended.

Talking should also be looked on as a learning process by the one who initiates it. Instead of just being used to express or reinforce one's own dogmas, conversation provides one with the opportunity to seek out correction or revision of ideas. Those beautiful but rare words, "You know, I think you're right after all," should be more common in everyday discourse. But if there is no controversy in the topic discussed, all the better for inspiring one to interest. If one can tap the well of another's interest for himself, he may add to his own enjoyment of life. Many an avocation begins in being stimulated by someone else's appreciation for a particular field.

Talk does not have to be argument. At least at its jumping off point, it is better to have tentative mutual acceptance of some aspect of the matter discussed, if this is at all possible. When a divergence of thought does occur, a head-on challenge can start a painful confrontation. The other will bristle in the face of contradiction. Voices raise; tonal acidity is heightened; tempers may begin to sizzle. Perhaps personal attack in the form of a veiled or overt insult is launched. At this point, further discussion has no value.

Even the neutral listener, moved by earlier logic, can be turned off by the later demeanor of the logician. It really pays to be the "nice guy" species of conversationalist. Being confronted with something one cannot accept is not a signal to wage a counterattack. Contradiction can be as graceful as agreement. A "Now that may be true; however . . ." is the perfect method of easing one's contradictory hypothesis into the conversation. If a stone wall is then thrown up, the subject may be gracefully changed if it is not necessary that it be pursued further.

Talking without first putting the mind into gear is a common error. Saying it without thinking—to wife, superior, subordinate—may exact a price of sleepless-ness, regret, and possibly, lasting insecurity. One would like to have the opportunity of a second chance. Consequently, the supervisor should follow the elementary and simple rule of thinking before he speaks.

The Static from Within

The tone of voice can distort communication drastically. Some vocal tones have all the moving qualities of the ringside gong that brings the boys from their corners. A voice can be as provocative as an alarm bell. It may be characterized by an irritating ring that immediately evokes annoyance, if not outright hostility. Feelings of insecurity and inferiority may be at the bottom of this deficiency.

Perhaps the regular use of caustic humor can blot out otherwise effective com-munication. Humor in itself is good. But humor can be a mask to cover real attack. Humor embedded in barbs can be a disguise for true feelings. However, that mask will not be impenetrable to the victim of sensed innuendo. Of course, there is the sensitive one who is not at ease when made the object of a joke, no matter how innocent it is. When this attitude is discovered, the communicating comedian should forever and permanently remove the sufferer from his list of potential straight men.

Then, too, there is the person who just talks too much. While listening efficiency tapers off with time, the nonstop talker may not realize that after a while he is talking to a deaf ear. A good point once developed can be undone by going into superfluous comment. In talking, as nowhere else, one should quit while he's ahead.

The best way to learn whether one is getting through is to see how the listener is responding. If his mouth is open with no sound forthcoming, it could either mean he is yawning or trying to get a word in himself. In either case, it means he has had it, "amen" should be uttered, and the pulpit abandoned. Unless he is insincere, the listener's repeated pleasant nod, probably reinforced with a smile, can mean that he is appreciative of, or at least agreeing with, what you have to say. A scowl without any indication of approval can be a sign of warning. He could be getting annoyed. Asking his views on the subject, calling it quits, or at least changing the subject, may be strategically sound.

The police supervisor should be aware of his own personality quirks which may distort the message he is trying to convey. If he realizes his subjective shortcomings, he should not rationalize them away, but try hard to overcome them. He always must be aware that feelings of inadequacy or hostility in particular will contaminate meaning. Perhaps it will be simple misunderstanding that is responsible for short-circuiting the message process. But misunderstanding is not something that always is independent of the person who is misunderstood. In almost every case, the communicator has laid the groundwork for misapprehension through a failure to make earlier self-appraisal.

Talking Down the Line

If upward communication in a police organization is a rare occurrence, it will be nonexistent without effective downward flow. The men want to know what is doing above. They want to know what the men at the top are thinking. They want to know what to expect in the way of new policy and procedure. They want reassurance that those so far removed from the battlegrounds of the streets know what is going on at the war front.

It is up to their first-line supervisor, the contact with the hierarchy, to carry the thoughts to them from above. Here he may encounter difficulty, however. It may be that a genuine fear of starting communication is more common in a police department than expected. There may be a traditional lack of confidence directed toward the top by the ranks. Concurrently, there may be feelings of administrative insecurity that make officialdom reluctant to do much talking.

If these management barriers to downward communication are evident, the supervisor has to work around them. He will have to get his own superiors engaged in more communication. His practical readiness to bring word up the ladder in turn may prompt a downward flow. His fellow supervisors should be brought into a group action of prodding officialdom into making more word available for the lower ranks.

When a police team leader does carry word to his men, he should not distort it just to get his own private thinking across, attributing his own thoughts to the hierarchy. He should not take the opportunity of grinding his own axes in the form of apparent downward communication. As an example, if he thinks the men are coming to work in street attire that does not suit his taste, he should communicate his feelings on this as being his own, instead of attributing it to the voice above in the finest tradition of passing the buck.

A common grievance of police personnel is that "there just doesn't seem to be any communication in our department." There is always some communication, even when it is being overtly avoided. Rumors, innuendos and confidential chats are also communication, though of a very unhealthy sort. It would be more valid to say that "there is poor communication in our department." If this allegation ever is voiced within hearing of the supervisor, it is his warning signal to get to work. It means motivation and morale may be tottering on the brink because of administrative silence. It means the men are craving talk. It means he must begin talking, and continue to talk. Silence may be golden, as the saying goes; but talk also can be.

Listening in Full Stereo

A police supervisor may be a poor listener because his idea of listening is that it is purely passive and effortless activity. He probably would define it as the state of not talking. He does not see it an an art. He thinks of listening as a mere gathering in of vocal sounds, while he ignores the variety of mechanisms that validate the listening process.

There may have been a more despotic day when listening was not considered an important task of a police supervisor. Quite acceptable in police discourse was the sterile "I'll do the talkin' and you do the listenin'" edict. To question, to contradict, even to suggest, particularly when exercised by the younger patrolman, actually may have been looked upon as a form of impertinence. Subordinates all too often were relegated to the ranks of little children who were to be seen but not heard.

Now communication is looked on as necessary regardless of the occupational or social level of either party. Even the most recent recruit has a voice to which a police superior must listen. Once thought of as a more singularly directed process, today communication is conceived of as flowing to and fro, side to side, upward and downward. To listen well is considered as important as speaking well. The roles of speaker and listener must be freely interchangeable if communication is to be worthwhile.

Of course, one may not as yet be able to talk back to his television set. But, alas, the day may not be far away when there will be a sort of reverse television available. Then you will be able to take your set to a football game and watch what is happening in your neighborhood bar! But the time is already here when the police supervisor has a duty to listen, as well as talk, to his patrolman—comprehensively, effectively and dynamically.

Using Fine Tune and Volume Controls

The setting is a sergeant's patrol car. At the superior's side is the dedicated reserve officer enthusiastically pouring out the exploits of his avocation. Now he is busily reciting the details of his most recent day at the range. He pointedly narrates the events of target practice all the way from slow through rapid fire. He culminates the tale with a proud boast of his sharpshooter's score. It is clear this triumph marked a major occasion of the volunteer's life.

The sergeant certainly is not being projected to the same heights of ecstatic satisfaction as the narrator. In the first place, he is completely uninterested in marksmanship. In the second, he cannot see why anyone wants to "play cop" when there are so many other things to do in life.

Now there is that other reserve officer who works as a stockbroker. Interested in the world of finance, the sergeant finds this man's company a lot more fascinating and profitable during a similar duty tour.

In the case of the sharpshooting volunteer the ordeal of listening is transformed into one of passive daydreaming. This is a grand opportunity for the supervisor to plan his camping trip in its fine details. Or he might muse over his own personal triumph as the life of that party last night. While he dreams, there will be the background humming of the bees in the form of his exhilarated rider's shot-by-shot account of the smashing victory of marksmanship.

In ignoring the man, the superior is not just making a choice he has a right to make. He is on duty, and there is an obligation that goes with his supervisorial function. He not only should tune in on his volunteer partner, but he should turn up the volume as well. As long as his department has a reserve unit, it is his obligation to keep the volunteer's interest elevated, to keep his morale propped up, to make him feel he is appreciated. The sergeant must try to experience interest in the conversation, and to show interest through gesture and word. Listening may be laborious, but the supervisor is being paid to perform the laborious. He will have to be deliberate in putting aside distraction, because he is obligated to gratify the unpaid worker and to feed the enthusiasm that will contribute to the volunteer's job performance. In the throes of purposeful distraction, the turned off listener may miss something very worthwhile through his distraction.

The Gratification in Being Heard

An age-old dispute centers around whether there can be sound if there is no ear to hear sound. The same question might be converted into another brain teaser which asks whether self-identity can be realized if there is no other person to perceive one's existence. The nature of talk may shed light on the query. As stressed earlier, all speech does not necessarily serve a utilitarian purpose. Thus language in a sense can be looked on as rounding out the need to establish selfhood, to give identity.

Therefore, when the enthusiastic reserve officer tells of his accomplishments at the firing range; when the young patrolman talks about the antics of his toddler; when the older policeman recites his crimebusting deeds of a distant past—there may be more of a compelling need to express, than just a desire to tell what happened. In fact, there may be pain in holding back something that can be given substance through becoming known. Loneliness can be very real, and its degree is not just a factor of the scarcity of people in the sufferer's company. Listening by the other lessens the acute pain one otherwise may feel.

Consequently, the introductory query, "Did I tell you about my grandchildren?"

in the spirit of true charity should not be met with a, "No, you didn't, and I appreciate it very, very much." In private life, it is simple courtesy that dictates an obligation to hear another out, within reason, of course. On the job, listening to a subordinate represents an integral duty of supervision, one which contributes to job satisfaction, motivation and morale.

Obviously, the need to communicate extends far beyond the realm of small talk. Anxieties, fears, pain—all find relief in being expressed. A patrolman may have a compulsion to convey job dissatisfactions, personal grievances, and creative ideas. If a superior will not listen, the subordinate will have to look for channels of communication outside the lines of formal organization. Then the man who seeks an ear invariably will turn to where an ear can be found. The labor movement experienced growth through its traditional willingness to hear out the worker. Similarly, the police officers' association fills the role of listener for sworn personnel. If a patrolman does not have a superior to stand at the receiving end of communication, he knows the employee organization will serve the purpose. It is not to the best interest either of individual or organization for the supervisor to avoid his role of listener.

Building a Picture from Sound Waves

Physical and psychological chasms separate the police supervisor from the man he supervises. Neither can enter the thought processes of the other. Each knows the other only in terms of the disjointed words and actions and demeanor that reach him in the form of transmitted symbols and signals. Each party is encased in a kind of armored suit, creating an impenetrable barrier to the other's scrutiny.

If he is to know his patrolman, the supervisor will have to capture and make use of every manifestation of personality projected his way. When he hears the man speak, it may not be the content of words alone that will be most revealing of the speaker. Voice modulation, movement, rhythm, and resonance all will tell something vital about the person.

Take the example of a patrolman whose voice is habitually belligerent and dictatorial. It may be suspected that the seemingly brazen one might be compensating for a deep-seated weakness. Rather than forcefulness, in a given case it may be frustration, insecurity and defensiveness that comprise the man's makeup.

Too much up and down exaggerated movement along the sound scales may unveil in the policeman a sarcastic nature designed to irritate people. Speaking in persistently high volume may be indicative of excitement that stems from insecurity. If the rate of speech is subject to rapid and unpredictable changes in the course of a brief verbal span, the erratic quality of the speaker's thought patterns may be reflected.

Of course, the standard, but important, warning against the police supervisor donning the psychoanalyst's smock must be voiced. It is not intended that the sergeant should translate the pitches and tones and volumes of a patrolman's voice into a psychiatric diagnosis. But he may be able to acquire some kind of tentative picture from speech habits which will become quite significant when coupled with the observed actions of the man in question. There can be supervisory value even in inexpert speculation on what makes a man tick. The amount of supervisorial confidence of which a patrolman is worthy, the determination of his aptitude and judgment, the prediction of impending disciplinary breach—all can be based on what is observed while listening to the subordinate in the squad room, business office, or patrol car.

The Filtering Factors in Listening

There are days when we listen better. There are people to whom we listen better. There are subjects of discussion which move us to listen better. In other words, listening is not a uniformly passive process. Sounds and tones and meanings are filtered out and acted upon by a variety of conditions. These may be either within or without the listener.

The very real physiological clock within one dictates that energy will be at a low ebb halfway through the midnight watch. Consequently, the policeman with a compulsion to talk at four in the morning may not expect to get the sparkling attention directed to his inspiring words at high noon. If it is a hot, muggy afternoon, the drone of the talkative patrolman will resemble the humming insects cavorting amid the foliage. Or if the supervisor is suffering from a headache, the chatter to which he is exposed hardly can be expected to serve as an aspirin.

Sometimes environment poses a filtration medium for both speaker and listener. Interviewing a patrolman in his more familiar patrol car can elicit unimpeded discourse not likely in the less familiar station office. However, if the car is parked in a way that the sun streams down against the policeman's face, the trauma of an old-fashioned third degree will dull the patrolman's attention. The physical setting of communication is a vital factor in generating its effectiveness. "Specify anything and you will have it," said grateful king to philosopher. "Please stand out of my light," answered the sage.

All the static in communication does not come from without. The mental set of the listener also is a primary source of interference. In receiving his patrolman's structured thoughts, a supervisor's own prejudice on the subject may put them in a different light. For instance, he may perceive a patrolman's proposal for policy change as threatening. His this-is-the-way-it-always-has-been-done perspective may block out any appreciation for novelty. Or due to his own cynical feelings that everybody is on the make, he unjustifiably may read selfish motivation into the communicator's mind when the proposal really is inspired by purely idealistic impulses.

Foremost in distorting what is conveyed is a misunderstanding of the words that are used. Or it may be tone of voice alone which stirs up emotions in the listener to block reception. The element of strong feelings in the speaker's voice will elicit similar counterstrains in the listener. Thus what might have been an unimpassioned conversation will be transformed into open conflict. Remember, it does take two to start an argument.

Listening from the Mountain Tops

A singular deficiency in the area of police administrative practice is the glaring want of upward communication. The policeman on the line is very much a reservoir of street knowledge. His associates and superiors alike respect his right to the information that has been acquired about people and conditions on his beat. However, this tendency does not provide for full dissemination of what he knows. Neither the data so valuable to coordinated effort, nor lower echelon attitudes indicative of how well management is functioning, pass up the ladder for the constructive guidance of the hierarchy.

Police administration traditionally has been deficient both in ferreting out information from the ranks, and encouraging its upward flow. Often it has been a simple matter of management not wanting to know that all was not well below. The men envision barriers to communication, and these cause group emotions to become dammed up. As a result, there is a kind of neurotic response to the function of management and supervision. Rumors flourish; discontents smolder.

If there is pathology in the ranks, the signs of the sickness must be made aware to those on higher levels. If hostilities, greed, and distrust are rampant, their presence must become known at the top—quickly. Prompt awareness of this kind of weakness on the operational front is necessary for designing the blueprints of correction. The primary duty of isolating the troubles, defining the difficulties, and getting knowledge of them to command lies with the line supervisor.

Much of what is learned about the field may be directed at the supervisor himself, for his own benefit and use. It is unreasonable for him to consider himself all-wise and self-sufficient in working knowledge. True, by virtue of his higher rank, he should know more about exercising supervision than the patrolmen who are supervised. But he still must depend on his men for acquiring knowledge of the environment in which supervision is to be accomplished. He has to seek out, coordinate, and transmit the data necessary for policing his area. He has to determine where supervision must be applied or intensified. The closeness of the men to the working scene will make it possible for them to pinpoint what is needed for getting the job done properly.

The man above has as much to learn from the man below as the superior has to teach the subordinate. It is much like what the physician said to his patient: "Let me know if these pills work. I have the same thing myself."

There is one circumstance that a supervisor must guard against. If the policeman finds that his past communication has been profitless, channels may become suddenly and permanently closed. If the subordinate repeatedly refers data to his supervisor, and it is unused; if deficiency is pointed to time and again, but is uncorrected; if proposals for policy are suggested over and over, but are discarded without implementation—the end result unquestionably will be a "what's the use" attitude of futility. The blatant supervisorial assurance that his door is always open will mean little if the back door is always found to be open too, allowing what comes in to flow out untapped. If the supervisor wants communication, if he wants to be the catalyst to its upward movement, he has to work at putting what has been communicated to use once it is acquired.

The Fine Art of Listening

If effort is to be put into listening, then intelligent effort should add up to better listening. First to be considered is seeding the flow of conversation. There is one way to get anybody to talk: Find out what he likes to talk about.

There is personal value in listening to someone tell us about something that fascinates him. While we hitherto may have had no interest in golf or rock collecting or gardening, our lack of concern may simply have been a matter of knowing nothing about these fields. One hardly can find interest in what one does not know. Listening to a person who is absorbed in a subject can allow some of his fascination to rub off. Now there is a feeling that we have been missing out on something all the while. So there may be personal profit in directing a simple, "How's your game been lately?" to the patrolman whom the supervisor wants to engage in conversation.

After the chatter has begun, one should not complacently sit back and expect the outpouring to continue automatically. The face should carry a look that denotes interest. This must amount to more than a blank stare. The simple movement of eyelids can convey concern with the subject under consideration. The facial muscles alone can convey shock, glee, surprise; and the sensed empathy will prime the pump of more discourse. But response, whether tonal or expressive in other ways, should not be carried to the point of artificiality. Not advocated is the forced "be sincere—even if you don't mean it" attitude in listening.

There is a place in listening for voicing approval, disapproval, opinion, suggestion, or just reacting in a neutral sort of way. If comment must be made on something unaccepted, without wanting to reject it at the time, a simple "oh?" with rising inflection of voice, represents a perfect noncommittal response which still satisfies the need of indicating interest. Without either condoning or rejecting a thought advanced, "oh?" with tonal upswing, means nothing more than "oh?" The main function of the brilliant monosyllabic comment is to give assurance the listener is still awake, and at the same time to serve as an adequate catalyst for keeping the conversation going.

It must always be kept in mind that the one who is speaking, if he is at all sensitive, will be particularly aware of the responsive manifestations in his listener. He may rightly or wrongly interpret boredom from a yawn, shifting about, or obvious uneasiness. If the listener stares into space, preoccupation may be sensed. Impatience may be recognized in a glance at a watch. Distraction may be validly conjectured when a question is asked to which an answer already has been given. The sensitive one may be easily though painfully turned off when he becomes aware the target of his outpourings is not keeping up with him.

Something must be put into listening to reap the rewards of what listening has to offer. To become proficient in listening, one must work at listening. If one is satisfied to engage in sloppy, distracted listening off the job, he will exercise inefficient, superficial listening on the job. The key to listening properly is a self-discipline that only can come through the repeated and structured expenditure of effort. Good listening is a good habit, and good habits must be derived from practice.

Finally, a police supervisor should not disregard the natural barrier which stands between team leader and patrolman. There is a sense of separation inherent in rank which may limit the flow of information. Concern with the peer group—perhaps just in the form of not wanting to be branded a teacher's pet, or, at worst, a stool pigeon—may be a restraining factor for the policeman. Breaking through the wall will call for all the more work on the part of the supervisor who wants to listen. In short, he has to instill confidence in the man he wants to talk if he is going to get him to talk at all.

However, more important to remember is that the uniform chevrons which may serve as a barrier to communication also may act as a symbol of refuge for the troubled patrolman. There is escape in sensing the presence of an empathic superior to whom he can turn, and in whom he can find relief from his on-the-job anxiety. Perhaps the sergeant is too close to the trees to see the forest of human concern in the ranks. He must always be aware that professional supervision implies human supervision—the men have the same compelling need for a receptive super-visorial ear as they have for the guiding supervisorial voice.

SUMMARY

A leader in Place of the Boss. • Contemporary norms have substituted the leader for the boss. • The supervision of the leader is superior to that of the boss. • The policeman of today is to be led—not driven.

The Identity of Leadership. • Real for the follower is the one who is close to him.

The Need of a Leader. • As social animals we are people oriented rather than abstraction oriented. • A leader offers a kind of force that rounds out a person's ego. • The leader gives identity to an idea by becoming the idea itself. • The supervisor is the embodiment of principles which make the agency function. • In both the large and small agency, the supervisor's nearness makes him the real leader. • The supervisor gives dimension to the working identity of the patrolman.

The Qualities of Leadership. • The supervisor must have a certain amount of vigor and drive. • The supervisor must be able to build up enthusiasm in the men. • There must be a quantity of physical and emotional well-being in the team leader. • A sergeant must be able to withstand pressures from within and without. • The first-line supervisor has need of an orderly and flexible mind. • The ability to lead is characterized by the ability to instill confidence. • The supervisor must be tuned-in on the perspectives of the men. • The leader has to be a really nice fellow.

Developing a Leader's Traits. • The value of friendliness is that it conditions men to be fashioned by another. • The man who wants to lead must undertake psychic conditioning. • The best form of leadership conditioner is to do things one dislikes doing. • Contagious enthusiasm comes from the deliberate effort to be involved. • The police leader must have a built-in sense of organization. • Keeping up with the organization gives the supervisor hints of what to learn. • The team leader must develop a sense of objective.

Thinking with the Men. • The way to develop a sense of objective is to plan and decide deliberately. • It is easy for the supervisor to stay abreast of what the men are thinking. • Authoritarianism must be avoided in tampering with the men's perspective. • The way to change attitudes is by conscious effort with conscious restraint.

Being Seen by the Men. • The first-line supervisor should work at being a nice fellow. • To smile, not to hurt, to listen, and make one feel good are the leader's tools. • The supervisor must be aware of the new forces that shape personnel attitudes. • Peer group attitudes can become stereotyped and paranoical from attack. • The better communication is that of demeanor instead of words. • Speech standing by itself is an inadequate leadership tool. • The supervisor must be seen as a man of courage. • The man who is led has to see the leader as able to carry him through trouble. • The policeman must see his leader as knowledgeable, reasonable, and confident. • The supervisor must be seen as friendly, fair and interested in the men.

The Voice of Leadership. • The supervisor must be seen as one to whom the man can talk, even bare his soul. • A supervisor's words should be pointed, frank, and devoid of doubletalk. • The police supervisor's discourse should not tear down, but construct. • The team leader's words should be positive in tone. • The language of leadership conveys the thought accurately and objectively. • The men fix the label of boss or leader on the man above them. • The supervisor will have to work hard, relentlessly, and sensitively at leading. • If one finds leading easy, then perhaps one is not really leading.

The Nature of Speech. • Man's talk is not just designed to fill a vital need. • Speech is the usual form of supervisory communication. • The way in which speech is uttered determines meaning for the receiver.

Reasons for Work Talk. • Two-way small talk can fill voids in the working environment. • Talk provides a way of knowing the man and establishing rapport. • Attitudes, ideas, people, and things should be discussed. • Mutual talking through of problems may be facilitated. • Casual conversation conveys a picture of each person to the other. • Comment on a bit of work performed implies it has not gone unnoticed. • Work that is recognized becomes the personal product of the craftsman. • The men will be suspicious if the supervisors huddle too much. • An air of secrecy is relieved by the supervisor's communication. • Talk promoted by the supervisor will stimulate cooperative enterprise. • Automatic exchange of information gives meaning to cooperation.

Rules for Talking. • The parties to conversation should be equal participants in it. • Conversation should be seen as a learning process. • At the start of conversation there should be a commonly accepted point. • Talk becomes valueless when tempers rise. • Contradiction can be as graceful as agreement. • When agreement becomes impossible, the subject might be changed.

Pitfalls of communication. • A supervisor should put his mind in gear before he talks. • The tone of voice itself can be a barrier to communication. • Humor can serve as a mask for assault. • One who is sensitive should not be made the object of a joke. • The monopolizing talker soon addresses a deaf ear. • Pleasure, displeasure, annoyance, or boredom will be reflected by the listener. • The supervisor should be aware of his person-ality quirks that interfere with communication.

Downward Communication. • There will be no upward communication where there is no downward. • The supervisor is the communication tie-line from officialdom down-wards. • There may be a fear of communication in a police organization. • A team leader's habit of bringing word upwards may facilitate downward flow. • The supervisors collectively may prompt management to communicate. • One's own message should not be passed on as communication from management. • When a man alleges "no com-munication," a supervisor should take notice. • Silence may be golden, but talk also can be.

The Place of Listening. • Listening is not a passive and effortless activity. • There are a variety of mechanisms that validate listening. • The old rule of supervision was that the subordinate did the listening. • Now it is considered as important to listen well as to speak well.

The Work of Listening. • There is a supervisorial duty to listen to the subordinate efficiently. • Daydreaming should be avoided while one is supposed to be listen-ing. • There is a supervisorial duty to show interest in the speaker's words. • Distracted musing while another speaks is a bad habit to cultivate.

The Satisfaction in Talk. • The use of language gives one self-identity. • There may be more of a need to express than a mere desire to tell something. • Listening contributes to job satisfaction, motivation, and morale. • Anxieties, fears, and pain find relief in being expressed. • To find a listener, a patrolman may have to go outside the formal organi-zation. • The labor movement has grown through a willingness to listen to the worker. • With no supervisor to listen, the employee organization will afford an ear.

Beyond Hearing Words. • To know a patrolman, every manifestation of his personality must be captured. • Voice modulation, movement, rhythm, and resonance reveal the person. • In conversation, words standing alone are not meaningful. • A tentative image from speech habits takes form through observed actions.

Conditions of Listening. • One listens better at certain times and to certain people and subjects. • Many conditions filter sounds, tones, and meanings. • The physical setting of communication is vital to its effectiveness. • Much static in communication comes from within the listener. • Misunderstanding the words is foremost in distorting com-munication. • Strong feelings in the speaker will elicit counterstrains in the listener.

Upward Communication. • A weakness in police administration is the lack of upward communication. • Often management does not want to hear from the levels below. • A neurotic response to management and supervision may arise from the want of chan-nels. • Signs of discontent in the ranks must be quickly carried upward. • Knowledge of operational weakness is needed for its rapid correction.

Learning from the Men. • The supervisor should not see himself as all-wise in working knowledge. • A sergeant must seek out, coordinate, and transmit work data from his men. • The team leader must learn where supervision needs intensification.

Encouraging Communication. • If past communication has been profitless, the men will withhold it. • A police supervisor must work at putting what is communicated to use. • Intelligent effort should contribute to better listening. • One's interest in a subject can rub off on the listener. • Facial expression and voice should give response to what is heard. • Response should not be carried to the point of artificial exaggeration. • Approval and rejection, opinion and suggestion form part of listening. • Monosyllabic comments serve as catalysts for keeping the conversation going. • The sensitive person will stop talking if he becomes aware one is not listening.

Improving Listening. • To become adept at listening, one must work at listening. • Self-discipline through effort is the key to good listening. • Good listening is a good habit acquired from practice. • A communication barrier between supervisor and patrolman may be expected. • A supervisor must instill confidence that he wants to talk to his men. • There is relief in knowing there is a superior to whom one can talk. • There is the same need for a supervisorial ear as for a supervisorial voice.

CHAPTER 2

Working with the Team

The policeman on the receiving end of a supervisor's direction and guidance is not just part of a person. The man who comes to work is not just a kind of automaton who has left his greater self at home with wife and kids. He is a whole and complete organism, replete with emotions and drives and capacities, who comes to work in his entirety.

The supervisor will have among the ranks of his subordinates the strong and the weak, the balanced and the neurotic, the ambitious and the lazy. On his team there will be the mature and the immature, the clear-thinking and the confused, the good—and even in the best of police organizations—the bad. Thus there will be a need to communicate with personnel—to counsel when they need direction and help, to praise when they have excelled, to reprimand when they have strayed onto a deviant path.

How to Counsel, Praise, and Reprimand

A policeman may be reluctant to talk when he most needs to communicate. He may be embarrassed. Or if he wants to talk, the supervisor may fear losing the label of "good fellow" if what he says to the man is construed to be negative. The supervisor may be hesitant to inject tension into a placid relationship between supervisor and supervised. There always is the hope that the problem will go away by itself.

However, it is not the supervisor's option whether he should communicate. Instead of being a personal choice, the election actually is an organizational one. There is a duty and obligation imposed by the higher office. The team leader must realize the necessity of counseling, praising and reprimanding.

The Notion of Counseling

A frequent boast of the police supervisor is that his men confide in him beyond the call of duty. They tell him about the quarrels with wives, or recite the worries about those older kids who may be heading for trouble. If he has a young-lady clerk or meter minder on his team, he may attribute to his magnetic charm the fact that a highly personal tale of a split-up with a boy friend is poured out to him.

What this readiness to confide means is that everyone has a driving force to seek out a patient and receptive ear. There is a need to relieve tension by letting someone share the burden, for the sympathetic listener may offer a word of reassurance in times of trouble. To be a good listener is praiseworthy. But the initial attraction of the troubled one to the person willing to listen may not necessarily stem from an unusual quality of personality in the receptor.

Emotions are of concern in the worker's supervision. Industry has learned that since it is the whole man who is on the payroll, if the company is not getting its fair share from the employee it may be a result of the emotions he brings to the job. It is the employer's business to become involved in a worker's private life if the job is being affected. Similarly, in the official family of the police agency, there too has to be concern with the inner man. The first-line supervisor is not always able to assert that a member's private life is none of the department's affair.

There are times when a policeman voluntarily seeks out counseling; at other times, the supervisor will have to seek out the man who needs counseling. If a policeman wants to talk to his sergeant about a personal struggle, the troubled one usually can be sensed unobtrusively trying to make contact. He will hint around the problem, probably proposing a question which is not supposed to refer to him. It usually will take little encouragement to get him to connect himself with the question's concern. Having allowed the identification to be made, the floodgates will be opened—and a soul will be poured out!

Instead it may be that a team leader will have to explore with a question of his own to find out what might be wrong. The supervisor, and the man's fellow patrolmen as well, may be aware of changes in attitudes that indicate worry, concern or doubt. The gesture of a sympathetic ear being available for the asking will trigger the tale.

However, the supervisor may have to call a problem to a man's attention when he appears to be unaware of his difficulty. Or it may be that he knows of it, but shows no apparent concern. This may present the supervisor with a difficult situation to resolve. There is an omnipresent desire that relationships with one's fellows, be they superiors or equals or subordinates, remain free of conflict. There is the fear that counseling may be rejected, or even outright hostility flare up, which makes a showdown imminent. Nevertheless, the supervisor's responsibility must not be shirked.

There are old and new forms of counseling. The old employed the direct approach. When a man was falling down on the job, he simply was advised to "get on the ball." When he was taking too many shortcuts, he was plainly and unequivocally told to "cut it out." If it was believed he could do better, he was decisively urged to put out a bit more. When he was errant in his ways, the correct path was unequivocally indicated.

Because they are dated does not mean these pointed methods of counseling are to be rejected. When the old-time police captain berates the young supervisor for being hesitant in facing up to a problem employee, telling the sergeant "he can't be a boss and an old lady at the same time," the sergeant may have something to learn from his archaic superior. A specific firmness in attitude and language is the only communication some people understand.

The unmasked direct approach of old may have to be blended into the more artful modern form of counseling. It may be simply a matter of drawing the errant one aside, and pointedly spelling it out for him. This in itself may amount to the positive approach of advising or explaining. A police supervisor must never forget that he is dealing with men who supposedly are accepted by the agency in part because of their superior emotional stamina. Therefore, he should not have to take an apologetic stance in confronting them with the rights and wrongs of performance and attitude.

This does not mean that he has to project a supervisorial image of jutted jaw and fearsome scowl. There may be times when a less directive approach to counseling should be employed. This involves bringing what underlies the problem to the surface, instead of waging war on the problem itself. The newer counseling technique lays bare the emotions, and subjects them to examination. Feelings are carefully analyzed and clarified with an opportunity for the troubled one to get things off his chest. This kind of counseling calls for greater skill, practice, and desirably, a little training. It allows a rapport to develop, which allows the counselee to understand why he feels the way he does.

The practice of this more subtle form of counseling is well within the reach of the police supervisor, even though at first it may seem complicated and forbidding. The best approach is to place oneself within the reference frame of the man being counseled. For example, Paul the policeman is abrasive with both clients and his peers. The supervisor may confront Paul with, "You have a tendency to come on a little strong, Paul. That's my weakness, too. It gives people the wrong impression, and that's pretty unfortunate. You and I really aren't that kind of person, Paul. I've had to put the brakes on after being burnt, and it's hard to do, Paul, etc." Getting Paul to recognize his deficiency may even lead him to discover that he has some strong feelings of hostility which are vented when he communicates. Perhaps a new introspection will even uncover some resounding undertones of insecurity and inadequacy in Paul. He may find out he is overcompensating for these by an aggressive harshness in making public contact.

This is not psychiatric practice in any sense. It is just a simple way of causing another person to subject himself to a little self-evaluation. If it fails, then a frontal attack may have to be undertaken after all. Then a more simple style of counseling might have to take the form of, "Paul, you just got to stop being a no good so-and-so, or people won't like you!"

The Verbal Lash of Reprimand

There is room for the old-fashioned reprimand. A police supervisor not only has the privilege—he is often confronted by the positive duty—of taking a team member over the coals for either a singular breach or ongoing inadequacy.

If a policeman appears worthy of being dragged on the carpet, there should be no reluctance to get the distasteful job done. The supervisor should subscribe to that first principle of reprimanding: the reprimand must be given at once when deserved, or it will be without impact. When Mother has the children wait for Father to come home in order to have the "roof pulled down over their monstrous little heads," she is missing the opportunity of exacting punishment with profit. For now Father is being put into a framework of artificiality that will make the paddling he administers completely meaningless. The reprimand must come at a time when the sense of breach in the offender is strong, and an indignant reaction can be appreciated. Then the vividness of the infraction has not been blunted by time.

Yet there is a danger of oversubscribing to this principle of immediacy. In leaping into the fray, a supervisor may be operating on an insufficiency of facts. He may have jumped to conclusions which are unwarranted. He may be misinterpreting something, misunderstanding something, or even imagining something. Consequently, the facts should first be assembled, and submitted to at least a rapid test. The wrongdoer always should be allowed to give his explanation of what happened. Regardless of the nature of the occurrence, the facts of an incident should be seen against the background of the policeman. Often the violation is a culmination of a long list of personal malfunctions that previously have gone unchallenged. If this is the case, the violation should not be considered in isolation.

When the supervisor has assembled all the facts, he should be ready to wield the verbal lash. Here another old rule comes into play: the reprimand should always be given in private. A public display of official wrath can serve no useful purpose. It will cause added embarrassment to the offender. It even may elicit sympathy from his peers, and this will put the superior on the defensive. Thus the sergeant should simply draw the errant one aside, and make his presentation out of earshot of anyone else on the team.

The choice of words will be dictated by the person of the offender, as well as by the nature of his offense. Again, different persons are attuned to different tones of language. There can be all of the verbal approaches from the subdued, "I am quite sure you didn't intend things to take this turn," to the more directed,

"If this ever happens again, you're fired!" What a supervisor should not use is self-defeating profanity or abuse. Nor should he give way to an emotional show which a more controlled subordinate will watch with contemptuous amusement. The supervisor should not do or say anything for which he later may feel it necessary to apologize.

A reprimand should be recorded in the personnel file for the use of another superior who some day may be confronted by a new incident involving the subject. Putting something in writing will also be a kind of trigger for getting rehabilitation started. The modern principle of discipline on the personnel level, as in the case of corrections on the criminal plane, calls for straightening out the one who has erred. The most important effect of the employee's reprimand should be that what happened will not happen again.

Of Orchids and Applause

Inasmuch as words of praise come easier than words of redress, a supervisor will be more comfortable in issuing a "well done" to the patrolman who has performed admirably. Knowing that one's work is appreciated is a powerful motivating force. There is strong satisfaction in recognizing that accomplishments will be noted and valued. That all-important self-image is beautifully enriched by a word of praise for effort and worth.

The supervisor must be careful to avoid being one-sided in recognizing what deserves praise. He may appreciate the aggressive arrest, but allow the cool-headed handling of situations without arrest go unnoticed. Or he may be an enthusiast for toughness, but permits the diplomatic processing of a confrontation to go unrecognized. Or he may never consider it worthy to compliment the man assigned to the complaint desk, but lavishly praise the field policeman for the most ordinary actions. The supervisor should evaluate the accomplishments of each man in terms of what he is achieving, rather than postulate admiration on the basis of his own pet interests and perspectives.

If "Nice going, Jack" is given for every routine action the job demands, it will soon lose its value. While not necessarily issued sparingly, praise should be given deservedly. Its worth should not be diluted by frequency. When it is rightfully due, it should be meaningfully offered, given when it is most expected, while the receiver has that good feeling of knowing he has excelled. This is the crucial time when the man will be disappointed if appreciation is not forthcoming. For this reason, the supervisor must keep abreast of what is going on, so he will not miss the praiseworthy incident.

Praise will mean more if others are aware it is being bestowed. Unlike the reprimand, praise should be rendered in the presence of others whenever possible. It will trigger a chain reaction of satisfaction as one's peers join in the acclaim. There also is the promise for the man on the sidelines that he too can receive such applause, providing he goes out and does likewise.

These are the simple forms of special communication called counseling, reprimanding and the giving of praise. In a sense they all tie in together, and are somewhat interchangeable. Even at the time of reprimand, something else may surface which is the proper subject of praise. Both reprimand and praise are actually forms of counseling; and counseling is not set apart from reprimanding and praise. Because all this is deep, penetrating communication, it is sensitive and fragile communication. What is sensitive and fragile must be handled with painstaking care, or irreversible damage to ego and self-image may be incurred.

How to Conduct a Team Conference

There is a certain police department that just has to be a good one! Each morning, following an unbending ritual, the Chief meets with the assistants and commanders who report directly to him. Together they have coffee, and talk. For the refill, the top rankers meet with their executive and middle management officers. More coffee is consumed, and they talk. So right down the line, until everyone from cadet and clerk-typist upwards has shared in coffee and conversation, according to an official pecking (or rather, sipping) order.

The coffee bill runs high, but it appears to be worth it, for everyone in that organization seems to know what is happening on both an administrative and operational level. Everyone has the chance of saying what should be done. While coffee consumption is sizeable, that of time is really not. While the usual unstructured morning coffee break period is eliminated, little is lost here. For much of the usual confidential and inaccurate chitchat of the customary private confabs now has become open and constructive. No one really minds, because the coffee is free. And communication in that hard (coffee) drinking and hard talking organization is unrivaled among the police agencies.

Whether or not his department subscribes to such officially sponsored pleasurable conversation, the first-line supervisor should take it upon himself to set up his own variety of regular staff conference. He can do it daily, merely by replacing the command "Fall in!" with "Meeting time!" or (and why not?) "Coffee time!" Not only will the duty tour start off on a morale enhancing warm and pleasant note, but this way important questions can be asked, and answers proposed. All the while there is that unmatched motivating force of mutual contribution. Along with this, there is that keen sense of satisfaction which comes from knowing one is not completely left to the whims of administrative circumstance, but has a real say in running the departmental ship on which he has booked passage.

Setting up the Conference

Since police facilities have often taken on the modern touch faster than the department it houses, most organizations have ideal physical settings for meetings. The only inadequacy of the typical squad room is that the seating arrangement may be poor. Traditionally, both chief and sergeant were supposed to meet in a setting where they could speak out to, and perhaps down to, the men. Consequently, a round table has not always been available as a prop for staging the most effective conference. The appropriate physical setting for "talking with" is substantially different from the usual environment designed for "talking to."

The supervisor must understand that there is an obvious advantage in conferring at a round table, or an oval table, a rectangular table, or even a square table. The impact from this geometry is that the contribution is mutual. There is no barrier between hierarchical ranks. An atmosphere for a smooth flow of conversation is provided, different from the usual barrier blocking the instructor from the instructed, characteristic of the typical lecture hall.

When the proper setting has been found, a program for conferences can begin. They may be scheduled on a regular basis—daily, for instance—or just called as needed. The purpose of the conference should be either informational, as "here's what's happening on the street, and here is an up-to-date list of the idiot trouble-makers we should know about;" or action-oriented, as "this is the way we can stop those daytime burglaries bugging us out of our wits!"

Adequate notice should always be given when the conference is to be called, and how long the session will last. It is disconcerting for a policeman to either have to cancel personal plans, or break his regular job routine for a meeting. Consequently, there is an advantage in having a set meeting time. But if the conference is called, a brief preliminary written notice along with a later reminder will eliminate the sting of an inconsiderate "command performance."

There is a more important advantage to the team conference than just to fill an immediate need. Anyone who has conducted a departmental meeting recognizes that there may be a built-in barrier to communication in the usual police group. There is a reluctance to incur hierarchical wrath. "If I stand up to the forces above," says the wary patrolman, "it might be my neck."

The concern with untouchable forces inside the organization is not the only blockage to free expression. Less acknowledged is the powerful factor of peer standards that must not be violated. There is a strong attitude of belonging which characterizes the policeman within a perceived frame of reference common to the vocation. This sense of group conformity may account for a reluctance to express himself within a group environment. When the individual does speak out in the presence of peers, it is more likely to be a unilateral attack on outside elements, which will safely attract his associates' backing.

The regularly scheduled conference will have the effect of breaking down this communication barrier. A free flow of thought becomes habit-forming when the men become accustomed to the give-and-take within the peer group and acceptance of disagreement among equals is seen as quite respectable. There is less fear of the accusation that one is identifying with a hostile hierarchy. An efficient, constructive, easy communication is set up which will have positive effects on discipline, morale and operations alike.

The Fine Art of Conference Leading

When the time and place for the team meeting have been set, the supervisor should take a good look at the environmental factors involved. The room should be tidied up, the chalkboard cleaned, and the chairs arranged neatly. Supplying a ruled pad and pencil at each place is a reminder that memories are short, and that there may be points of the meeting worthy to record. Providing stationery also indicates that preparation has gone into the conference, and implies that the agency considers it important enough to spend a little on writing materials.

Then again there is the matter of coffee. The social significance of the brew should not be disregarded. It represents a liquid version of the symbolic breaking of bread that brings people together. In the cup there is the idea of the gift, a satisfaction of the unconscious, primitive need for someone to care. As the aromatic fluid is sipped, there is a good feeling which puts everyone in a more congenial mood to talk. The financial outlay for a pot of coffee will be well worth the positive spirit it will stimulate.

After the men have entered and taken their places, a warm smile will help to set the favorable tone. Having displayed his dentures pleasantly, the supervisor should lose no time in getting the conference started. The first order of business will be to familiarize the participants with the purpose of the meeting.

This means there will have to be an agenda. It should always be made clear that the men are free to contribute discussion topics by making their subject proposals for the next meeting. If possible, copies of agenda items should be distributed prior to each conference. It is important that discussion be organized so that the agenda may be covered systematically. This implies that a time limitation should be established for the session. The participants need not be shifting around uncertainly in their seats, with no idea whether the ordeal is half over or just getting started. When adjournment is announced, the time and place of the follow-up should be specified. This allows the policeman to see discussion as a continuous process.

What the supervisor as conference leader should remember is that his role is to preside. He does not force ideas or outcomes. His function is only to keep the ship on course—to prevent the participants from straying off into deadend channels. As both good and bad ideas are tossed into the fray, his job is to maintain structure. Without blocking anyone's contribution, the supervisor has to be subtle in guiding considerations gently back to the roadway after they have drifted off onto the shoulder, or become bogged down in fields at the roadside.

The best way to maintain direction is to interrupt in order to summarize, to formulate, and to point out significances. In every group a chairman is needed to block the introduction of inanities, and skillfully create meaning where a contribution would otherwise be devoid of meaning. "I see what you're trying to say, Joe, and it's a great idea," followed by a loose summation which makes a little sense, is an excellent way of salvaging utter hogwash.

The one-in-every-crowd usurper bent on monopolizing the stage has to be kept in constant check. The direct approach, "Will you please shut up!" is not recommended. It can be tactfully accomplished by apportioning time to talk equally. That feared raised hand—after it has been raised for the fiftieth time—can be beautifully ignored, simply by recognizing other raised ones, or forcibly directing the discussion to some less talkative participant.

There will be policemen who sit back either complacently or timidly and contribute nothing. If this exponent of the Silent Sphinx is encountered, thus forfeiting his unused time to a talkative associate, he may have to be dragged with graceful force into the deliberation. The old techniques of "You had an experience like this from which we might learn, Harry;" or simply, "I'd sure like to hear what you're thinking about this, Pete," are icebreakers.

The conference leader should overcome the temptation of doing all the talking himself. If he hogs the show the men will probably let him monopolize. Particularly when he tosses out a point and no one picks it up, there will be a tremendous temptation for him to carry the ball personally. This he should not do. If no one responds to a general question, he should let it hang as the silence gradually becomes deafening. This is like trying to look the other fellow down by staring into his eyes. Somebody has to give, and it should not be the conference leader. Or, the question may be directed so that it will force participation.

A policy decision need not be formulated from the team conference. Policy in an area that embraces more than the team may have to be formulated on a higher level. But the opinions and suggestions of the men from the unit meeting should be referred to the policy maker on the next higher level. If the men are going to participate with more than tongue in cheek, they must be reassured their participation is not mere window dressing. Otherwise, they will be fast to smart under the notion that they really are impotent, obsessed by a gnawing self-image of powerlessness arising from the sham of a purposeless group conference. When a formula has been designed, when a consensus has been shaped, when good ideas have been born—the results should be passed upstairs. The first-line supervisor has to be dynamic in his upward referral, not a hat-in-hand apologist who simply goes through the motions of representing his men to management.

The Making of a Good Conference Leader

The supervisor in the conference director's chair should give the semblance of working rather hard, without at the same time making his team members feel that they themselves are working too hard. He should sit erect. He should maintain an unforced look of eager interest on his face. When he talks, he should convey the impression of having given the subject a lot of thought, of knowing what he is talking about. He should be alert, avoid the earmarks of distraction, and display inspiring enthusiasm over the matter at hand.

It is easy to show disagreement with another's conflicting idea. There may be a natural tendency to bristle, become defensive or argumentative. It is not uncommon for a participant to emote, to become belligerent, perhaps to engage in sarcasm. When this happens the conference leader must keep cool, change the direction strategically if the going becomes heated, and avoid the fatal mistake of pulling rank to overcome opposition. Tact and poise have to be maintained at any cost, and always with a smile—a fringe benefit for the group which costs little.

Smiles are associated with humor, and humor has a place anywhere. The ability to employ humor does not mean one has to be a comedian. The would-be comedian

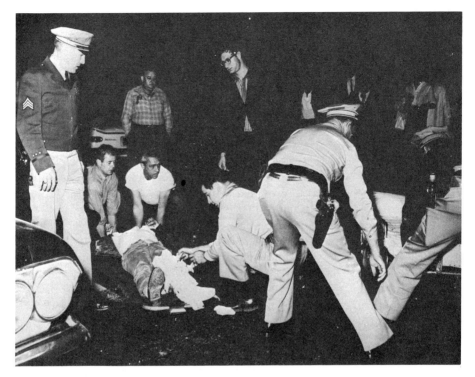

Photograph courtesy of Berkeley, California, Police Department.

who feels compelled to ply his trade can suffer from a bit of artificiality as his well runs dry. But a sense of humor, seeing how funny the grotesque can really be, can work wonders in keeping the fingers of team members away from each other's throats. Sometimes an outright laugh or smile, even when there is little that is humorous, in itself can suggest the soothing notion that the situation must be very funny after all.

The supervisor has to incorporate adequate timing in his conference leadership. He has to know when to cut off debate, when to call for a consensus, and when to synthesize the findings into a tentative or final decision. He must do this without assuming an autocratic stance. He has to convey to his team members that it is they who are producing the action-oriented solution; that they are formulating policy for the whole department.

If it is finally up to him to present his own decision, the supervisor should do so while analyzing all the factors that went into it. Even if the men must turn decision-making over to him, they still should be allowed to see their contributions as the building blocks of his final determination.

Policemen should have full opportunity to participate in the team conference. If a question is asked, the questioner should be guided into suggesting his own response. If a decision is to be made, the ones who will have to implement it should be the first to present a choice of alternatives. If policy is to be established, those who will be controlled by it should offer its solution. The supervisor is the man who assures the right of participation to all. The supervisor taps the ability, know-how, and experience of the men who are on the line of confrontation in the field.

How to Delegate Authority

The most glaring weakness in functional supervision is not doing too little. The supervisor scoring the lowest is the one who tries to do too much. He is the one-position football team who does his own running and blocking, his own passing and receiving. He is the one who does not know how, does not want, to delegate authority.

Why One Hoards Authority

When corruption once ran ingloriously rampant in some cities, the patrolman may have spent his day off and his vacation on his valued beat. While this may have showed a real dedication to duty, it might have been his financial stakes that needed protection from a claim-jumping replacement. The private policy of this extinct species of patrolman really represented a failure to delegate something, which probably could not be identified as authority.

The modern supervisor who must do it all himself represents another brand of insecurity, but one that may be related to that of his distrustful predecessor. He may be fearful that someone, somehow, may be stealing a prerogative that rank has bestowed on him alone. He may feel inadequate before his subordinates, or there may be a political fear that one who overshadows him will move ahead when advantage is to be gained. The authority-hoarding supervisor may represent a brand of avarice that is directed toward power rather than money.

The supervisor who refuses to delegate authority simply may not know his job. Unfamiliar with the basic principle that supervision consists of planning, directing, controlling, he does not see himself as the coach on the sideline, but as some superman who is covering every position on the field. He sadly misses the point of what supervision means, and instead represents just another sailor on the crew while the ship flounders without captain or rudder.

The excuse of a supervisor that it will take him so long to show somebody how the job is to be done that it will be easier to do it himself, is a factual admission of inadequacy. The police supervisor is first of all a teacher of men. For him to announce his inability to teach means that he holds himself incapable of fulfilling his primary responsibility. The reluctance to parcel out authority to those on a lower level represents a weakness rather than a strength.

The Need for Sharing Authority

There is a timeworn principle of administration that holds that authority should be commensurate with responsibility. In an occupation earmarked by authority, the validity of that principle is all the more glaring. A policeman's work is one of reasoned constraint, and constraint may not be exercised without authority first being conferred. Otherwise it will be the unqualified letter of the law that blindly dictates all action, while he unwisely ignores particular modifying circumstance.

However, nothing in law differentiates authority on the basis of individual police rank. The rookie patrolman immediately after taking his oath of office has rights of arrest and force identical with those of the thirty-year chief of police. It is elementary that a supervisor cannot restrict the exercise of a patrolman's legal authority when the need for taking action arises. This is not to say he is without power to establish policy on the application of law—for example, at the scene of a mass disturbance. To make all necessary legal actions taken by a patrolman subject to his supervisor's ultimate review and approval is not in accord with law. Authority goes with a patrolman's duty, and the first-line supervisor has no option to reserve it.

Leaving aside the legality of the issue, the practical import of sharing authority is readily apparent. Self-image is most important in the world of work. There is the stimulus of pride in getting the job done. There is the reinforcing push of confidence in performing the task. In a field of employment that emphasizes hierarchical rank, it is all the more necessary to promote a sense of worth in the worker. Thus in the police field a supervisor should nurture self-pride and instill confidence by allowing the men to exercise initiative. Wherever possible he should share his own authority with the patrolman charged with doing a specific job.

To perform best a man should get pleasure from the performance. Satisfaction should be derived from the doing. This means that he should have the right to perform through his own motivation and his own election. To be himself he has to be endowed with an authority to act—to follow through as needed. For a policeman to have to seek approval from his sergeant for every act shuts off the possibility of gaining the satisfaction that goes with doing police duty. Otherwise, he is continually acting only in the name and authority of his supervisor, not his own. He is a craftsman, but cannot share the joys of craftsmanship. The supervisor is depriving him of the very motivation it is the supervisor's duty to provide.

The patrolman is not the only one who is disadvantaged when authority is not shared. The authority-hoarding supervisor also is being victimized by his own unwise tendencies. The most prominent factor in any work role today is the economy of time. More and more it is being realized that the bigness of the environment and the increase in demands make time a very rare commodity. A supervisor has to apportion out his time as well as his effort in the accomplishment of purpose. He has patrolmen working for him, and he should use their services. The formula of operation holds that the first-line supervisor has the responsibility to see that a job is done, and the patrolman alone has the ongoing responsibility for the actual doing. Graceful adjustment to a fast-moving age, when it is almost impossible to keep up, is required on every level of endeavor. This adjustment may be made by a supervisor in meting out authority to perform, while he reserves the right of review from the sidelines.

Authority must be delegated if the team is to perform with efficiency. Without authority at the operational level, activity will be restrained, hesitating, timid. If efficiency is lacking in the team, responsibility for the inadequacy will fall on the team leader. If he noes not delegate authority, he cannot now transfer responsibility for failure. He is left holding the proverbial bag which he was unwilling to share before the roof fell in.

The Hidden Play in Authority Delegation

The best formula for delegating authority is to set specific limits and responsibilities for patrolmen. As far as possible, guidelines approaching exactitude should be defined. The varieties of situations and the nature of contingencies encountered by the line policemen make it impossible to spell out his authority in specific terms. The degree to which the supervisor's authority may be shared has to be done in a situational sort of way. He indirectly will indicate the rights and powers a subordinate may exercise without calling for a supervisorial decision.

This indirect method of delegation entails referring real and hypothetical situations for the patrolman's consideration. There should be a continuous calling for his ideas as to what is optional in the proposed cases. Where authority is not shared, this should be indicated. As an example, decisional action may be barred where an off-duty policeman has been involved in an altercation. Another may be the release of an arrested person without booking in an instance of borderline legal privilege. If policy so dictates, these are cases where it should be specifically determined that a superior must be called in to decide disposition.

Getting the patrolman to think ahead—to plan his activity in the light of contingencies—will give him a clearer notion of the extent of his authority. Thinking through hypothetical patterns will bring into focus the limits of his right to act. Perhaps the overriding consideration should be a superior not being there to take responsibility in sensitive cases. In talking through the make-believe occurrences, the patrolman should be encouraged to summon the supervisor whenever practical in a touchy situation. Where authority must be assumed on the spot owing to an urgency to act, the policeman should boldly make the decision himself. This case method of presentation is the best way of setting down authority lines, formulating the principles to be invoked in assuming authority, and for recognizing the limited situations under which authority must ordinarily remain exclusively in supervisorial hands.

Frequently asking the patrolman for his suggestions and advice is a good way to get him to realize he has been delegated authority. Approving his thoughts on the conjectured situations, and encouraging him to take his proposed action is the best method of eliciting initiative and recognizing delegated powers. To reinforce further the notion of conferred right, when a supervisor is at the side of a patrolman on an assignment where the policeman regularly has the right to act, the patrolman should be allowed to do so without having to await a go ahead from the superior officer.

What is most important is that the policeman should not have to answer for his every action. A sense of jeopardy for making the wrong move should not be constantly held over his head. It should be implanted in the patrolman that judgment must be carefully exercised, but marginal error may be excusable.

What the patrolman should understand is that the extent of authority granted him is maximal, while the limitations are minimal. Restrictions will be founded only on the basis of legal and organizational needs. Where there are dangers of legal or critical sanctions; where potential disciplinary action against a peer is inherent in a situation; where policy determination to suit a particular circumstance is required—then the authority of the patrolman to make a choice of actions may have to be limited. But beyond this, if there is responsibility to act, then there should be full authority to act. Perhaps it is more practical to impress upon the subordinate this *spirit* of authority delegation than to spell out the *rule* of authority delegation.

SUMMARY

The Need of Counseling. • The policeman at work is a whole man—a composite of drives and emotions. • A team is composed of many types of men, of differing strengths and weaknesses. • A man seriously in need of help still may be reluctant to talk.

Supervisor as Counselor. • The supervisor has a positive duty to counsel, praise and reprimand. • Structure and timing will make it easy to counsel, praise and reprimand. • A supervisor will find pride in having his men confide on personal matters • Tension is relieved by finding an ear when trouble engulfs one. • A letdown in working efficiency may be a product of personal problems. • It may be an employer's business to become involved in a man's home life.

Undertaking Counseling. • A man in need of real help may merely hint around the problem. • Changes in attitude that indicate worry and concern may be evident to all. • A supervisor's false desire for serene relations may cause him to avoid counseling. • The old form of counseling involved the direct approach. • Some persons only will respond to strong and pointed language. • A supervisor need not take an apologetic stance when he confronts the member.

Kinds of Counseling. • At times a less direct approach of counseling may have to be used. • The newer form of counseling involves uncovering and examining emotions. • Nondirective counseling may require more skill, practice and training. • The new counseling aims at leading one to learn why he feels as he does. • One should place himself within the reference frame of the man being counseled. • The new counseling is not to be considered psychiatric practice.

Reprimanding. • There still will be times when the old fashioned reprimand should be used. • A reprimand must not be given so fast the facts of the case are lacking. • The facts underlying the need for reprimand should be submitted to test. • The reprimand always should be given in private. • Before a reprimand, a man should first be allowed to give his version of the affair. • A reprimand should not include any speech or actions for which a supervisor must later apologize. • The aim of the reprimand must be to prevent repetition of what has happened.

Praising. • There is a strong motivating force in sensing one is appreciated. • The supervisor must extend his praise to a wide area of virtues and values. • To retain its worth, praise should be given only when really deserved. • Praise should be given in a way that it will mean something to the recipient. • A supervisor should know what goes on to know when praise is deserved. • Praise should be given a man in the presence of his peers. • Counseling, praise and reprimand can be readily intermixed.

Scheduling the Conference. • The supervisor should set up a program of regular squad conferences. • Conference participation assures one he is involved in decision-making. • Most agencies have good physical settings for the conference. • The round table usually has not been available for the police team meeting. • The idea of mutual contribution is reinforced by the round table. • The round table gets rid of the barriers inherent in hierarchical rank. • Before scheduling a conference there should be something to discuss. • The conference agenda should be informational or action oriented. • A conference should be announced well in advance.

Meeting Participation. • There may be a reluctance to talk because of a fear of command. • A hesitancy to talk may be caused by a fear of violating peer standards. • Regular scheduling of conferences will break down communication barriers.

The Conference Environment. • The room should be tidied, chairs arranged, and blackboard cleaned. • Pencils and paper should be provided. • Coffee contributes a social atmosphere condusive to communication.

Conducting the Meeting. • An opening warm smile by the conference leader sets a favorable tone. • Men should be allowed to suggest agenda items for the next meeting. • Copies of agenda items should be distributed before each conference. • A time and place for follow-up should be set at the time of adjournment. • The sole function of the conference leader is to preside and guide thinking. • The way to direct is to summarize, formulate, and indicate significances. • A man who usurps the floor annoyingly should be checked politely. • An opportunity to talk should be apportioned among all. • One who is reluctant to participate should be drawn into the talk gracefully. • There is a temptation, which must be avoided, for the conference leader to carry the ball himself. • To get participation an overhead question should be asked, and a reply awaited.

Conference Production. • A policy decision does not always have to be a product of the conference. • The meeting should provide the building blocks of a policy decision. • To get contribution, the men should not see their involvement to be an empty gesture. • The supervisor must refer thinking the men have produced upwards.

Working at Conference Leading. • A conference leader must extend effort to lead the conference. • The supervisor should sit erect, and keep an unforced look of interest on his face. • The leader should show alertness, avoid distraction and maintain enthusiasm. • The conference leader should avoid pulling rank to overcome opposition. • Humor has a worthwhile place in running a conference. • Humor can keep tempers in check when emotional feelings rise. • The leader must know when to cut off debate, call for consensus, and summarize. • If the supervisor must make the decision, he should explain all its factors.

Group Contribution. • When a decision is made for them, the men must still see their participation. • Adults like to participate, and the conference provides this opportunity. • The man who must implement a decision should have the right to offer alternatives. • The conference leader taps the ability and knowledge of the participants.

Group Contribution. • When a decision is made for them, the men must still see their participation. • Adults like to participate, and the conference provides this opportunity. • The man who must implement a decision should have the right to offer alternatives. • The conference leader taps the ability and knowledge of the participants.

Failure to Delegate. • The supervisor doing the poorest job is the one who tries do do too much. • Doing too much by oneself represents feelings of insecurity in the supervisor. • A supervisor's failure to delegate authority may mean he fears being superseded. • Not delegating authority simply means the supervisor does not know his job. • A supervisor who hoards authority falsely sees himself as a superman. • It should not be said that one must do it himself because it is too hard to teach another. • If one has the responsibility to act he should have the authority to act. • A patrolman's enforcement action is in no need of constant appraisal.

Benefits of Delegation. • Delegating authority nurtures self-pride, and instills confidence. • Satisfaction is derived from doing when one can act on his own initiative. • A patrolman cannot perceive his craftsmanship when denied authority to act. • The efficient supervisor's time must be conserved through authority delegation. • The patrolman's action will be restrained and hesitating if without authority • A supervisor who does not delegate authority must assume responsibility for failure.

Conferring Authority. • Guidelines of limits and responsibilities should be set for the team. • The contingencies possible make exacting delineation of authority difficult. • Limitations on authority should be spelled out through hypothetical posited cases. • Getting the patrolman to think through situations confers the idea of authority. • Frequently asking a patrolman for suggestions gives him a sense of authority. • A patrolman should not be made to answer for every decision. • Initiative should be encouraged in the team. • Authority conferred should be maximal and limitations minimal. • It is better to instill the spirit of authority than to set up its restriction.

CHAPTER 3

Developing Policemen

How to Teach without a Classroom

Knowledge is not something delivered nicely packaged, and in lifetime supplies. Continuing education in a variety of diverse fields give evidence that learning is a lifelong quest. In law enforcement, continuing education is found in advanced and refresher courses for sworn personnel given under the auspices of both academies and colleges.

Not yet established on the high note of these instructional programs is the instruction of the team leader on an even more continuous basis. The police supervisor's education of his unit may actually be of higher quality than the department's, because his is often directed to a more defined need. Too frequently department-wide programming begins with "Let's give them some in-service training," immediately followed by "What do you think we ought to include in it?" The supervisor who perceives advanced education for the men as necessary to get his own job done, will develop instruction on the more logical "this is what they need training in, so let's go" blueprint.

While he may not see himself as being in the education business, the police supervisor is a teacher. His classroom may be the squadroom or the front seat of a patrol car. Perhaps it is behind the complaint desk. Or it might even be on the sidewalk casually chatting with his foot patrolman. Wherever his halls of learning may be improvised, he is just as much a teacher as the professor in the elaborate lecture setting. The first-line supervisor may be even more effective than the certified educator, particularly if he adheres to the simple and basic principles that are the foundations of the ancient art of teaching.

Photograph courtesy of Livermore, California, Police Department,

The Supervisor as Teacher

The job of teaching is fundamentally easy, and for a police supervisor the task should be even easier. Policemen want knowledge. They want to be able to do a tough, dangerous job well. Also, there is that big beautiful glow of advancement in rank on the future's horizon. At least at the present time, promotion is achieved through the standard playback of knowledge in the form of a civil service quiz. So the potential test-taker is greedy for the tidbits of information on what may loom up again in the form of multiple choice questions in the examination.

Thus the supervisor-teacher may be able to skip that first step of instruction, where the learner has to be motivated. He is dealing with somebody who genuinely wants to learn, and has come to him to learn. The sergeant-schoolmaster will be revered and appreciated by a policeman who has turned learner, even by the previously uninspired.

The traditional kind of instruction the police supervisor will have to impart is on-the-job, individually directed, practical teaching. The most common pupil is the patrolman who has to be shown how to perform the new assignment. Or perhaps another policeman's finished report is not up to standard. Maybe a certain officer's use of the radio leaves something to be desired. Or it might be that increasingly frequent rumbles are heard about a particular man's lack of tact in handling the police client. Or he just may be that ordinary rookie who never emerged from recruit school a finished product.

The police supervisor has only to schedule his time for working with the patrolman who needs help in doing his job. He will have to outline how much time to spend with this unit member, and must decide on what form the instruction will take. He will have to plan how to impart principles. Then he will use the opportunities of field duty for applying these principles. There even may have to be a form of testing at the end, to make sure the man is on his way to accomplishment.

A good subject for group discussion is the new information periodically available to the men. It may be a new state statute, or a significant case that has come down from the high court. Perhaps the department has invoked a new procedure. Or it just may be a more sophisticated technique of doing an old job—for example, taking over at the crime scene, handling the psychotic subject, or operating a new piece of police equipment.

This kind of group instruction may be easier to plan than more formal programs. Classes may be held on a rollcall basis, and be of just a few minutes each. Or an occasional one-hour training period may be set up at the start of a normal watch. After selecting an available time, the supervisor can begin by designing a miniature course outline. Then he will supplement this rough blueprint with more detailed individual lesson plans. At this time he will select his method, and perhaps look around for visual aids, or maybe decide upon a qualified guest assistant. Whatever he does, this mini-instruction will be real instruction, carrying as much educational impact as the best academic programs.

Perhaps least subscribed to in the police service, but offering the greatest potential, is to allow the men to profit from an experience where something unfortunately went wrong. Because of the usual bureaucratic fear of criticism, police have been adept in burying their mistakes. When a case was badly handled, when somebody unwisely let himself open to a major complaint, or when a policeman was injured or even killed; there usually is something in the regrettable incident from which everyone could learn. Instead, silence falls and the books are closed on what all would rather forget. In contrast, the supervisor should watch for, and even uncover, the unfortunate occurrence in everyday practice, and allow the team to dissect and unravel in conference what happened. If human failure played its role, if bad judgment was used, or if just plain negligence was at the roots of the mistake, the incident which found its way to the debit side of the ledger may be constructively moved over to the asset column. This can be done if the occurrence provides any opportunity for education to prevent what happened from happening again.

The first-line supervisor should not be timid about entering into a makeshift classroom setting. He should live up to the principle that the supervisor is a real, full-fledged teacher with the highest credentials. He should seek out the subject matter, and look for the opportunity of time and place to practice his role of pedagogue. For him the audience will be captive, but willing. His classroom will be the world of work, with its built-in laboratory for transforming all that is taught into full dimensional realism.

Teaching Tools for the Asking

As any artisan, the teacher needs tools to do his job. Many of the larger departments produce their own instructional literature, in the form of information sheets, bulletins, and newsletters. Closed-circuit television is available in some instances for police on-the-job classrooms. Thus the police supervisor's task is made relatively easy, inasmuch as the technical devices for teaching are at his ready disposal.

Even where these elaborate implements are not available, it is not difficult to improvise. For example, there is always a movie projector, and free films pertinent to police work are not hard to come by. Almost every supervisor has his own camera and slide projector at home, and with a minimum of imagination can make transparencies for teaching use.

Every police organization has typists and duplication equipment. A note of caution, however. If he tries to be too elaborate in his written work, the supervisor-author will probably never get his text materials completed. But if he is satisfied with creations which may lack finished polish, he can be prolific turning out good, working handouts.

Some of these productions may be designed for the home use of the men. There may be a kind of problem set, with brain teasers to be thought about at home, though not necessarily solved there. There may be a question-answer format closely akin to the latest self-pacing learning devices. The more imaginative supervisor can develop his own form of correspondence instruction in the form of takehome lessons.

Even if he has nothing else in classroom equipment, there will still be the chalkboard on the wall of the typical squad room. The blackboard is the poor man's visual aid, and it can be employed with skillful simplicity. However, it is not always used to advantage, even though it is indispensable to teaching. The points at issue may be analyzed, outlined and recorded on this oldest classroom tool. After a teacher gets in the habit of using eraser and chalk, he will feel as if his hands are tied when he stands before his group with no board available.

The Rule Book for Teachers

There are four steps in teaching. Whether the first-line supervisor is offering a bit of tutoring to the individual patrolman, or giving classroom indoctrination to the entire team, the process will still involve the same four steps. This is the standard way of driving home an idea, to complete the function we know as learning. It is a progressive method of making an abstract idea part of the real person who is doing the learning.

The first step is the introduction. The learner is told what there is to be learned, why it should mean something to him, and the use to which the newly acquired knowledge may be put. Thus the fires of his interest are stoked. He is told how his learning will be acquired, what will be done to help him, and what aids will be put at his disposal for mastering the instruction. The introduction will let the learner know all about his undertaking, providing a blueprint for achievement.

Then comes the presentation. This is not mere talk. The novice instructor must recognize that 85 percent of learning is acquired visually and only 15 percent through hearing. Manipulative learning is achieved more readily through seeing the performance than by being told about it. Instruction should be interspersed with plenty of examples, and all the while the language must be simple and clear. In addition, the best teachers cultivate the ability to transmit an enthusiasm for the subject matter.

Application, the third step, comes after the principles have been set down in clear, concise form. Now what has been learned is put to work. It becomes a living thing, adapted to real here-and-now situations. When the learner has the opportunity to actually do the thing being taught, then the learning process is tremendously enhanced. For example, if report writing is the topic under consideration, subjecting the learner's actual reports to application of the principles set down in the lesson may be used. Or if the matter considered is a physical manipulation, such as using a riot gun, experiencing the feel of handling the weapon impresses both theory and practice.

Finally, testing completes the classic four steps of learning. The notion of testing is too often falsely identified as threatening. This is especially the case in a vocational area where advancement is based on the civil service examination. The idea of a test should be a positive one, a highly productive part of the teaching process, rather than its mere supplement. Testing provides positive rewards for both student and teacher. It allows the students to see the range of what he should know in a given subject and provides him with feedback on what aspects he needs more work in. Testing is also a device that allows the instructor to know whether he has succeeded in getting the instructional job done. Through it he knows whether more work is necessary, whether he should try a new approach, or whether his policeman now can do a certain job better. This evaluation may be accomplished through oral questioning, offering a few written questions for response, or just watching the learner perform the task.

Thus, ordinarily one who knows the subject matter and who understands the four steps of teaching it is able to be an effective teacher. If the supervisor knows how to introduce the subject, how to present it, how to apply it, and how to test it, then he knows the essentials of how to teach it. Putting oneself wholeheartedly into the role, allowing his enthusiasm to rub off on the learner—these are the earmarks of a gradually mastered teaching skill.

The Methods of Teaching

A standard portrayal of the teaching process probably entails somebody standing before the class and expounding wisdom. This is the lecture system of instruction, unduly maligned in the trade. The lecture still has an effective place among the many teaching methods, provided it is used by one proficient in the lecture.

When new material is offered, unfamiliar in its entirety to the student, lecturing is probably the most appropriate teaching method. When used it must have a definite scope. There should be an attention attracting introduction, and a summarizing conclusion imbued with punch. In between there must be a logical, point-by-point development of material. Plenty of illustration ought to be interspersed with the content. Ample time should be allowed for question and comment. The lecture method may not only be the best—it may be the only method suited to accomplishing a particular teaching task.

There are other forms of presentation. The conference method, with its variations of panel and informal discussion, has long received the nod as a superior form of indoctrination. It allows full participation that is particularly satisfying to adults, because grown people want to engage actively in the instructional process to which they are subjected. The conference is particularly suited to in-house police education because of its appeal to those who are brought together with the same kind of problems and experiences. In conference, the difficulties and happenings of work are thrashed out by veterans of the battlefield, coming up with commonly conceived problems and solutions.

The superiority of the discussion or conference is that it is more than teaching. It has been pointed out that the difference between a college and a university is that a college teaches, while a university learns. Analogously, it might be said that in the lecture situation there is teaching, but in the conference one learns. In the conference, the hodgepodge of collective experience is refined into principles applicable to real situations. The difficulties that arose in a real setting are solved by the people who experienced them, later thinking them through and resolving them together.

The conference leader has to be much more skilled than the lecturer. With the method designed for the small group, discussion is ideal for the police team. The leader is in a position to keep communication closely personal, a prime characteristic of the effective conference. His foremost task is to keep everyone involved in the discussion, and to hold in check those who want to monopolize the proceedings. The chalkboard can be used advantageously. The problem should be concisely defined, cases analyzed, and alternative courses of action considered and evaluated. While the supervisor is struggling to keep contributions from the group general, he should avoid the error of taking over himself. The answers have to be developed by the team, and not independently imposed from above.

There is a particular appeal to policemen in the conference discussion. They like its practicality. They are stimulated to think. It has the important side advantage of being another way of getting them to see themselves as a team. When the students do come upon a solution to a difficult problem, they will share that pleasant glow of group accomplishment. It is truly a learning experience; not just the passive process of being taught.

Perhaps the most common method of instruction the first-line supervisor employs is the tutorial. Here the individual is taken under the pedagogical wing, and guided almost affectionately to accomplishment. It obviously requires more time than the indoctrination of a group. Self-pacing is the most important advantage of this method. The continuous opportunity to test is the master control at the tutor's disposal. In the police environment, the supervisor can take advantage of moments of inactivity as well as the laboratory conditions of field activity to drive home the needed points. The patrolman can work through the situations by himself, yet under the guiding eyes of his mentor.

The most desirable quality of the turor is the ability to enter the mental framework of the learner. It is easy to presuppose knowledge and personal ability in the student which are really not there. This may develop into a loss of patience in the teacher, having the fatal effect of discouraging the learner.

The teacher has to be constantly engaged in measuring his students' ability to perform. Encouragement and advice have to be given on a continuous basis. Not only should questions be encouraged, but the teacher must stimulate the learner to think through the answers himself. The steps of introduction, presentation, application and test apply to individual instruction as well as to a group. He should begin by teaching what is easy, and gradually work up to what is more difficult. Where there is room for demonstration, it should be liberally employed.

There are many other methods of teaching. The lecture-discussion, the directed conversation, the laboratory demonstration—these are just a few of the other prominent ways of doing the job of instructing. However, the supervisor can be remembered by his patrolmen as a veritable "Mr. Chips" simply by using the lecture, conference and tutorial systems, selecting one or a combination according to need and objectives.

This is not to play down the need of long preparation and hard experience to develop into a proficient teacher. It is to suggest that when one knows, loves and lives his field of vocational endeavor, he may find it possible to convey his enthusiasm, knowledge and skill to another for his use and edification. Teaching can be as easy as that!

How to Get a Policeman to Observe

Observation is not a purely passive activity. To smell, to taste, and to touch may not be dependent on will. Nevertheless, generally one sees what he wants to see, and hears what he wants to hear. Most observation is perceived with the eyes, and the bulk of the rest with the ears. If one sense is missing or impaired, the other compensates for the defect.

For the policeman, part of whose function is to observe, contact is made with the environment of his work through sight and sound. The somewhat hackneyed truism that a patrol force represents the eyes and ears of the police organization recognises the patrolman's mandate to see and hear. Thus, a pertinent role of the police supervisor is to ensure that his subordinates are seeing what they should see, and hearing what they should hear. The team leader has the responsibility to teach them so that their observation is comprehensive and acute.

Observing Through Unfocused Eyes

Let us consider a hypothetical example which illustrates the hazards of lax observation. A patrolman has just made the arrest of a lifetime. His world is one of congratulatory handshakes and flashing photo bulbs. He is the center of a ring of reporters who eagerly pen his acount of the big case. Relatives and friends will read of his exploit in tomorrow's newspapers. The hero policeman relaxes happily in the warm and pleasant glow of a great achievement!

On the following morning he visits the prosecutor. Again there are handshakes, and the official stamp of recognition is placed upon a job well-done. Then counsel begins questioning the arresting officer. What exactly was the position of the suspect when he was first seen? What specifically was he doing? What were his spontaneous utterances? What was he wearing? The queries become more intensive in their demand for evidentiary exactitude.

A bit of uneasiness begins to replace the policeman's glow of self-satisfaction. After repeated admissions of uncertainty, the condition is one of pure embarrassment. The hero has become a bum and a beautiful bubble has burst.

What happened, of course, is that the policeman relaxed at a time when he should have been alert and about—looking sharp and staying sharp. Instead, his gaze was one of admiration directed inward, when all the while he should have been looking analytically to the outside. What was said, what happened, have vanished. Up to this point he had taken for granted what had appeared simple and self-evident. Proof? What proof? Everybody knows what happened!

Now there are legal barriers to surmount, having to do with what is called, "beyond a reasonable doubt." In the adversary game about to be played, an underdog defense will use every card in the deck to prevent the prosecution from justifying the legal requirement of proof. Included will be an attempt to make a dummy out of the star prosecution witness—the man of accomplishment, the arresting officer. Even as his success in the field was narrated on the front page for his many admirers to behold, so will his clumsy failure in the courtroom now be printed in bold relief for the same people to read in his time of defeat.

Could supervision, or, rather, the want of supervision have contributed to this breakdown? Perhaps a sergeant had not thought it necessary to condition his men for the big case. Perhaps he had never prodded them into staying on their toes. So he too has to share the responsibility for failure with his man.

Cultivating the Power to Observe

Like most skills, astute observation develops from practice. One learns to see simply from doing a lot of controlled seeing. One learns to hear through a refined practice of structured hearing. One learns to remember from engaging himself as often as possible in the act of deliberate remembering.

Some people possess more acute eyesight, and some are more proficient in hearing. Defects can be remedied easily by eyeglasses which now are invisible for the vain. Even the new spectacle-frame hearing aids can be most inconspicuous. But aside from the physical, one person may be more psychologically attuned to a world of seeing, while others are more given to a universe of sound. Here too, deficiencies are as easily correctable as those of the sense organs, providing the proper exercises are taken.

An example will be found in the way one participates as a spectator at a football game. It is well known that the amount of enjoyment experienced in the stands is proportional to how much one sees going on in the field. Watching the guard who has pulled out of the line may indicate immediately the direction the play will take. Noting that a particular linebacker has missed a couple of tackles will be anticipatory to his substitution. Observing that a defensive flanker is playing too deep could mean a vulnerability at which the offense will strike. While the more scientific spectator is watching something other than the quarterback's hand-offs and passes, he is developing habits that will lead to more satisfaction and pleasure in watching a football contest.

Similarly, habitually concentrating on the people, places and things of a beat can sharpen the patrolman's identifications and evaluations. That fellow in the closed service station looking under the hood could be a lookout for a burglar working in the office. That car parked for a day or more in the same spot may be wanted. That pair of fellows parked near the bus stop could be waiting for some lone female victim to start home. A furtive glance or interrupted conversation of loiterers as the policeman approaches can be significant. Comparing the passer-by's facial characteristics with those on a wanted poster can turn up the long-sought fugitive.

These patrol activities are commonplace, and part of good police practice. But they are not always accomplished to perfection. It is not unusual for the off-duty officer to pass a uniformed associate who fails to recognize him. Or another will sit in a car on a surveillance mission, only to find patrolmen who drive or even walk by the vehicle repeatedly without once recognizing the plainclothes occupant. Almost every police officer has entered a courtroom a day or so after an arrest without being able to readily identify a bailed defendant seated among the assembled spectators.

All this means that policemen will not always observe with the full powers of their faculties. In addition to the resulting less efficient work performance, side benefits of value may also be missed through this inattention. It is extremely satisfying to many persons to be recognized by someone on official levels. The police-community relations value are obviously great when a patrolman is able to assign the right name to the right person in casual meeting.

Consequently, a policeman should go out of his way to see and to hear, and beyond this, remember vividly what he has observed. If criminal subjects and other objects of police attention are not readily available for the exercise, a dry run practice is desirable. For example, looking at any person selected at random, picking out identifiable characteristics of appearance and manner, and then mentally recording a sharp image of them, affords an excellent practical exercise in observation. A special mental compartment for the unusual should be consciously cultivated. Frequent recall will give longer life to the stored images.

Mental Sets That May Distort Observation

While the will to see and the will to hear are fundamental in determining how well one sees and hears, there are factors which reduce the effectiveness of observation. Preconceptions of the observer often give final shape to the mental images formed. Because of reinforcement through common acceptance and traditional thought habits, what is observed may not conform to reality. Contrary to popular belief, that dumb blonde may really be a smart brunette!

A common example of distorted observation is to take the unusual appearing person as the one who is the potential lawbreaker. The bedraggled young fellow with long hair and beard may be well worthy of police attention, but so is the smooth-shaven, well-dressed sharpie. The black pedestrian in the lily-white neighborhood in a given instance may be properly singled out for observation by an alert patrolman. But the less conspicuous white burglar may be simultaneously escaping scrutiny as he passes along the same sidewalk, blending well into the environment. Thus, because of their rigid structure, built-in reflexes for identifying the unusual and unexpected may respond falsely, or at least incompletely, to the persons and things about one.

Mannerisms similarly may be misinterpreted through entrenched thought patterns. Thus the hostile, impertinent youth may be seen by the policeman as the sure criminal delinquent. The deferential lad, polite and friendly, may be dismissed from the officer's attention with everything short of abject apologies. However, the rough-speaking youngster might not be the one who is criminally inclined, while the well-spoken and congenial lad could be a worthy suspect to a logbook full of offenses.

While not necessarily urging a patrolman to rid his perspectives of all stereotypes, the supervisor should use every opportunity to warn his men of the dangers in oversubscribing to their prejudices. The team leader should urge his subordinates continuously to make their observations total in scope. He should caution them against failing to subject their preconceptions to question or test. The men should be prompted to incorporate a quest for both the positive and the negative in their observations. What is right in any given person or circumstance should be sought out along with what is wrong. For that bottle may not necessarily be half empty. The perennial optimist may see it as being half full!

Prodding the Man to Observe Well

The learning process is facilitated by the teacher's gentle and well-planned shoves. If an occasional question directed at a student is anticipated during the lecture, better attention from the group may be expected. In assigning problem sets after a theory has been propounded, the application results in a conditioning that reinforces the principles. While teaching observation techniques in the classroom, the presentation of a check list to complete after brief exposure to some person or thing is a well-known practical exercise.

In the classroom that the patrol car itself provides, it may obviously not be possible for learning techniques to be too elaborate. But simpler methods may be very effective. This laboratory on wheels presents real life opportunities for learning which could be only simulated at the police academy. The settings on a patrol beat are changing constantly, and the objects for consideration are many and varied.

There is plenty of opportunity for a supervisor and subordinate to talk together while on patrol, particularly when things are not too busy. During these quiet moments the supervisor can direct practical questions at his man. Did you see that fellow back there standing at the building line? The thing that chap walking down the sidewalk was carrying—could it have been a lady's purse? Isn't this the third time we passed those kids cruising in that Chevie?

When the supervisor accompanies a patrolman on an assigned run, the time for staging a little exercise on the way back is opportune. What was that the complainant said when you asked him such-and-such? Did you see that painting hanging on the wall in the living room? Did you notice a sort of chemical smell in the house? What kind of dog was that the woman put in the kitchen as we arrived?

At first, subjecting the patrolman to these little workouts in observation may be made to appear as casual conversation. There will be no reason why he should not be permitted to see through his superior's intent and design later. It actually may be profitable for word to filter throughout the team that the supervisor is using a deliberate technique to prod the men into good habits of observation. Then the men will be motivated to prepare for their turns by looking and listening more sharply regularly. Awareness of the supervisor's methods may stimulate in the policemen a consciousness of the value of good observation.

When a court case is anticipated following an important arrest, helping the potential patrolman-witness set his memory in order will be most worthwhile. Do you remember how the fellow was dressed at the time the arrest was made? What were the exact words he blurted out when he saw you? How did he react to the complainant's accusation? How far was he from the gun you found? What was the make, color, type, and model of the car he got out of before you grabbed him?

In coaching the officer, he should be reminded to compartmentalize remembered facts. They should be preserved vividly, and ready for instant retrieval during the course of questioning in court. Comprehensive notes should be made while everything is fresh in his mind. The supervisor should point out that listening to others after his personal observations have become blurred by time will tend to influence his recollections unfairly, and perhaps with distortion.

The very practical matter of felt embarrassment because of memory failure should be brought to his attention. It should be pointed out that the patrolman may wrongfully feel pressured into perjuring himself through hesitating to testify he does not know what should be known. Thus the supervisor rounds out his role of a tutor who seeks to develop an observant patrolman. Or he may be thought of as an instructor in a laboratory course in practical observation. All of this is accomplished by using commonplace field occurrences as the means for drilling his patrolman student. Basically he simply is pointing out the pitfalls of inadequate observation, and instilling in his officer a sense of the value in observing better.

Finally, what can be more effective instruction than setting up oneself as model? In teaching the fine art of patrol observation, the supervisor's role should be that of an instructor who is masterfully proficient in observation himself.

What to Look For in His Report

When the Navy skipper issued his terse statement, "Sighted sub—glub—glub—," he was making a report. It was a good report because it satisfied at least one essential of good reporting: it made perfectly clear what happened. While more detailed data might have been of value to high command, the five syllables basically filled the bureaucratic need for knowing what had occurred.

Reporting is basic to line, staff, and auxiliary operations. In law enforcement, the teamwork required to accomplish a job calls for making information available to a variety of people. Something must be known of an incident, and of those involved. Reams of paper will move into the files of the larger departments daily. Some of the pages will be read, reread, and have supplementary sheets attached. Others will be fed into computers or transferred to microfilms. Much of the paper will never be referred to again.

It must be assumed that a lot of the data so recorded will be indispensable to intelligent and efficient police operations. Because a piece of paper containing a policeman's words may have to satisfy a specific present or future organizational need, it should tell all that will have to be known—clearly and accurately. If the recording is bad, a sergeant who let it get by will have to take the blame. A first-line supervisor must know what to look for in his man's report when he receives it for the official files.

The Rule Against Putting It in Writing

There are unwritten norms that are not covered in the usual classes on police administrative practice. One of these relates to the unformulated rule subscribed to by a surprising number of agencies: "Don't put it in writing!" The considerations underlying this informal tenet at first appear quite worthy. By leaving it unsaid, one is not obliged to explain away something contradictory that turns up later. As it might be under the evidentiary discovery laws, an investigator's hand is not shown to the opposition when left unrecorded. A man is not put in jeopardy by an assertion made earlier that will take on the semblance of error, misinterpretation, or neglect at some future time.

While these reasons for recording sparsely may appear good, some counterbalancing arguments should be considered. In the first place, it is not possible to determine what implies the possibility of future jeopardy. Secondly, incurring jeopardy through reporting happens so infrequently that an old-timer will have difficulty remembering when he had to be sorry for having put something in writing. Finally, the practice of only selectively recording facts may be simply a neglect of official duty.

Consequently, the supervisor should insist on a positive reporting rule of relevancy, rather than on a negative one of secrecy. If a detail of the circumstances being described is pertinent, it should be put in writing. The policeman should have no option to leave a fact of potential relevance unrecorded. If a man is permitted to labor under extreme caution about what he puts in writing, it is certain that he will occasionally miss a point of great importance. One can be equally sure that sooner or later data will be needed that is irretrievably lost because of its ommission.

However, a man should not be forced into a strait jacket of reference that drives him to feel that every thought, occurrence, circumstance, and utterance he encounters on the job must be recorded. It is impossible to lay down an exact formula which can invariably dictate when a report should or should not be made. There must be some professional discretion left to the officer in deciding whether he should record something he comes upon during the duty tour. He must not have to labor under an immobilizing fear of censure because he did not report something that unexpectedly proves of consequence at a later time. But this needed degree of freedom must not be interpreted as a right to disregard report-making when it is otherwise needed. A supervisor should determine that a man uses common sense in exercising discretion.

How To Say It Clearly

Affected and convoluted writing is hard to understand. Simple and direct language is more easily understood as well as being easier to write. Reports are written to convey information, not to impress with literary style. The aim of any style should be to make the facts of a report concisely understandable to the reader. Many police reports include poorly chosen words that do not readily convey the idea that is intended. Clauses may be so badly structured that the meaning is obscured in a welter of confusion. Sentences may be haphazardly strung together so that there is no clear sequence of thought which adds up to a clear story.

Very simple words can get an idea across better than deluxe five-syllable monstrosities. Simple pronouns help. Unless an official rule directs otherwise, "I" should be used in place of a clumsily formal "the reporting officer" in telling what was seen, heard or otherwise learned.

Just as words should be short, likewise sentences should contain as few words as necessary to get an idea across. If sentences are too long, the thoughts trying to be expressed will be tied up in knots. Sometimes even several readings will fail to get them untangled. While the use of the passive may be gramatically correct, "it was told to me," rather than "he told me," has a tendency to make understanding a bit more difficult. Report writing should be to the point, and pivoted on the "do"—telling who did it, why it was done, where and when it was done, and how it was done. The easiest way to convey these thoughts is the best way. Writing easily makes understanding easy. "Relax and write" should be the basic rule for report style a first-line supervisor impresses upon his men.

The Structure of the Report

The purpose of police reporting—whether relating to an occurrence, an investigation, or administration—is simply to recount information in a way that is understandable and usable. The policeman making a report should keep one commanding guideline in mind: his reader should get a reasonably good facsimile of what the policeman has learned through first-hand experience. While a picture still may be better than a thousand words, that picture is seldom available. If words are properly chosen and strung together, an amazingly accurate likeness can be obtained.

Police report forms usually provide prepared boxes for inserting detailed facts. They also ordinarily have space for a free account of what is being reported. If the policeman has nothing but a blank piece of paper on which to tell his story, he may have to start a bit ahead of where he would begin when using the narrative space of a prepared form. Then his initial paragraph must tell what this report is going to be about. Regardless of how complex the occurrence reported, he must first lay down a concise statement telling what happened, and what he did about it.

Now that the reader knows what is being reported, and has been provided with a summation of what he is going to be told, he is ready to be fed details. There is a basic rule for relating these: they should be strung out in one-two-three order. Using cardinal numerals to label the separate assertions will add clarity: "I went to such-and-such place where I met so-and-so, who told me one, two, three. I then did one, two, three. Learning the identity of the suspect I went to one, two, three. Apprehending the perpetrator, he told me one, two, three. I found evidence in the form of one, two, three. I booked him on charges of one, two, three."

Before setting down thoughts in this readable way, a blueprint will always be helpful, and often indispensable. A supervisor should suggest that his patrolman form a habit of taking a few moments to jot down a pattern. While the sketch does not have to be so elaborate as to include all the indentations of roman numeral to paranthetical small letter found in the standard outline, a simple listing of successive words or phrases that stand for the individual points will suffice. Then when he dictates or types his report, he need only expand each of these to put his story together. Because a plan has been made, there will be a logical one-by-one presentation of thoughts, devoid of needless repetition. The building blocks of narration will be placed neatly one on top of the other, and a sharply defined and understandable picture will gradually emerge.

It is important to make a distinction between what is a fact; what is said to be a fact, but may not be; and, what is conjectured to be a fact, but will have to be proven a fact. There should be no scarcity in the report narration of "he said," "I found," and "it is believed." The first and third person pronouns should be used freely. What has been done in handling the case, and what still has to be done in processing it should stand out distinctly. It must be clear how much is already known, and how much has still to be learned. If a person's specific words are best for telling something, these should be used, set off by proper quotation marks. A report is not judicial testimony. Thus relevant opinions should be given freely, providing they always are labelled as such.

In the end, a conclusion should be drawn up that leaves no one dangling in the air. Here is from where we have come, here is where we are, and here is where we must go. The reader, whose first question was, "What's it all about?"

should not now have to ask, "Well, so what?" The significance of an incident should be made clear. If the matter is not closed, if there must be some kind of investigative or administrative action still to be taken—this must be set down as a formula for action.

The Importance of Accuracy

The girl in the police record room is already far behind on her Monday's filing load. But she has had to spend an hour looking for a report that must be there! By chance she decided to check under the complainant's first name instead of the last. And there it was! "But," explained the errant patrolman, "anybody could make a mistake when the guy's last name is Edward."

An expensive watch may have been missed in the pawnshop check because the wrong case initials were listed in a stolen property report. After all, it is easy to write "NVK" instead of "MBK." Take a look at the typewriter keyboard, and there they are, "V-B-N-M." You can't blame a policeman for making a little slip like that when he's not paid to be a professional typist!

A great many police reports contain inaccuracies. But a pharmacist cannot afford to make one error of filling a quinine prescription with strychnine. Nor can an engineer escape responsibility for a ten-inch mistake in structural design with a "darn those decimal points!" show of concern. Policemen should not continue their chronically careless report writing attitude that puts a burden on the clerical staff, the assigned investigators, and the subscribing public.

The facts in a report must be correctly stated, and a supervisor is responsible for their accuracy. If there is doubt concerning an assertion, it still should be made if pertinent, but must be modified by indicating the uncertainty. Speculation should always be labeled speculation, and established fact should be called established fact. There are many words which properly denote something that is less than certain fact. "Alleged," "believed," "presumed," "thought," "may," and "probably" are all examples of modifiers which allow room for the contrary to be later proved. The caution of the press in avoiding libel litigation should be taken as an example. As in news copy, the report's reader should be made aware of what degree of certainty goes with every bit of information conveyed.

The supervisor must insist that the policeman be scrupulously accurate in giving every item of routine data. It is intolerable for "Smythe" to be spelled "S-m-i-t-h." Routine entries have to be correctly made regardless of how immaterial the officer may consider them. He should think of himself as being open to lawsuit if a mistake is made, just as the physician has the threat of malpractice litigation hanging over his head with every diagnosis. Accuracy should be practiced deliberately by the report writing policeman, with a double check of each item before it is recorded.

The Supervisor's Follow-up Function

Sloppy police reports are seldom brought to administrative attention. Another officer who has to use a bad report will not complain of someone else's inaccuracies to a superior. Even if a civilian clerk would want to make an issue of a policeman's carelessness, his less-than-sworn status may attract less-than-full concern from a superior.

The primary check point in report processing is the report writer's first-line supervisor. There is a limit to how much he can know about the actual details in order to subject reports to close scrutiny. But he can still maintain an intelligent surveillance of his team's reporting function. First he should play the role of one who needs to know what is contained in the report. He should see himself as the investigator who is to work on the case, or the newspaper reporter who is to prepare a column from its content. If he cannot get the story from the first reading, something probably is wrong with the report. If it is found the narration is at fault, and not the supervisor's slow comprehension, the report should be rewritten.

The inaccuracy of details sometimes is so glaring, personal knowledge is not needed for their detection. A name may be spelled differently in two instances of use. A listed time will be seen as improbable in view of an assertion made elsewhere. An incident in the narration may contradict a later statement of fact. If something fails to make sense, the supervisor should return the report to its author for revision.

Even though the spelling of words and the mechanics of grammar may not necessarily affect meaning, the patrolman must be held responsible for correct spelling and proper grammar. There are many handbooks that serve as practical guides to better spelling and it will be proper for a supervisor to assign a little home study to a man with a glaring spelling deficiency. It has been observed that policemen were better spellers in the day when simple spelling was included in civil service entrance examinations. But today's demand for paper work still requires that a police officer spell well. The supervisor should be the ongoing examiner of the man's spelling skill, and must insist on reasonable standards of proficiency.

There also should be adherence to at least the simple rules of grammar. Improper punctuation may be the most common report weakness, and one which definitely affects the understanding of the reader. The comma is a very useful tool for keeping thoughts in individual packets and making comprehension easier. If sentences are kept short, fewer commas are needed, because the concise thought groups are kept apart by periods. Knowing when to end a paragraph also helps to arrange thought packages in a way to make them digestible at a single reading.

The key to understandable writing is the proper grouping of thoughts. Running ideas together without separations may be a proper stylistic device for a stream-of-consciousness novel. But for a report which relates detailed information for immediate comprehension by the reader, the punctuation tools for setting thoughts apart must be used. The policeman who does not know how to paragraph, and does not comprehend the use of the comma, is a particular candidate for a little instruction. His report may legitimately be defaced by the supervisor's red pencil to indicate where a comma should have been used, or a new paragraph started. A red-marked report will have to be done over, and having to rewrite enough reports may prod the deficient one into doing the job right.

The people who really know how badly reports are made are the employees of the record room. They are the ones who have to read an item three or four times in order to extract a key thought for the keypunch. They are the people who have to make sense out of a pitiful welter of confused details. They are the ones who have to spend precious time tracing the data of an inaccurate report. In the larger departments good management calls for the assignment of a regular follow-up officer to oversee report writing. Regardless of the kind of record division organization, the first-line supervisor can maintain a practical liaison with that unit to learn who are the deficient members of his team.

After the supervisor has singled out the poor report writers, he can work with them constructively. First some gentle instruction, and then an observation period to detect improvement will be in order. Their reports can be subjected to intensive scrutiny, and returned with each detection of continued deficiency. The police supervisor can call attention to how content might have been better arranged, and how something could have been better said. In the long run, a policeman is more apt to conform to the call for improvement than to buck the demands his supervisor imposes.

How to Motivate the Unmotivated

Once upon a time, there was one clear motivating force in the employer's book. It took a rather simple form: "Get to work, or you're fired!" In a time when the worker is looked on as a very human being, both manager and supervisor acknowledge and respect the inner and outer drives that prod the employee to accomplishment.

This new perspective of humanitarian character is not just a product of some "let's be kind to the poor working-man" movement. It is well established that work output is a factor of worker satisfaction—satisfaction with the job, the working environment, the people he works with, and the people he works for. Put these together, and their sum spells out the idea of motivation.

Motivation is not something that is uniform in intensity. For example, there may be little at the start of a new effort, but it builds up as one goes along. Or there may have been a lot of motivated and inspired activity for a while, but suddenly the worker slides into a lethargic inactivity of alarming proportions. Has anyone other than the worker himself control over this drive? Good supervision may be thought of as synonymous with good motivation.

The Drives Within

To understand his team members, the supervisor should be aware of the range of basic needs that make up the emotional anatomy of people. At the bottom of the scale are the physical appetites which serve as the primitive forces behind human action. These predominate the animal's existence and manifest themselves to different degrees within each individual man.

Hunger caused Pavlov's dog to salivate, and hunger has caused man to kill.

Photograph courtesy of Livermore, California, Police Department

Countless human beings have spent their lifetime's energy just staying alive. The basic motivation of millions was found solely in warding off starvation. Work afforded the few pieces of silver for conversion into something that could be eaten. The foodstuffs obtained afforded the means of nourishment, nourishment needed to be able to work. The vicious circle went on from hungry childhood to early death.

The thirst and sex drives take their place with hunger as essential motivational drives. However, in a nation where survival is more or less guaranteed by a benevolent state, these basic urges of biological origin have little reference to the study of employee motivation. Other forces of more psychic and social origins are relevant, however.

The supervisor should understand the full impact of these higher needs. They are the desire for security within a group, for esteem derived from a group, and for self-realization within a group. The failure of these needs to be satisfied underlies the feelings of defeat and deprivation that are translated into a loss of motivation.

The police supervisor must recognize that these drives are not developed with equal intensity in everyone. The events of early childhood contribute, and later in life, the influences of family, friends, and fellow workers play their role of alteration or reinforcement. But all along there is a variable scale of intensity. The forces may increase with time, and the need for ego-satisfaction will grow as one becomes older. Take the increased concern with security that comes with aging. Or look at the inordinate sense of pride the elder citizens displays when he wins a bit of small-scale recognition from some petty official. So in rookie and veteran alike, the supervisor may expect to find a common drive to be somebody in the crowd, and to have that recognized place in the crowd assured.

Man does not work for bread alone. To perceive work in its proper perspective, labor should not be separated from living. The supervisor ought not to overlook work's time dimension—almost a quarter of one's adult hours may be spent on-the-job. While it is not customary to identify a man by his physical dimensions, his religious affiliation, or by the size of his family; we do label the individual by the kind of work he does. Every policeman will know that in his home neighborhood he will be referred to as Mr. So-and-So, "the policeman." What is more, he is equally a policeman while patrolling his beat and while sleeping peacefully in his bedroom.

Nor is being identified by occupation something independent of the labelled subject. When the police officer goes home at the end of his shift, he will think police work. There is a feeling of possessiveness about the job environment. It is *his* beat, *his* squad car, and *his* department. He may hang up the uniform at headquarters, but he carries his role home with him every day.

It is not enough for the police supervisor to know that his man has an awareness of belonging. He should capitalize on it. Dynamic supervision nourishes this vivid sense of participation. The team leader should keep his patrolmen informed of what is happening in the department. He has to make his subordinates aware of the purpose of every assignment, and the significance of every policy. The patrolman has to be guided into knowing the import of the segmented part he plays in the total operation. The one who puts all departmental relationships into focus for the patrolmen, who gives reason to their being and activity, is the first-line supervisor of the team.

What Goes into Job Enthusiasm

If the supervisor is to promote job satisfaction among his men, he should have some idea of what attracts them to police work. It has not been established that only one type of personality is drawn into the occupation.° Unlike the tenets of that oft recited hypothesis, it has not been shown that police recruits score higher than the rest of the working class of authoritarianism.† Certainly, from his own experience the supervisor can testify that there are many kinds of men who comprise his organization.

Why, then, do men become policemen? Considering the more tangible attractions of a police career, it cannot be ignored that in most areas salaries are now good. In addition, security plays a very prominent part in recruiting police officers.°° Tenure is conferred almost automatically on the patrolman. The number of forced

°Arthur Niederhoffer, *Behind the Shield: The Police in Urban Society* (Garden City: Doubleday, 1967), p. 104.

†*Ibid.*, p. 150.

°°*Ibid.*, p. 141; Richard Blum and William Osterloh, "Keeping Policemen on the Job," *Police* Vol. 10, No. 5 (May–June, 1966), p. 28.

separations after probation, and perhaps even during the trial period, is exceedingly small. Unlike many other fields, a man is not under the threat of having to produce to hold his job. Strikes are uncommon, and layoffs nonexistent. Ordinarily the pension system is far better than elsewhere.

In the less tangible areas of occupational attractiveness, the typical police recruit is imbued with a strong sense of morality.° The determined zeal with which he comes to the aid of the crime victim and confronts the perpetrator, dramatically demonstrates his acute sense of right. It also is found in the unconcealed satisfaction he shows when he apprehends the wrongdoer. A clearly visible drive to assure that justice will be done is sometimes even strong enough to introduce overreaction.

There is also the excitement of the chase. He wants little routine to fill his working day. He has no taste for the quiet night on patrol. He looks for the action-packed radio call. He actually seeks out the incident that promises excitement.

It is readily apparent that the aspirant to a career in law enforcement is in search of adventure in the truest sense.† Skolnick points out as significant that 50 percent of his sample indicated detective work as a choice, which he looked on as a desire for danger and initiative, and 37 percent wanted patrol or traffic. Only 4 percent wanted administrative work, and none had in a bid for jail duty.°° Excitement has to be seen as a common and legitimate attraction for the man who wants a career of police duty.

There are many more features of the occupation that cause young men to become policemen. The work represents a life outdoors. People are more interesting to deal with than things. There is also a very real satisfaction in public service—in helping the person in trouble. Not to be disregarded is what Niederhoffer refers to as "the appeal of the uniform and the authority it connotes."°°°

When the Motivated Become Unmotivated

A primary concern of the supervisor is to detect any drop in motivation. When a man who has been enthusiastic suddenly begins to show his interest has fallen off, the supervisor should not consider the change to be freely selected. Something has gone wrong, and it is up to him to find out why.

It may be that the officer is thinking of leaving the field. Perhaps the firehouse is beckoning enticingly, with its good working hours, lowered responsibility, and freedom from the public hostility faced by policemen. Or it may be an opportunity to take up that old trade again; or maybe a teaching post, putting a credential to use; or his brother-in-law who needs a partner in a new enterprise. If it is simply a matter of moving to another job, perhaps there is nothing the supervisor

°Blum and Osterloh, p. 30.

†Ibid., p. 28.

°°Jerome Skolnick, *Justice Without Trial: Law Enforcement in Democratic Society* (New York: Wiley, 1967), p. 47.

°°°Niederhoffer, p. 133.

can or should do—other than to remind the policeman that the pay goes on until the day of resignation, and pay has to be matched by output.

It may be some personal difficulties that are being reflected in job performance. Perhaps it is the prospective divorce, with the financial treadmill that will follow. Or maybe it is the mushrooming overload of debts, with a bleak fiscal future. "So, the heck with the job!" he says. "What's the use of trying to get ahead, when it all amounts to a futile struggle to get out of a trap!"

Perhaps he is becoming frustrated with the kind of people who are his clients. In groping for the concerns of the police, Skolnick found that about one-half of his "Westville" simply listed "relations with public" or "racial problems and demonstrations" at the top.° This was even before police became a firing target for terrorists.

Then it may be those old gnawing pangs of disappointment at not getting ahead on the job. The supervisor should be well aware that what the policeman wants more than salary and conditions is the opportunity for advancement. He wants to step up a rank, or maybe just get out of uniform and into the detective's role. There may be real frustrations over which the patrolman has no control. Perhaps the testing process is primitive and poor, and the one extra miss of a badly designed question will be the difference between promotion and waiting another four years for the next contest. Or it could be politics in the selection process. Or it may just be a matter of not really having the intellectual ability.

Weak administration may have caused motivation to plunge. Things in the agency are run in a stumbling, inefficient way. Incompetents have been promoted and now relax, perpetuating the incompetence. Or political favoritism, not personal ability, pays off. The disillusioned member finds escape by retiring into lethargy and resignation.

These are just some of the mental sets that may be lowering motivation of the individual and team. The cause may be simple or quite complex. It may be valid, or without substance. Whatever the roots, the supervisor may not just sit back, and tell himself with a sigh that this is the way it has to be. It is for the supervisor to isolate the cause, find out why it is happening, and then set up a plan to restore the job enthusiasm that has been lost.

The Restoration of Job Enthusiasm

The supervisor is not in every case urged to coddle the dissident in the ranks. When a man resorts to the easy way in meeting every demand of the job, to the disadvantage of both the taxpayer who pays the bill and the fellow officer who is faced by a consequent double load, the old approach of "Get in the ball game—or else!" may still be valid. There is a contractual obligation to do a job that may not be overlooked.

Many of the complicated factors that contribute to a drop in motivation can and should be met by the police supervisor. If there is something below the surface

°Skolnick, p. 50.

trying to escape, it may not be hard to get the man to talk. It must always be expected that the man with a problem is looking for the opportunity to communicate his troubles. Whether he is under assault by off-the-job or on-the-job difficulties, a willing ear may be the welcome medication in a time of trouble. What counts is that there may be some tangible cause for the loss of motivation that the supervisor might be able to cope with, and even correct, if he knows about it.

This is not to say that all the supervisor will have to do is engage in some soft talk to adjust a warped attitude or unreasoned fear. The problem may be long-standing, firmly embedded in causes outside his or the officer's control. Perhaps it is suited only to clinical solution. What matters is that the cause be clearly identified and isolated, and corrected if possible. If it is not adjustable, perhaps it can be worked around by the supervisor in an effort to restore motivation.

If the emotional trauma is caused by administration or management, the supervisor should avoid automatically postulating that the agency is right and the man wrong. He is under no compulsion of blind loyalty to try to convince the disgruntled one that his grievance is fancied. But the supervisor does have a responsibility to contribute towards the correction of weaknesses that are causing the dissatisfaction. If this can only be done by referring the matter to a superior, then he should take that course. If prevailing practice and policy are at the root of the deficiency, and he has reason to believe that going to management will be ineffective, perhaps enlisting the moral aid of other supervisors to pressure administration can be a start to attaining the needed adjustment.

However, there may be systemic deficiencies and voids which are by now too reinforced to be corrected through any supervisorial or even managerial action. Then the supervisor will have to work around the barriers in restoring motivation. It is entirely possible to have a motivated squad, even though there is imperfection in the platoon, company, battalion, regiment, or, perhaps, the whole army. The team is what is closest to the patrolman, and consequently most real for him. What counts most is at the team level. It is up to the team leader to exploit this team-centered perspective of the policeman.

First, one of the best and easiest forms of motivation is of primitive psychological origin, but it is of perennially practical validity. The supervisor who never misses the opportunity to acknowledge a man's accomplishment will soon get to know the magic power of a little recognition. Making the difficult arrest, locating a stolen automobile, or preparing a good report, are all occasions for a bit of commendation. Whenever this can be done within hearing distance of the group, or relayed for all to know, the supervisor should put himself out to complete the communication process. This gesture is not forced, nor should it be looked upon as an adult version of a "That's a good boy, now" artificial stimulus. It is an adult display of appreciation that will in turn be appreciated; one that promotes the efficiency of the team and makes the team leader's own job easier.

Allied to the consideration of praise is the question of whether a kind of box score is appropriate for fostering a spirit of competition. There is a motivating pride in having one's production compare favorably with that of his peers. However, individual police effort and accomplishment are not always adapted to comparative measure. The box-score technique of management prodding has led to undesirable practices, such as concealing an investigative lead from an associate, or the wholesale issuance of traffic tags for borderline violations. If they can be used gracefully, tables or charts showing the comparative output of the men may serve to spur them on to superior accomplishment.

There is a pride of ownership one enjoys through knowing that he is doing a job that has worth. If the supervisor makes his man aware that there is a real purpose for the assignment, that it has a concrete objective, and that all the difficulties and problems are well recognized, the motivation for accomplishing a task will be enhanced. Then allowing the patrolman to plan its fulfillment, to make his own decisions on follow-through, and giving him a chance to test the outcome is a good way to make him feel that it is his own personal job.

If there is a constant threat of censure for doing the wrong thing, the resulting fear will lead a man to choose to do nothing, rather than risk doing something. This discourages him from sticking his neck out and taking action. The supervisor can promote motivation by making it clear that initiative is what he wants, and that honest error in itself will not cause one to be taken to task.

The policeman has become the target of assault in this age of conflict and animosities. There is a growing disillusionment on the part of policemen occasioned by the danger and abuse he faces. It has become quite commonplace in the police ranks to bemoan the "public disrespect" and "lack of public support" that go with a restless world. This verbalization has a contagious effect, with a consequent negative impact on police motivation.

The veteran supervisor who has observed public attitudes over the years is in a good position to neutralize this new masochism. In his before-and-after perspective, he may suggest that there is more generalized respect and support for the police today than he ever knew in his earlier years on the job. The supervisor may propose that with few exceptions, the majority of citizens very much appreciate the police—one reason being that the populace is genuinely fearful of crime. There is a great deal of support for the local police, and this is not just a product of pleasing bumper stickers and sponsored billboards. The team leader should combat any blind tendency of the men to accuse the citizenry of letting them down. He may validly dispel negative feelings that affect motivation by positively stimulating a recognition that there is actually strong backing for the police today.

Probably the strongest motivating force in a police agency is in the peer-group bonds that are so strong between policemen. Study after study points to the solidarity in police ranks, to the spirit of near social isolation that predominates the vocation. Skolnick proposes that the cooperation among policemen is not so much a factor of administrative policy as a product of the teamwork that is valued so highly by policemen.° When asked what they liked most about police work, former officers told the researchers that the fellowship in police membership ranked high.°°

The supervisor should fully exploit this solidarity by making it a prominent

°Skolnick, p. 59.
°°Blum and Osterloh, p. 28.

motivational drive. It is for him to give significance to the natural ties that bind together the men. When a policeman is neglecting to shoulder his share of the load, the first-line supervisor can gently but persistently interpret the failure as letting the unit down. In turn, it even might be brought to the associates' attention that they are being overburdened by one man's neglect. When this failure of the part to participate in the whole is brought into focus, the isolation from group rapport can be a tremendous motivational force.

Finally, as a matter of tradition, leadership is described in terms of what followers would do for their leader. Thus, the man who is at the head of the group can rightfully be seen as the living embodiment of motivation. In the realm of police activity, it can mean that what the officer does in the way of a little bit extra can be thought of as a personal favor to his supervisor. The supervisor offers the best of direction; in return, those who are directed offer the best in performance. The best motivation is a good supervisor—a simple find at the end of a complex quest.

Helping the Officer Attend College

Higher education is no longer confined to the preemployed. Particularly since World War II, the young worker—and very frequently the older employee—has sought to advance in the field he had already chosen. His eye may be directed to outside opportunity or simply to the tremendous personal satisfaction that learning for its own sake can bring.

The Policeman Who Goes to School

The patrolman-student has become increasingly common because of the mushrooming of programs for police on a collegiate level. The 1966 President's Commission spelled out advanced education as an integral part of its formula of job requirements.°

To facilitate school attendance, there may be problems for the supervisor to resolve. The officer carrying a full program of college units still has to put in 8 hours on the police job each day. He has to make court appearances. He must be ready to fill emergency details. All the while college overcrowding makes it difficult to select the most favorable classroom hours. Consequently, duty shifts may have to be drastically rearranged.

In the interest of the men and the department, school attendance by police personnel must be given a high priority. Every commanding officer and each supervisor should encourage registration in college courses sincerely and enthusi-

°Task Force on the Police, The President's Commission on Law Enforcement and Administration of Justice, *Task Force Report: The Police* (Washington, D.C.: United States Government Printing Office, 1967), pp. 137ff.

astically. If satisfactory completion of a specified number of units is set as a condition of promotion, all the better. Also, there should be close liaison with colleges offering administration of justice, police science, criminology, or the like as a major.

There may be concern whether a policeman will remain with his department after getting a college degree. Is he using the police job merely to work himself through school while he aims for another career? A department must be reconciled to accelerated turnover of personnel. It should recognize particularly that there will be a continuing loss of college-trained police officers until the organization learns how to use education effectively. Perhaps police service should accept lateral transfer as an earmark of professionalism, and try to implement this professional notion. So the police supervisor need not pivot his attention on whether the man intends to stay in the ranks following graduation.

The Involvement of Supervision

What may have to be a matter of supervisorial awareness is the patrolman's interest in his police role during the school year. Will his patrol car be parked regularly in some quiet spot between calls, while he pours over his textbooks? Will he look for a couple hours of on-the-job slumber each midnight watch? In other words, does he intend to see his duty tour as of secondary importance while his full priority is given to his student career? In all fairness to the agency paying his salary, there have to be some controls to assure a fair return for its monetary output.

Thus a supervisor has the dual responsibility of making school attendance possible, while guaranteeing that the job will still be done. He should learn the man's academic objectives, the description of courses taken, and the classroom schedule. When he finds out what working hours will best suit the student's needs, everything possible should be done to arrange an accommodating shift. Here there may be a reluctance to interfere with traditional notions of working shifts. The standard has been to set up work tours in neat symmetrical packages, a practice not always condusive to operating efficiency. Restructuring time schedules for the advantage of the student may set a pace of flexibility which will be of more benefit to the department.

In exchange for this paternal accommodation of his officer's needs, the supervisor certainly has the right to look for continued satisfactory job performance. It is not anti-intellectual for the supervisor to pay careful attention to the man's work habits and output during the school year. If there are indications that the police job has been given lower priority by the patrolman in his dual pursuits, he should be quietly consulted on the deficiency.

The requirement for appearing in court may present a special difficulty for the policeman attending school. The supervisor should not be reluctant to confer with a prosecutor when any given incident of gross inconvenience confronts the officer. Subscription to an orderly program of court days for a member will largely resolve this difficulty.

Following Through on Education

The supervisor's involvement in the man's academic pursuits should not be merely one of administrative control. He should display constructive and constant interest in the student's aspirations and achievements. Occasionally asking about progress and grades may serve as motivating warmth. When the educational goal has been achieved, the supervisor should promote the best use of the service by the department that the graduate has to offer.

A supervisor with an advanced sense of values can do much to convey to administration what education should mean to the organization. Learning does not merely represent the acquisition of knowledge. The purpose of higher education is the development of a creative, inventive, dramatic perspective—one which every police organization badly needs. This may be the administrative key for becoming able to do an old job a new way, at a time when demands on the police are so great. The supervisor can serve as the man's agent in voicing an implied warning that if a department does not wish to buy what he has to offer, it may be expected he will vend his wares elsewhere.

SUMMARY

Growth of Police Learning. • Continuing education for the professions has become widespread. • In-house training given by the supervisor is not common in police practice. • Plans for in-service education too often omits determining specific needs.

Supervisor's Teaching Role. • A police supervisor's role incorporates true teaching responsibilities. • The men want to learn the best way to do their jobs. • An added motivation for police learning is the strong desire for advancement. • The traditional form of supervisory instruction is individually directed. • A supervisor has to schedule his time for the man who has learning needs. • New information is continuously needed by the men. • A supervisor's group instruction on an "as needed" basis is easy to plan.

Teaching Tools. • Case studies of what went wrong are the neglected area of police instruction. • It is easy to get access to visual aid equipment for teaching. • Trying to prepare written work too elaborately will prevent its completion. • A supervisor can develop a simple form of correspondence type instruction. • The blackboard is a highly effective visual aid.

Steps in Teaching. • The four steps of teaching are introduction, presentation, application, and test. • The four steps have not been substantially improved upon by time. • Introduction includes what is to be learned, its meaning, and its use. • Presentation should include demonstration, examples and inspiration. • Application calls for putting to work what has been learned. • Testing should be seen as a non-threatening learning experience. • Anyone should be able to teach who knows the subject matter and the four steps.

Methods of Teaching. • The lecture still has an effective place in teaching. • Entirely new material may be presented best by the lecture. • The conference method of instruction may be seen as a superior device. • The participation allowed by conference is appealing to the adult learner. • The discussion format is ideal for the small group, and so for the team. • Policemen like the practicality of the discussion method. • The supervisor most commonly uses a variation of the tutorial method. • The most important advantage of the tutorial is that it is self-pacing. • Using the tutorial method, the supervisor can enter a man's reference frame. • A supervisor should begin by teaching what is easy, then move to the difficult.

The Nature of Observation. • One usually sees what one wants to see, and hears what one wants to hear. • The policeman makes contact with his environment through sight and sound. • It is simple for a supervisor to demand that his men observe well. • Following an arrest, a policeman might tend to relax when he should observe. • One learns to see and to hear well through controlled seeing and hearing. • One may be psychologically attuned to a world of either seeing or hearing.

Improving Observation. • Habitually concentrating on people and things can sharpen observation. • Learning to call a citizen by name has strong community relations value. • A policeman should go out of his way to see, to hear, and to remember. • Good exercises in observation may be of the "dry run" variety. • A special mental compartment for the unusual should be developed. • Frequent recall will give longer life to stored images.

Observation Distortions. • Subjective preconceptions often give distorted form to mental images. • The person who is different may be invalidly seen as the potential lawbreaker. • A person's mannerisms may be misinterpreted through one's thought patterns. • The supervisor should warn against oversubscribing to stereotypes. • What is right in a person sould be looked for along with what is wrong.

Teaching Observation. • A practical exercise in classroom observation is the model and check list. • A patrol car provides an ideal classroom for instruction in observation. • The supervisor can drill his man in observation while with him on patrol. • The emergency handled can later be used as an exercise in observation. • The exercise in observation can first be disguised as casual conversation. • Being aware of the supervisor's drills may motivate the man to observe better.

Advice on Observation. • When a court case is expected, a supervisor should urge remembering details. • A policeman should be taught to compartmentalize remembered facts. • Listening to others will distort memories that are blurred through time. • A policeman should be warned of the likely embarrassment when memory fails. • Comprehensive notes should be made while facts are fresh in mind. • A man should be cautioned against perjuring himself when memory fails. • The supervisor may be thought of as laboratory instructor in observation. • The best instruction in observation is presenting oneself as model observer.

The Police Report. • Much report data are needed for efficient police work. • A report should tell clearly and accurately all that may have to be known. • A first-line supervisor must take the blame if data are recorded badly. • The supervisor should insist on relevancy rather than secrecy in reporting. • Each pertinent bit of information should be included in the report. • Overguarded reporting will lead to omitting important facts.

When to Report. • An exact formula for knowing when and when not to report cannot be drawn. • Ultimately it must be left to the discretion of the patrolman to decide when to make a report.

Simple Writing. • Poorly chosen words may not convey the intended thought. • Badly constructed phrases and clauses lead to confusion of ideas. • Sentences roughly strung together will not add up to a clear story. • Simple words get a story across more easily than ornate ones. • Pronouns are not used enough in police reporting. • Excessive use of the passive makes understanding more difficult. • The narrative report should be pivoted on the word "do."

The Report for Reading. • "Relax and write" should be the basic rule of report styling. • The purpose of the report is to tell something someone must know. • A word-picture can be a worthy substitute for the photograph. • A concise statement of what is to be reported must precede the details. • Facts should be strung out in clear one-two-three order. • Cardinal numbers may be freely used to label thoughts. • A man should be encouraged to make an outline before writing the report. • A simple outline will promote a logical presentation of thoughts. • The writer should indicate clearly what is factual, and what is uncertain. • It should be clear what has been done in the case, and what must be done. • If a person's words will tell something best, they should be quoted. • A good conclusion should make all significances and necessary future actions clear. • A formula for action should be laid down at the end.

Reporting Pitfalls. • A great many police reports contain inaccuracies. • A policeman's reporting errors emburden the clerks and investigators alike. • A supervisor should insist that facts be correctly stated. • All routine data should be accurate, regardless how immaterial they seem. • The writer should double-check the correctness of each detail.

Report Surveillance. • Sloppy police reports seldom may come to administrative attention. • The first-line supervisor is the initial checkpoint for inadequacies in report writing. • A supervisor should see himself as the reader who has a need to know. • Something is wrong if the report's meaning is not clear at the first reading. • If something is unclear, the report should be sent back for revision. • A patrolman should be held responsible for grammar and spelling. • The supervisor should direct the poor speller to engage in home study. • Improper punctuation is common in reports, and affects reader understanding. • The key to writing for comprehension is the proper grouping of thoughts. • The comma keeps thoughts in neat packets for absorption.

Dealing with Inadequacies. • The policeman may need instruction on paragraphing and punctuation. • Having to rewrite enough reports will prod a man to reporting better. • A supervisor may use a red pencil in reviewing poor reports. • Record room personnel know the facts on report deficiencies. • A supervisor will uncover poor reports through liaison with the record room. • Instruction and inspection should be used with the poor reporter. • The deficient report-writer's work should be singled out for scrutiny.

The New Motivation. • Early motivation lay in a reminder that the choice was work or be fired. • Now inner and outer drives are recognized as basic to motivation. • Today work output is seen as a factor of worker satisfaction. • Motivation exists on different levels for different persons. • What makes up good supervision is synonymous with good motivation.

Work Motivation. • A desire for security, esteem and self-realization in the group predominates. • The drives for security and position are not uniform in everyone. • Past experience and development play a role in shaping individual drives. • Man does not work only for purposes of survival. • Work plays a part in life which makes it inseparable from living itself. • A man is labelled by the kind of work he does.

Police Motivation. • Even off duty a policeman lives his police work in his thoughts. • A police officer feels possessive about his job environment. • The supervisor should nourish in his man a sense of participation. • There are many types of personality in every team. • Today in most places police salaries are good. • Superior job security is conferred on the policeman. • The typical police recruit is imbued with a strong sense of morality. • There is an attractive force found in the excitement of the chase. • Police work is attractive in being a life outdoors. • Police work embodies satisfaction in that people are more interesting than things. • The uniform and authority make police work particularly appealing.

Signs of Motivation Loss. • A supervisor has the duty of detecting a fall in motivational levels. • When a man is determined to go to another job a supervisor can do nothing. • Personal difficulties may be reflected in inferior job performance. • A fall in motivation may be found in a disillusionment with clientele. • There may be great disappointment in not having achieved advancement. • Weak motivation may be primary in causing motivation to decline.

Handling Motivation Loss. • A supervisor must find out the cause, reason, and remedy for motivation loss. • The supervisor need not in each case coddle the unmotivated. • It need not be ignored that there is a contractual obligation to do a job. • The unmotivated subject may be seeking the opportunity to talk. • The cause of motivation loss should be painstakingly isolated. • A supervisor should accept a man's dissatisfaction with the agency. • The supervisor may enlist the moral aid of his peers to fight agency defect. • A team may be well motivated despite the deficient larger body.

Promoting Motivation. • Giving recognition for worth and accomplishment is a motivational tool. • Individual effort and achievement are not always adapted to direct measure. • A box-score display of accomplishment has advantages and disadvantages. • When a job is looked on as important there is a pride of ownership. • Allowing the patrolman to plan and make decisions injects worth into the job. • A supervisor should remind the men that the public actually offers much support. • The peer group solidarity should be used as a motivational drive. • Leadership is determined by what the followers will do for the leader. • The best motivation is a good supervisor.

Difficulties Attending College. • A growing number of policemen are taking college courses. • Working hours may conflict with classroom hours for the officer. • A supervisor may have to resolve time conflicts for the policeman.

Encouraging Education. • A police officer should be urged to increase his education. • Liaison should be set up with colleges offering police courses. • A police agency must learn how to use education.

Facilitating Education. • The student's interest in his job should be of supervisorial concern. • The supervisor should learn the student's academic program. • Favorable working shifts for the student should be arranged. • Good job performance by the student should be demanded. ● Provision for suitable court days should be arranged. ● A super-visor should show interest in the man's educational aspirations.

The Agency's Benefit. ● The supervisor should encourage the agency to use education profitably. ● Command should be familiarized with the member's educational achieve-ment. ● A man's learning gives him a perspective that will benefit the agency.

SECTION II

CHAPTER 4

Discipline Dissected

If praise is directed at a first-line supervisor, the beneficiary of the men's admiration might be referred to as "one helluva boss!" Dual interpretations might be given to this. It could mean one of those masters of the fine art of personnel supervision—a superior who has the ability to run a tight but contented ship. This is the one who does not have to hold the threat of negative sanctions over the heads of his crewmen.

On the other hand, "one helluva boss" could refer to the less proficient, "anything goes" species of supervisor. He is the superior officer whose only positive stance is a loud and continuing proclamation that his man must be right—regardless! He'll stand behind the man—no matter what! All the while anything does go, to the ultimate ill fortune of organization and team alike.

How to Be a Well-loved Disciplinarian

Discipline is one of the qualities practiced and wielded by the successful police supervisor. Like so many other terms, "discipline" is construed as negative and punitive, confined usually to the formal pages of the rules manual.

But when something goes wrong, and the sergeant must explain why somebody committed the breach, discipline will be retrieved from its verbal storage place for emergency use. A "breakdown in discipline at the supervisory level" now may be solemnly charged. Then the full flavor of negativism compounds what has been understood as a traditionally negative word. Yet this charge of supervisory

Photograph courtesy of Berkeley, California, Police Department.

failure may not be without substance. The administrative crisis occasioned by the offense might have been averted if "discipline" had been used to mean something positive, acceptable, constructive, and rewarding for those who submit to its dictates.

Discipline for the Good of All

One of the first things to be learned by the newly-appointed police supervisor is that he is doing no favor to the team by filling an exaggerated, distorted, and misconceived role of perennial good guy. Discipline is not something that can be done without; it is the cement required to hold an organization together. The corner stop-and-go signals represent a form of traffic discipline that do not penalize the motorist who has to wait 60 seconds for the light to change. The half-time -congestion at the stadium refreshment stand makes the thirsty customer long for the orderly line he found at the ticket booth before the kickoff.

Police discipline is the essential means to assure order, efficient operations, equitable distribution of work load, and cooperative effort. It is the defensive mechanism to ward off dishonor and scandal that will have to be shared by the composite membership when it occurs. Without the restraining force of discipline there will be unfairness, confusion, and lack of teamwork which is destructive to initiative, morale, and the personal satisfaction of everyone. The regulatory controls of discipline are all the more needed in an enterprise where individual effort is not subject to real measurement. Police work is typical of this kind of activity where true output is not measurable.

Thus when the field sergeant ignores the suspiciously long out-of-service intervals of the member who has a reputation for not sharing the load, he is far from being the "good boss." Here the supervisor is tolerating a clear injustice to the patrol car operator who is trying to do a job. When the same permissive supervisor escapes into the out-of-sight shelter of a sidestreet when the team drunk staggers in his direction, he is doing no favor to the other men who are consistently jeopardized by their tippling associate. This means the desire to be a good fellow results in being a bad supervisor—one who penalizes the group through a failure to challenge the shortcomings of the individual.

Rules That Are Bad

Traditional police rules may often be faulty. For example, a paragraph may prescribe authority with empty qualifiers, as when each paragraph spelling out delegation ends with an emasculating "pursuant to approval of the Chief." Regulations may be years out-of-date, as the item directing that an arrested streetcar motorman be accompanied to the barn, saying nothing about the buses that long ago replaced traction. Or a rule may be unintelligently worded, as that which directs that the officer in charge of department vehicles "be notified immediately when any defect in motorized equipment is encountered." (Imagine the ingratitude of this specialist at being awakened an hour or two before sunrise to learn about a flat tire that has been changed!)

Frequently authored by scientifically uninspired police management, rules may be clumsy, vague and contradictory. They may better represent a technical catchall for defining the nondescript breach of the policeman, rather than concise formulae of proper conduct. Consequently, it is not unusual to hear conferring superiors ponder over the questionable act of a subordinate with a probing, "Now isn't there an order about that somewhere? Wasn't there an order one time? Well, I know there's a rule somewhere!" Thus police regulations should not be just negative tools to suit the technical needs of legalistic control over personnel. They should be instruments of constructive, positive, productive discipline.

Even if the rules are relatively well constructed, they still may lack built-in flexibility which would make them more applicable to the infinite variety of police field experiences. Their rigid legalism is not always suited to the demands of the situation a patrolman actually encounters on the streets. There, circumstances may force him to engage in a purposeful violation just to get the job done. No matter how necessary the departure from a particular regulation, an ill-conceived rule will force the policeman in the field to act unjustifiably at his own peril when there is no authorization for exception.

Rules were subject to little challenge in the past. However, recent studies have indicated instances of strong reservations on the value of the regulatory codes.

Thus, in his comprehensive study of police cynicism, Niederhoffer's questionnaire answered by a sample research group revealed: "Less than 10 percent of the patrolmen believe[d] that the rules are fair and sensible."° McNamara's sample heavily indicated "that efficient police work cannot be accomplished by adhering to the letter of the Rules and Procedures."†

In other words, the supervisor may be faced with the dilemma of having to enforce rules that are not completely enforceable. His is a compound jeopardy of having to observe rules himself, and having to demand others observe rules that are actually unsuited to the requirements of dynamic and imaginative supervision. In view of the need for flexibility in applying standards of police practice, this kind of absolute and total compliance will be impossible to demand.°° However, when a man commits an infraction of which disciplinary notice must be taken, all attendant infractions, no matter how technical and irrelevant in substance, will be taken into account. Then not only the violating patrolman will be held responsible, but the sergeant who failed to prevent the secondary violations will also be held to account.

Consequently, department administration should be prodded into spelling out the regulatory enforcement latitude for supervisors, providing for departures from strict compliance. If it fails to do this, the first-line supervisors should propose a definition of policy on enforcing individual rules. Or the supervisors may prepare model revisions for the department executive's ready adoption. Then, even if final administrative action is not realized, management will have been put on notice that existing regulatory provisions are inadequate. Thus, a later unjustifiable move to hold a sergeant liable for less than full enforcement of a rule or a patrolman at fault for incomplete compliance, will be avoided.

The Continuing Attitude of Discipline

The preoccupation with disciplinary rules, a product of the legalistic orientation of police, may make disciplinary control less than efficient. The exercise of discipline should be seen as more than a ready stance to pounce on subordinates who have erred. The function of discipline should extend beyond the rigid demand for compliance with a code. The common failure to appreciate the significance of discipline may cause the supervisor to leave unchallenged the questionable act or attitude of a patrolman merely because he cannot perceive how it relates to the substance of a formalized rule.

The supervisor should think of discipline as a total attitude he continuously conveys, rather than as his manner of meeting a particular situation. He must understand that he can be a disciplinarian without issuing an order, conveying

°Niederhoffer, *Behind the Shield*, p. 218.

†John H. McNamara, "Uncertainties in Police Work: The Relevance of Police Recruits' Background and Training," in *The Police: Six Sociological Essays*, ed. David J. Bordua (New York: Wiley, 1967), p. 241

°° *Ibid.*, p. 185

a warning, or imposing a reprimand. Discipline is expected by the patrolman. It makes his job safer, easier, more efficient, and self-satisfying.

When the supervisor gives an order for a patrolman to perform a particular task, it should first be determined whether the specific job can and should be done at all. What the supervisor is demanding of his patrolman should be understood clearly. It must be made plain what the detail requires and just how much in the way of accomplishment is expected of the policeman.

The superior's follow-up should not be that lurking, "ah, ha, I gottcha!" type of supervision that implies expectation of the patrolman's breach. Instead it should be undertaken in a way indicating genuine help to the man. The attitude of the supervisor should be one that shows the task jointly as his own *and* his subordinate's. If the policeman fails, so does his supervisor. Instilling this awareness of a supervisor-patrolman joint enterprise represents positive discipline in its purest form.

The Dignity of Discipline

The formal type of military separation between supervisor and subordinate, and between manager and supervisor, does not really exist in the police field. There are no official social barriers imposed between personnel. All supervisors were once patrolmen. First-line supervisors may continue on a first-name relationship with the men after promotion. The traditional close familiarity means there is no protective mask to screen the personal weaknesses of superiors from the view of subordinates.

A realization of the ordinarily deficient selection processes involved in civil service promotions may make the patrolman doubt the competence of his supervisor. He may remember him as the patrolman who never missed an opportunity on the job to hide away with his books to prepare for the examination. He may see him as one whose rote technical book-learning is not matched by the personal qualities needed for effective supervision and command. A patrolman's memory does not have to be too long to recall a superior's less than exemplary conduct when he wore a patrolman's uniform.

Reflecting on his own blurred, if not tarnished, hierarchical rise, the police supervisor may be uncertain as to just how much dignity he should project. How far can he clown with his subordinates before the prestige of his rank becomes diminished? Will condoning the common use of his given name or nickname undermine his authority? Will permitting himself to be seen in too informal a light affect his disciplinary stance?

The supervisor should establish a standard of dignity by setting up expectations of respect without demanding it in words. As an example, when mentioning to his patrolman another supervisor or command officer, he should use the formal title. Also, while humor has a perfectly good use in all communication, the supervisor should not carry it to extremes. As to squad room horseplay, he should keep out of it altogether.

The supervisor may not be free to set his own whimsical standard of dignity. Rank is something that is both identified with organization, and flows from organization. It exists independent of the individual. A man's own contribution to lowering the status of rank adversely affects the organizational concept, and this is beyond his right. If one supervisor permits a breakdown in respect for himself, it potentially extends to a loss in dignity for all supervisors. Thus he has an obligation to maintain dignity at an appropriate level, and can do so without ever voicing a specific demand, or without singling out the subordinate's individual act or attitude for correction.

The Degree of Control to Be Exerted

While the supervisor may instill in the patrolman a feeling that he is there to share responsibility, it does not mean that the subordinate must be led around by the hand. Good supervisory practice does not include covering every police call to check on the way the assignment is handled; or to ask repeated questions on whether there was compliance with orders; or to demand an accounting for each duty hour spent in the field. This hounding will stifle initiative by making the policeman dependent on direction for everything he does. The subordinate will become so preoccupied with the possibility of error that he will be afraid to make a decision. He will lose confidence in himself because no confidence is being bestowed.

Accordingly, the sergeant should apply the guiding principle of minimizing his verbalization of control. The supervisor should observe the process in which the patrolman is engaged without interjecting himself into it. His questions on accomplishment of assignment should be blended into the context of a discussion, rather than being pointedly asked. What he expects should be so well known from his attitude that he only infrequently should have to formulate specific demands.

As an example, when he covers the radioed assignment where the patrolman has the situation in good control, he should assume the stance of a bystander. If a citizen, attracted to his rank, directs a comment or question to him, if possible it should be redirected to the officer assigned to the incident. Similarly, when he visits the man on fixed-post assignment, his nondescript "What's doing?" can elicit as much information on task performance as clear-cut queries. If in either case a question on how to handle a situation is asked by the patrolman, he should attempt to guide the man into formulating his own answer.

The patrolman should not be forced to do his work dogged by his supervisor. He must not be made dependent on prompting and guidance in every one of his actions, decisions, and judgments. Consequently, the first-line supervisor should perceive his basic role as one of discreetly observing, inconspicuously prodding, and quietly reviewing the patrolman's work. His necessary inspection for rule compliance should consist of random spot checks, rather than a through-the-keyhole variety of observation. It will be his nonphysical, constructive presence at the duty scene, coupled with his implied assertion that he will share both the success and failure of performance, that will legitimize his desciplinary demands.

Doing as I Say and Do

A tendency to mimic is universal in normal personality expression. Whether we give it the technical designation of "ego ideal," or the more commonplace tag of "hero worship," consciously or unconsciously one selects a model for himself. Watch the way a baby mimics its mother's laugh while she chats on the telephone. Similarly, every police veteran has found the recruit noticeably adopting the attitudes of his admired senior partner.

In police supervision the instrumentality of words may be exaggerated to the point of not perceiving the power of communicated demeanor and habit. The sergeant will order; the sergeant will instruct; the sergeant will counsel. All the while it may be overlooked that the most dynamic message of supervision is example. In his enthusiasm over new jobs and associates, the young patrolman in particular will adopt models from among those who make up his world of work. The first-line supervisor, the superior with whom he has continuous contact, will symbolize for him the entire command structure. If the supervisor proves himself worthy of this ideal role, the subordinate's tendency to imitate him will be extraordinarily strong.

Consequently, the supervisor's craftsmanship should include a planned effort to take advantage of the imitative propensities of the men. The superior's neatness, his precision, his competence will be consciously or unconsciously copied by his subordinates. The way he holds himself and the way he acts will be adopted by his team as norms of bearing and conduct. If he looks for compliance, his own compliance will communicate the order; in fact, it will create an inspiration to comply. If he calls for discipline, the demand will be reflected in his own discipline of self.

How to Inspect and Follow-up

The notions of spying, eavesdropping, and keyhole peering carry a traditional cultural condemnation in our society. Unfortunately, however, the natural feelings against what is considered violative of fair play may be extended unreasonably. Thus a supervisor may feel that it is wrong to inject his probing nose into the finished work of the patrolman. The superior may distortedly think of inspection as a kind of punitive function that will incur the disapproval of his team. Likewise, he may look on the follow-up exercise as a display of distrust for the patrolmen he has never ceased regarding as his peers.

Inspection and follow-up are not forms of internally directed espionage. They are not punitive, nor are they threatening. They are control devices and necessary administrative tools just as legitimate as any other form of supervision. More importantly, they are designed to work to the full benefit of the men to whom they are directed. This is why the supervisor must see them in a very positive perspective.

An Introspection into Inspection

Opening a gift is always accompanied by anticipation. If it contains clothing, will it fit? If it is mechanical, will it work? There is invariably a bit of reassurance when one finds a little tag inscribed, "Inspected by——." This means that someone has checked on somebody's double check, and it infers the promise of satisfaction.

In the service fields, inspection may be a little less likely. In fact, it is more difficult to evaluate personal enterprise than material production. Besides, some friction may be expected to pervade the relationship between the inspector and the inspected. Consequently, one is less likely to find the supervisor peering over the shoulder of the service worker, listening in on his telephone calls, or watching him relate to the customers.

Police inspection is a neglected area of administrative endeavor. An inspector general of military counterpart has been slow to be adopted by police agencies. Nor has real inspection by line supervisors been a traditional function in law enforcement. Sergeants' visitations to the men have often been set according to a fixed schedule. ("I'll see you at 2:00 AM at the park ring-in box, Joe.") Verifying checks of activity reports relating to assigned investigations have been rare. And it has been unheard of to ask clients for their reaction to the service received when they requested police service.

In order to supervise well, there must be a confirming check on the action of the men. There has to be a follow-up on the work assigned. To inspect does not imply a suspicion of widespread goofing off, or scandalous boondoggling. To follow-up does not infer one necessarily suspects neglect of duty or disregard of responsibility.

What is implied by inspection and follow-up is that good order demands the personal stimulus inherent in evaluation and review. Effort is spurred by demands for quality. In other words, one is bound to put more into a task which he knows will be subject to examination. In fact, the man who is trying to produce will actually *want* his work to be subjected to inspection. Similarly, he will consider it in the interest of fairness to have the deficiency of his less enterprising associate uncovered, since an added burden will be placed on him through his confrere's neglect.

But inspection and follow-up are not functions that have to be legitimized by apologizing for their impact on police personnel. More important is that there also is a tax-paying public to consider. If the people are footing the bill for policing their cities and counties, they are entitled to get a dollar's value for a dollar spent. Inspection is a mechanism for determining that this balance of input and output is being achieved. Follow-up is a device for ascertaining that the man is putting out the effort that productive operations demand.

Thus inspection and follow-up should be seen as positive instruments indispensable to achieving positive ends. They are not mere threatening expressions of negative discipline. They are supervisory processes that provide necessary quality control in police operations. They are functions of supervision that will actually make tasks easier and more rewarding for the men doing the work.

The Objects of Inspection

The traditional police supervisory inspection of bygone days may have been directed simply to the question of whether there was a body on the job. This being determined, the next primary concern was whether that body was alive and kicking—soberly, of course. A sergeant checked whether the patrolman was on his beat, and then relaxed. Finding a man on the assignment fulfilled the supervisorial inspection function, and the supervisor then went on his way in complete satisfaction.

Only recently has the question of how the police job is being performed become a matter of concern. With new administrative perspectives in police endeavor has come a realization that more is important than the mere assurance a patrolman is on patrol at a given place and time. A responsibility has been assumed to guarantee that the individual policeman's effort is efficiently geared to the total enterprise of the group.

One of the primary objects of inspection is that a task is being performed within a proper block of time. This refers primarily to the response and processing factors of the called-for service. An opportunity to "goof off" is always available to the patrolman sent to handle the incident or take a report. For instance, a minor complaint may be inordinately time consuming, while a more serious occurrence may call for considerably less of the patrolman's time. Without inspection, only the policeman himself will know the actual time demands of the incident.

Of course, there are the out-of-service and return-to-service notations in the log. While the out time is accurately set, the return is obviously left to the option of the officer who responded to the call. Sometimes there may be a temptation to delay returning to service, particularly if the end of a shift is nearby. Perhaps the patrolman feels that he is forced to perform an excessive workload because of his gold-bricking associates. Besides, there is always an advantage in remaining out of service until a choice call is heard. Then he will blurt out an "I'm available for that one" when the hot assignment is being given to another unit.

The thoroughness of complaint processing deserves inspection. Will the occurrence call for report and follow-up, or will it be satisfied by a "no merit" or "party advised" logged catchall? Has the dispute really been adjudicated, and has a disturbance been returned to a real condition of equilibrium that will last? And was the minor complaint actually abated, or was the case abruptly closed by a careless or work-evading "unable to locate" or "civil matter advised" log entry?

If a report has been prepared by the policeman, how adequate is it? Are names inserted accurately? Are spellings correct? Are spaces filled properly? Does the narrative portion tell concisely what is involved? Is there a clear indication of how much follow-up must be accomplished? Will the girls in the office be able to key names, modus operandi, and other factors from its content? Simply, is it a good report?

Then there is the question of whether an ongoing job is being performed. Is the patrol exercised between calls structured and constructive? When a policeman is seen with his car parked beneath a tree, is it for reasons of task performance, or is the purpose a shady one? And does the theater visit while on foot patrol carry a truly official objective, or is the current feature just too good to miss?

Perhaps the most neglected object of inspection is the way the public is being handled. Is the manner of dealing with a complainant courteous and pleasant? Does the patrolman instill confidence that the processing of a complaint will be adequate? Is the policeman able to keep his cool when the citizen is on the borderline of nastiness? Does the patrolman communicate effectively with the excited client?

As a summary concern, the supervisor should be looking at the personal attributes of his team member. How is his appearance? Does he give the semblance of efficiency, or is his bearing sloppy and listless? Is his manner one of poise and composure? Is his personality characterized by smiling ease, or by scowling irritibility?

All of this may convey a mistaken notion that the basic object of inspection is to uncover what is negative. Not so! Weakness and error should be sought out by inspection, of course. But what is right and proper about the policeman are equally within the focus of the inspecting supervisor. From inspection there is just as much confirmation that things are going well as there is a realization that things are going badly. From inspection there arises the same amount of cause to commend the officer as there is to prod him on to better accomplishment.

Making the Spot Check

Observation has to be accomplished by a sampling process. A little of this is isolated for study, and a little of that segregated for analysis. Thus, by sampling, we rely upon the rules of statistical probability to project a conjectured whole from the part. Consequently, the spot check is the device used to examine the activity of the worker.

The spot check should not be carried on with a cloak-and-dagger semblance of intrigue. The supervisor should let the men know what inspection implies, either through explanation, or by letting his own process of observing be observed. The team should understand that its activities are subject to examination as an ongoing function of supervision. The policemen should see inspection as a positive process, implying benefit for both organization and public, and for the men themselves.

Spot checking is something more than a random acitivity. To be effective it should be structured. Otherwise it is likely to be unbalanced and directed towards an unrepresentative segment of personnel. Consequently, inspection should be carefully planned; checklists should be designed; and a time schedule of inspectional activities should be prepared.

The checks should be directed to both field work and paper work. In the office, logs and incident summaries should be read on a regular basis. The individual patrolman's calls should periodically be subjected to analysis. The number and kinds of complaints he has handled, along with any pattern of disposing of a particular variety of incidents will be indicative of his activity during any given period. These activities may be compared with the work of other patrolmen. Then any variance with group workload or disposition will probably suggest an individual's performance is wanting.

As referred to above, most important is the study of the time spent handling calls. While in themselves out-of-service and return-to-service record listings may not carry built-in significances, they may provide the basis for determining either the wasting of time or not giving enough time to processing complaints. A spot check which includes a sample of comparable calls handled by another may reveal the complaint processing efficiency of an individual officer.

Examination of offense and service reports is relatively easy. Better than picking out a single specimen at random for consideration is periodically to take a sample collection of one man's reports for study. Boxes on the report forms should be checked for proper entries. Narratives should be read for ascertaining clarity or confusion. Particularly difficult names may be checked against telephone or public directories for correct spelling. This is the best way of finding out whether sloppiness in name-handling may be making life miserable for records bureau personnel. Of course, if there is a supervisor in that specialty unit charged with the responsibility of report processing, he should be able to point readily to members whose paper work is inadequate.

Personally responding to a man's calls as cover should be widely practiced by the supervisor. While giving the semblance of random selection, a team leader actually should plan his backup response. The better practice is to spread this kind of inspection over a single watch. However, if one man appears to need a bit more supervision than another, the attention afforded to each unit need not be equal. Neither does inspection have to be visual. Talking over the situations after they have been handled will serve as a function of learning for the patrolman as well as inspection for the supervisor.

In finding out how a man relates to his public, the supervisor may use a device rapidly becoming common in business. He may go directly to the client who has recently asked for police service. It is a simple matter to ring the doorbell of a person who lately has submitted a report, or otherwise has asked for assistance. Making a smiling inquiry on whether the customer was satisfied with the attention he has received will not normally open a can of worms. If minimal time has elapsed since the event, there still will be enough emotional impact to make the account the supervisor receives factual. And besides getting a profile of a team member in action, this bit of inspection will carry a public relations import that private enterprise exploits eagerly. This improvised form of a public opinion poll should be somewhat structured. In addition to obtaining an idea of the demeanor and attitude displayed by the patrolman, this follow-up visit will contribute to revealing the thoroughness of effort as compared with the filed report.

All in all, spot checking a man need not be evenly distributed. Inspection has to be planned according to actual need. It has to be directed to individuals in proportion to the inspection they require. It should be focused mainly on particular group weaknesses that have already come to the supervisor's attention; for example, the quality of reports. Most of all, the spot check should be directed to accomplishing a particular goal. And finally, the results of inspection should be put to use.

Following-up the Follow-up

Calls for police services do not comprise a mere strung-out line of completed tasks. While the large majority of calls and incidents are handled promptly and then relegated to record cards, many require additional action. Routine assignments too, such as the service of warrants, obviously call for follow-up.

In an age of unlimited demands and very limited time to meet them, neglect of duty is not always based on unwillingness. Procrastination and simple memory lapse may be responsible for a want of follow-through. Police jobs that extend in complexity from a check of a vacation house to seeking out a murder suspect require much routine effort of an officer that may be neglected in the face of job overloads.

Consequently, the supervisor should keep a running account of what has still to be accomplished. He has to give priority to the greater needs, and deemphasize the lesser. He has to ascertain that there is proper investigation of an assignment. He has the responsibility of seeing that the job is done and he must assume the responsibility for failure if there is in fact a failure in performance.

Thus the supervisor should structure his routine follow-up exercise. If a warrant is tendered for service, there should be a check made within a day or two if no activity report has been submitted. On the other hand, it may be more difficult to follow up on vacation house checks. Even the notation "premises visited" may not imply proof that a harried patrolman actually checked the vacant cottage. While certainly impractical to park at the residence and wait for a patrolman's visit, studying the physical premises and discussing them with the beat man may demonstrate an embarrassing lack of familiarity on the part of the negligent policeman.

Paper work always makes follow-up easier for the supervisor. The report that calls for continued attention to a complaint, or for the arrest of a suspect in the criminal occurrence, usually makes the progress check possible even while the sergeant remains at his desk. Then, too, repeated incidents may serve as indicators of deficient attention. Or the absence of a clearance report will amount to a file flag announcing that the case is still open.

The follow-up workload of the inspecting supervisor will be no lighter than the operational workload of the inspected patrolman. Thus the team leader will not be able to give full attention to all follow-up needs. Priorities will have to be assigned, and after this, spot checking of what has been given priority will be required. Recognizing that only so much can be carried in the head, tools for remembering will be essential. Therefore, the supervisor should periodically make a list which includes every incident requiring follow-up. This list should contain cross references to complaint records. Items will have to be checked off and crossed off as cases are closed, as cases call for the inactive tag, and as the workload simply becomes too great. What is equally important, notations should be made on what follow-up processes disclose. If deficiency on the part of an individual comes to light, then there should be what amounts to a follow-up on the follow-up. The supervisor has the task of determining that the job is being done. Consequently, his own failure to correct any deficiencies revealed amounts to a failure to follow-up on himself.

This illustrates an anticipated weakness in inspection and follow-up processes—the findings are not put to use. Unless the results of inspection are used constructively, unless the product of follow-up is converted into a force to get the job completed well, then the time spent in inspecting and following-up will be wasted. When correction has to be made, correction should be demanded. When a bit more effort is needed, effort should be elicited. The supervisor must let it be known that inspection will be an ongoing function of his office, and that there will be follow-through on this inspection. He has to make it clear that inspection is not just an initial step in the programmed harassment of his men, but that harassment there will be if this is the needed prod for improving habits or methods. Inspectional results may have to be passed upwards, as well as downwards—and even sideways. And all the while, a supervisor's own inspection and follow-up may reveal that basic deficiency is not outside himself. It may be an offshoot of the way he is doing his own job of supervising. If there is to be adequate follow-up on follow-up, the team leader's inspectional attentions may have to be pointed inward.

How Far to Insist on Appearance and Presence

Stated simply, appearance is what a person sees first at the time of making contact with a police officer. It means the grooming and attire, the cleanliness and neatness that the policeman projects. Along with the passive element of appearance is the active one of presence; that instantaneously conveyed totality of a patrolman's demeanor and attitude. While the rule book may be able to dictate the norms of appearance and presence only in vague terms, the supervisor can have exacting notions on how much of each is to be demanded.

What May Not Be So Picayune

The life of a policeman calls for a gradation of value in his many kinds of tasks. Thus the bank robbery rightfully ranks higher in priority than the domestic dispute. This sense of differentiation may extend to excluding from attention small matters of appearance. Little things add up. The trivial expression of careless attitude can forbode the important occurrence of a careless act—or, what is worse, an act that is simply bad. The supervisor may fail to see that an inadequate self-image in his man may be surfacing in the form of inadequate appearance and presence. If the superior neglects to consider the public's interest in the grooming and bearing of its police officers, at least he should be aware of the impact a sloppy looking and carelessly dressed patrolman can have on a fellow officer who does shave and polish his shoes.

There is nothing petty about the supervisor who is interested in the way his men look, and carry themselves. The haircut and the nicely starched shirt collar both contribute to the working environment which relates to the organization's effectiveness and the individual's satisfaction. The supervisor must realize that the little items of dress, grooming, and bearing make up a language of their own. The vocabulary they have created is one of good order.

The patrolman's snappy salute when his sergeant appears may be developing into a museum piece in many organizations. An old-time superior officer would cringe to see a cigarette dangling from a policeman's lips as a supervisor or a citizen addresses him. The little signs of respect and courtesy which were once prevalent have been relegated to unimportance in some police agencies.

While no one suggests that a policeman should adopt the stiffness of a palace guard, there still is room for bearing of the kind traditional in the Armed Forces. A prominent reason for identification with the military lies in the law enforcement agency's readiness for immediate emergency group-action, accomplished with command precision. The required potential for instant organized movement makes the levels of military-type authority necessary. It calls for an atmosphere of readied obedience in anticipation of emergency. This military trademark particularly takes the form of appearance and presence among personnel.

While not continuously looking for personal defects, it will not be out of place for a supervisor to require at least a modified military bearing of the team. If a patrolman is standing, he should do so without the support of the curbstone light standard. If he is riding, he should sit upright and alert. If he is talking, speech should not be impeded by a wad of gum. If he is walking, the gait should be deliberate and purposeful.

The examples of bearing that have been cited should not be looked upon as merely imitative of a soldier. The supervisor who calls for them need not see himself as a kind of poor man's Wehrmacht Offizier. He is demanding a form of communication which is universal in meaning, and which still fits into good supervisory practice.

Personal Grooming That Matters

Accepting the policeman as a professional person does not rule out that police supervision should include a daily check for beard stubble, a crooked tie, and perspiration odor. It should be remembered that the intern who reports to surgery with dirty fingernails; the lawyer who enters his firm's office well-overdue for a haircut; and the engineer who carries a few calories of last week's lunch on his tie; will rapidly be called to account by their supervisor.

A police supervisor has the right—in fact, a professional duty because of the military flavor of his work—to make a continuous survey of his team's appearance. The traditional way of starting a duty tour used to be to fall in, and then to open ranks. The military formality may have been an empty one, but at least the idea of inspection was there. Whether or not today's supervisor sends his team into the streets with this ceremony, he cannot be accused of subjecting his men to an unprofessional indignity by checking the unit first as to whether they are presentable enough for public contact.

His inconspicuous, unvoiced inspection can still be thorough and systematic. It should start at the top of a man's head and work downwards, each momentary pause of the eyes used to focus on something in particular. Whether the cap is straight and its visor polished can be determined at one time, as well as the amount of excessive growth of hair at the back of the neck. It may be difficult to determine standard sideburn length, or what should be a conventional hairstyle. Perhaps department regulations should include a formula for tonsorial grooming. Wanting this, the supervisor's judgement should be centered around the long-standing conservative norm. There must be no reluctance to suggest a haircut, when, in his opinion, a haircut is needed.

As for the shave, the evidence should be clear that a razor had been used this particular duty day. If the man explains away the excess stubble with an account of how he accidentally broke his shaving mirror, it might be suggested that his memory for faces could have been called upon to get the job done. The chore should have been well enough performed to get all those little clusters of beard hair, which are liable to be distracting to the client making field contact.

Facial qualities can carry long-range inspectional import. It is not for the supervisor to tell the homely one that a face like his should be thrown away, and the cap worn on the neck. But it will be proper to make reference to the ugly gap left by a pair of adjacent teeth which could be filled by a partial denture. Also, in an age when the advertising media have done so much to educate the world on the evils of bad breath, it will be both understood and appreciated when the supervisor does tell the unsuspecting outcast.

Only minor eye shifts will be needed to scan both the shirt collar for fray, and a necktie for morning yolk. Shirts that show neckline grime and ties that are noticeably faded should not be worn. Meanwhile, the offensiveness of underarm odor is by no means exaggerated by the television commercials. In a day when deodorants are about all that can promise complete protection, their use may be confidently proposed by the supervisor. The aging policeman in particular may be an offender in this regard, and the defect, if present, usually is combined with increasing signs of other kinds of sloppiness. But earlier retirements are probably making problems associated with senility less common in supervision.

Hands are bound to come into focus during the course of a contact, and can serve to attract or repel the confidence of the citizen decisively. While a professional manicure is not to be a personnel requirement, keeping the nails clean and trimmed is not an unrealistic demand. Ugly yellow nicotine stains on the fingers appear to be a less common adornment now, but if there is this kind of discoloration the supervisor's comment will be in order.

Although a police agency boasts that its admission requirements are directed to top physical fitness, the department may continue to be rather unconcerned about what happens to its recruit after he completes his probation. As a related matter of long-range supervisorial concern, the man's figure most certainly should come into review. When it begins to be realized that according to the height-weight charts he should be 19 feet tall, it will be proper that his unattractive corpulence be brought to official attention. The supervisor should direct the rotund member's concern to his unbecoming figure, suggesting that medical advice be sought.

The Uniform Does Make the Man

A uniform may be identified with the policeman more than the wearer realizes. When the friendly watchdog licks the hand of the burglar, but then bites the leg of the officer investigating the burglary, he is giving vivid testimony to the symbolism official garb implies. A uniform makes the man stand apart, and it represents society's act of conferring authority on him. Clothes make a man, and so does the police uniform.

While cap visor or protective helmet should shine, uniform cloth should not. Trouser seats cannot be replaced, and when high polish appears in this area, it means that a new pair of pants should be acquired. Trouser cuffs may be trimmed if they become frayed, but there is a point where this operation can no longer be effectively performed. Blouse and coat may last a little longer, but neither do they have the quality of permanence. Leather jackets may take on a particularly sloppy appearance when wear and fading begin to predominate.

The supervisor's parental concern may cause him to take his man's anticipated financial outlay for job clothing into consideration. Perhaps his takehome pay is not the highest; there are hungry mouths to feed; how he meets those high monthly house payments will never be known! While a sympathetic interest in the man's domestic struggles is in keeping with good supervisory practice, departmental priority for nurturing a presentable looking force cannot be obscured. The supervisorial energy spent in sterile sympathy might be better devoted to helping the man balance his budget, if he appears deficient in this economic aptitude. If the department makes a uniform allowance, which is now increasingly customary, this particular kind of financial problem largely vanishes.

Finally, shoes are a particular focus of attention while making any personal contact. If heels get worn down, this noticeable defect in dress will detract from total appearance drastically. Also, it takes but a moment to buff shoe leather before the duty tour, and the polish which may have to be applied is not expensive. Shoes themselves are by no means cheap, but except in some remote equatorial locales, it appears that they will continue to have to be worn by on-duty police officers.

The supervisor should not feel ill at ease in calling the team member's attention to something wrong in his appearance. He might use his regular conferences and conversations to let it be well understood what he requires in the way of good grooming. There should be widespread knowledge that inspection will be continuous. When a deficiency is detected, the immediate filing of disciplinary charges does not have to be undertaken. Reference to an undesirable condition can be made tactfully, nicely, even humorously—at least in the first instance. If there is a persistent sloppiness, and the unkempt look becomes chronic, a supervisor's tact and humor may have to be tempered to meet the situation more forcefully.

Assuring the Integrity of the Team

The subject of corruption need not be banned from discussions of police administration. Today's policeman has no responsibility to conceal the wrongs of his vocational forefathers. He is under no compulsion to deny that bribery may have been an accepted part of a system in certain places at one time. But the topic need not be relegated to ancient police-history. In some places, the police may still be invoking extralegal licensing processes and petty shakedowns that became largely extinct long ago. If there are still the makings of a corrupt system in a given locale, condoned by political bosses and their appointees at the top of a police administrative structure, then the first-line supervisor might as well recognize the difficulty of insisting that there be total integrity in the ranks. But if the town is "clean," the working responsibility for keeping it that way lies with the patrol supervisor.

Why Corruption Disappeared

The disappearance of traditional corruption from the local establishment where it had flourished may not have been due solely to a dramatic change in human nature. The transformation was probably accomplished primarily by a combination of both governmental and public enlightenment. Federal internal revenue statutes played their part as well. There was a growing concern with administrative efficiency, demanded by the taxpayer who had become aware that he was entitled to a dollar's return for his tax dollar. Police salaries had become better too, removing what may have been considered a need to supplement the income of underpaid officers.

There was also a newly exercised centralization of government, featuring a growing boldness to carry agency authority into local areas of enforcement. With World War II looming, the federal government insisted that prostitution be abolished within set distances of military installations. State attorney generals moved into territories of local jurisdiction with unprecedented vigor, and closed up "open" towns. Simultaneously, the new concepts of outside intervention and control were accompanied by an upswing in the professional and ethical standards of local law enforcement.

It may be assumed that today, in most places, the demand for integrity among police ranks can be voiced without administrative hypocrisy. A supervisor is able to warn his team against being on the take without having to be eyed with an accusatory "Who's that big thief trying to kid?" look from the patrolmen. The supervisor is now able to rely on the support of command when he stands up to the infrequent symptoms of greed and corruption in police ranks.

Detecting Corruption

Greed has a symptomatology that impresses the onlooker in different ways. We are amused at the demise of the ragpicking recluse who after his death is found to have concealed a quarter of a million dollars in his mattress. We are less entertained by the fellow whose fascination for horses leads him to complain that his wife squandered all his paycheck on rent, groceries and clothes for the kids. Greed, whether practical or pathological, is the stuff from which corruption is made. Corruption is the implied offer to cast one's official eyes away from an illicit activity for a price. Seller meets buyer, or buyer solicits seller, and a felonious business enterprise has begun.

In the larger police departments, internal-affairs units exercise the primary function of assuring integrity throughout the organization. Regardless of organizational structure, the immediate supervisor should be able to control corrupt tendencies at the lower level. To become aware of the financial status of the team member need not be considered out of place for a supervisor. Does the man live over his head? Does he have a reputation for "playing around?" Does he have an excessive liking for cards, horses, and pools? Is he fond of money for money's sake—never missing the opportunity to acquire or save a dollar through a practice of low-grade chiseling?

While certainly not inferring that a man who falls within one of these listed categories necessarily becomes prone to bribery and extortion, when money means much to the individual in public service, some mental quirk or desperation could trigger corrupt ways. The regular work practices of any team member should be regularly watched for signs of illicit income. How accurate is his accounting when he books the arrested drunk? When he discovers an unlocked store on a midnight watch, does he always emerge with empty hands? Is the roving bookie more apt to set up business in his official domain?

Reputation has a way of becoming known when a policeman is "on the take." Even though a superior may have been unaware of the man's corrupt practices prior to the big disclosure, afterwards he will hear about it from many who could have told him long ago. Well-developed channels of communication will be likely to carry rumbles of wrongdoing while it is happening.

Confronting Suspected Corruption

If the makings of a case seem to be evident, the problem must be resolved in just that way—as a criminal case. Command should be advised. Surveillance might have to be established. Perhaps preparations for an arrest will have to be made.

If the insinuations are vague and broad, the matter will have to be handled with less decisiveness. Detailed investigation might have to be started with only skimpy allegations at hand. Regardless of how sketchy the indications of wrongdoing, in most cases it is wise to investigate and survey the man's activities intensively. Confrontation concerning the suspicion should be withheld until conclusive findings through investigation cannot be attained. It may seem undeserving for the supervisor to act in a way which appears to involve a prejudgment of wrongdoing. However, the evaluation of facts is objective, and equally disposed to exonerate as to indict. It is not uncommon for the man ultimately convicted of graft to have been considered far above suspicion by his superiors.

If a full investigation must be undertaken, a high degree of secrecy will have to be invoked. The supervisor should first bring the matter to the attention of his superior or the commanding officer only. Then it will have to be carefully determined who will participate in the investigation. In their customary defensive stance on behalf of the accused, the suspect's fellow officers will often voice displeasure over the secrecy which accompanies the investigation. But it must be understood that the matter is one of criminal dimensions, not mere breach of rules. There is no option for police management to handle it in any way different from any other suspected or known crime. Misguided protectiveness inevitably will result in alerting the suspected associate. It would take only a coin in a pay telephone and three words of anonymous warning to nullify a case. In offering this clarification to his questioning officers, a supervisor might remind them that the criminal act of one member hurls all of them into jeopardy. Respect for the police and the striving for professionalism are set back years by the action of one.

The Prevention of Corruption

The arrest of a member of the force might have been averted if there had been continuous supervisory concern with corruption. Seldom considered as a factor towards corruption is the folklore of the peer group. This usually consists of a widely voiced thesis that a lot of money is being made illegally by a lot of policemen. This theme can cast a spell on the younger officer who may be led to believe that a sign of vocational accomplishment is that "you've learned to make yours."

While not to be expected in an organization where general integrity is well known, if this kind of gossip is brought to the supervisor's attention he must act on it decisively. He should disprove what he hears, if disproof is merited. Or he should pass on an account of the overtones to his commanding officer if validity is probable. Allowing this kind of influential rumor to continue unchecked will produce attitudes in the novices which will ultimately be converted into action.

It is not intended that the supervisor continuously shake a warning finger in the faces of his policemen. But he should repeatedly make it clear that corrupt practices will in no way be condoned.

There may be propensities in a patrolman which are not criminal, but which later may take the form of illegal pursuits. These are expressed in his constant endeavor to get something for nothing. The prestige of the job will be used to full advantage in his greedy quest. Some call it chiseling, others refer to it as mooching. It was this kind of enterprise that inspired the legal pundit who said stealing an apple from the sidewalk fruit stand was not petty theft; the correct charge is "impersonating an officer." When a supervisor begins to recognize a member's preoccupation with using the job for his personal gain, he should consider it worthwhile to have a talk with the entrepreneur. Without indicating that it must happen his way, the continuous quest for a free pack of cigarettes may mark the start of a path to big stakes in illegal licenses on the beat. The best time to ward off a breakdown of integrity in the team is at its earliest manifestation.

Preventing the Brutality Charge

Policemen have a right to be fed-up with hearing that brutality is their occupational trademark. The most persistent charge comes from low-income neighborhoods. A follow-up of the allegations ordinarily finds them largely vague and unsubstantiated. In most cases they are based on hearsay and pure will to believe. It seems more likely that the police officer's unrestrained use of fists and night stick went out with discriminatory enforcement patterns of long ago. But two realities remain when the nebulous claims of universally club-wielding cops fade for want of support: the important consideration is that the mythical image of the brutal policeman does exist; and there may still be enough isolated instances of physical brutality to give shape to and reinforce that image.

What is Brutality?

Actual brutality probably never takes the old form of converting a station house basement into a medieval dungeon, where every interrogation began with, "And now tell me, do you bleed easily?" Where physical brutality does occur, it probably will be the occasion when a couple of blows to the abdomen are administered in the back seat of a prowl car; when the recalcitrant prisoner is slapped around a bit in the hidden confines of a jail elevator; or when a mighty shove is given to an obstreperous drunk as he is led into the jail, sending him plummeting against the booking counter.

Probably in almost every case there were attitudes and actions on the recipient's part which drew the policeman's punitive response. With no outside witnesses about and no telltale bodily marks, the supervisor who is present may find it easier to ignore the incident. After all, he may tell himself, the fellow was a wise guy anyway, and he asked for it. Then with a little more invalid supervisory reasoning, he tells himself that his men are doing a good job, and taking a lot of guff. What kind of a heel will he be if he makes an issue out of something like this?

Confronting Aggressive Tendencies

In taking what he believes is the most graceful and easy way out, the supervisor has fallen into the trap of disregarding several truths. The incident does not stand by itself. The aggressive patrolman who uses his fists quickly and unnecessarily did the same thing last week, and perhaps the week before. He has developed quite a reputation of being a tough guy. He even may have a few shortsighted admirers among his peers. It pleases him to be thought of as a "guy who'll take no bum weight off anybody."

But there may be many associates who do not like the fearless one's propensities for using fist and muscle. He is putting them all on the spot by his strong-arm tactics. If there is an investigation after someone is crippled, a partner will feel compelled to either put in a false report or perjure himself in the course of a cover up. If another patrolman does not like what he sees, how can he say anything when stripes or bars are wanting? How can another patrolman take on the fellow when a gutless sergeant is conveniently looking the other way while he is roughing up somebody dangerously?

So the condoning superior may not be quite the good guy he sees himself to be. He may not be winning the universal admiration of the men. He may not be that courageous superior who stands behind his men when they decree "not to take any bum weight from some fresh punk." Instead he is seen as placing his men in a jeopardy they do not welcome. He may have unintentionally generated a feeling in them that when there is a charge that brutality did occur, he will leave them holding the bag.

Propensities towards unnecessarily rough treatment of prisoners are not difficult to control if a supervisor understands his role well. The number of team members who believe that excessive force has a place in getting the job done is small. It is not difficult to identify the policeman who regularly subscribes to this approach. It should present no problem to suggest that a particularly aggressive craftsman restrain himself. It can be made quite clear that the supervisor will be intolerant of any unnecessary roughness. This principle should be enunciated for the entire squad without waiting for an incident that may make the warning too late.

Curbing Rough Ways

Observation suggests that it is usually not the policeman able to handle himself admirably who is the one inclined to brutal tactics. The less capable officer, flabby in muscle and inept in defensive arts, appears to be the one more likely to use unnecessary force on his prisoner, when reinforcements are close by, of course. His limited strength and inability to defend himself are the reasons for being that way. His aggressive acts represent overcompensation, and are designed to make up for underlying feelings of insecurity.

The supervisor must frequently impress on his members that they are without the right to respond physically to verbal abuse they receive on the job. Defend themselves if it becomes necessary, by all means; but attack punitively, never. What might be looked upon as virtuous in the unwritten code of manly human conduct will be totally out of place in police effort.

When a supervisor is driving home the lesson of self-restraint in the exercise of official duty, he may find graphic illustrations more effective than abstract urging. Would that tough policeman be just as courageous outside the sheltered confines of his headquarters? If his associates are unavailable, would his aggressiveness be tempered by their absence? Perhaps a sergeant would not be hitting too low if he suggested that the man would respond with less vigor if he were in sport shirt rather than uniform.

The counseling supervisor should interpret station house heroics as unpraiseworthy. What is missing in them is the real courage a man must invoke when handling trouble alone on a dark street. The pushing around of a defendant when site and strength are on one's side strongly resembles the boast of the little neighborhood lad: "I can lick any kid on the street—except the boys!"

The Warped Victim of Rough Play

One final word on brutality. There is little question that many of the wild men who shower hostility and verbal abuse on an interrogating or arresting officer may be emotionally ill. An officer who overcompensates for the show of aggression may be receiving a bit of personal satisfaction. "Wacking around" the defendant on his way to the lockup may be considered innocuous and a kind of necessary education. But this may not be the last time the police service will hear from the sick suspect.

This person's reaction to police confrontation may fit the response of the paranoid. His display of hostility may indicate he is dangerous. The retaliatory action of the policeman will not be forgotten. No physical mark may be produced, but there could be a permanent scar on his warped mind. He may brood over the incident. Each time he sees a uniformed police officer there will be an automatic reaction of hate.

Then one day he may be stopped for routine questioning by another police officer, perhaps a thousand miles from the scene of the earlier confrontation. With the unsuspecting officer completely off guard, the subject will irrationally draw a gun and kill the patrolman. The other policeman long before and far away, who did not know he was dealing with one who was seriously sick, might be looked upon now as the unwitting principal to murder.

SUMMARY

Positive Discipline. • Include the word "discipline" in your supervisorial vocabulary. • Discipline is not basically punitive. • Avoid being a permissive "good guy" supervisor. • Overlooking the capers of one member can penalize another.

Discipline and Rules. • Potential weakness exists in many formal regulations. • Management should be prodded to spelling out the amount of latitude allowable in regulatory enforcement. • Administration should be sold your improved rule formula. • Misconduct may not always involve exacting rule violation.

Discipline of Orders. • Before ordering a task, first determine that it should be performed. • Make it clear how an ordered job is to be done. • Don't follow up your orders with "ready to pounce" surveillance. • Follow-up by showing your desire to help getting the job done. • Lead your man to think of you as being with him while he does his job. • Make it known you share the responsibility for doing the job right.

Dignity and Respect. • Your demand for moderate respect need not be verbalized. • When referring to other superiors use their titles of rank. • Humor should be subjected to timing, and should not be carried to excess. • Dignity of rank should be maintained as an obligation to the organization.

Discipline of Control. • A subordinate should not have to be led by the hand. • Too close surveillance destroys initiative. • Minimize verbalizing control measures. • Observe performance without interjecting yourself in the process. • Pose your questions on performance within the context of discussion. • If a patrolman has a task assigned to him, let him do it. • Avoid hounding a subordinate. • Observe discreetly, prod inconspicuously, and review without severity. • Use spot checks for rule compliance, not keyhole inspection.

Discipline not Verbalized. • Capitalize on the imitative propensities of the young patrolman. • Set yourself up as a model of aptitude and performance. • Assert a demand for discipline through the practice of self-discipline.

The Real Meaning of Inspection. • The superior may wrongly look on inspection as punitive. • Inspection and follow-up are control devices as legitimate as any others. • Inspection and follow-up are directed to the interest of those they concern.

What Inspection Achieves. • Inspection may be less common in the service fields than in production. • An inspector-general activity has been slow to come to the police realm. • One is inclined to put more into the task that will be examined. • Inspection is used to determine the balance between input and output. • Inspection and follow-up are mechanisms for making the task easier for the men.

The Things to Be Inspected. • Old-time inspections was concerned only with whether a man was on the job. • Only recently has the question of how the police job is done come into focus. • Inspection should be made of the time block in which service is rendered. • The thoroughness with which a complaint is processed should be inspected. • The completeness and accuracy of a report are worthy of inspection. • Inspection is directed to patrol between calls for service. • A neglected part of inspection concerns the way the public is handled. • An objective of inspection is a member's fund of personal qualities. • What is right about what a man does is also an item of inspection.

Inspectional Techniques. • As there is too much to inspect individually, sampling must be used. • The supervisor should let the men know clearly what inspection implies. • The men should be led to understand the positive side of inspection. • Spot checking should be structured, rather than accomplished at random. • Inspectional checks should be directed to both field work and paper work. • Inspection should extend to the study of records on the time spent on calls. • Periodic samples of a man's reports should be scrutinized. • A supervisor should cover a man's calls for the purpose of inspection. • A person who called for police service should be interviewed on its quality. • Inspection should be directed to a man in proportion to the attention needed.

Following Through. • A man's failure to follow through may result from memory lapse or a delay in action. • A team leader should keep a running record of follow-up needs. • The supervisor is responsible for determining the job is done. • The sergeant should structure his exercise of the follow-up function. • Report examination will make follow-up easier for the sergeant. • Paper checks will reveal the need for field follow-up. • Priorities will have to be assigned to follow-up needs. • The supervisor should make a written record of each case requiring follow-up. • A weakness in inspection and follow-up is that findings are not usually used. • Inspection reports may have to be passed to others for use. • A team leader will learn that inspection should ultimately be directed inward.

Appearance and Presence. • Outward appearance is likely to reflect inner qualities. • Appearance is that which first comes to another's attention. • Presence is the totality of demeanor and attitude immediately conveyed. • Appearance and presence are not to be looked upon as unimportant.

Military Significance. • A working associate will be affected by another's poor appearance. • Grooming and bearing make up a language of discipline. • Military perspectives may be less emphasized in the police culture today. • A policeman should display modified military bearing. • The communication of presence is a universal one.

Personal Inspection. • It is not unprofessional to be inspected for appearance. • Effective inspection for appearance can be inconspicuous.

Areas of Inspection. • A policeman's hair styling should be conservative. • A hair cut should be suggested when neglected. • Shaving should be looked for as a daily operation. • A referral for dental work should be made when appearance is involved. • Bad breath and body oder are realities for supervisorial concern. • Frayed shirt collars and soiled ties call for replacement. • Hands are bound to come to the attention of the public. • A man's overweight condition is a matter of supervisorial interest. • The uniform is identified with the man more than is realized. • Cap visors should shine, but uniform cloth should not. • Shoes that need polish and worn-down heels detract from appearance.

Manner of Inspection. • A supervisor should not feel ill at ease in calling attention to defect in appearance. • Defective appearance can be pointed out tactfully and nicely. • Expected standards of grooming should be voiced in conversation. • It should be understood that inspection will be continuous.

Detecting Signs of Corruption. • Some knowledge of the member's need for money should be acquired. • The man's abnormal spending habits must be recognized. • Keep an ear to the ground for gossip of corrupt tendencies. • Watch for persistent practices of "getting something for nothing.". • Look for incidence of vice violations on a beat. • Observe how the man handles his contacts with money or valuables.

Dealing with Suspected Corruption. • Allegations of a breakdown of integrity should be passed on to a superior or commanding officer. • Initiate investigation and surveillance when suspicions arise. • Investigations should be conducted in strict secrecy. • Confront suspect with allegations when an investigation is at a dead end.

Discouraging Corruption. • Remind the men repeatedly that the days of a corrupt system are gone. • Challenge any peer group folklore that many are on the take. • Be loud in voicing a demand for absolute integrity in the team.

Detecting Brutality. • Physical brutality may largely be a phenomenon of the past. • The policeman's actions in processing prisoners should be observed. • Watch how an officer responds to verbal abuse. • Listen to comments on an officer's reputation for toughness.

Preventing Brutality. • Warn the men to show propensities toward roughness. • It should be made clear the use of unnecessary force will not be condoned. • Instill an awareness that empty toughness is not to be admired. • Hostility that comes from one officer's abuse may be directed at another.

Incidence of Brutality. • The charge mostly arises in the low income neighborhoods. • Allegations of brutality are ordinarily vague and unsubstantiated. • The important fact is that the image of the brutal policeman persists. • The image is given shape and reinforced by the isolated instance.

Reasons for Brutality. • A brutal act is usually accomplished when it is unwitnessed. • Brutality may be an act of retribution for verbal abuse. • The brutal act will jeopardize the other patrolmen present. • It is reprehensible for a superior to avoid purposely seeing the brutal act. • It usually is the man without physical ability who is the brutal one. • Using undue force may be compensation for feeling of inadequacies.

CHAPTER 5

Matters of Morale

Since World War II, the word "morale" has been indispensable to any study of organization. Just as with many other words of highly abstract meaning, this one too has been loosely tossed around in both complex treatise writing, and in just plain talk on organizational theory. Frequently it is bandied about as a nondescript catchall, much in the way that the nebulous expression "dissension" is regularly suggested when talking about a ball team taking its recent plunge to the league cellar. Contributing to this obscurity of meaning are the many definitions assigned to the word. Each of these is probably correct, depending on the particular vantage point of the definer.

One use of the word stresses the individual as its subject; the other gives emphasis to the group. Take the case of the shipwrecked sailor on the desert isle. When the bottle he set adrift two years earlier floats back with its unopened envelope inside marked "postage due," it may be said he will suffer a drop in morale. But if the word is used without illustration, the image spontaneously evoked will not be of a person, but of a football team—or perhaps a police team—or some other form of group endeavor. Thus morale seems to carry a more natural significance when it refers to a group phenomenon, or, at least, to a personal perspective of some larger organization to which the individual belongs.

When morale is applied to the organization, its ingredients vary in complexity from group to group. Thus much more goes into police morale than into that of a football team. So complex is the morale of a police force that every first-line supervisor should acquire a good working knowledge of its nature. The sergeant or team leader has to understand the key role he plays in building, maintaining and restoring the morale of his squad.

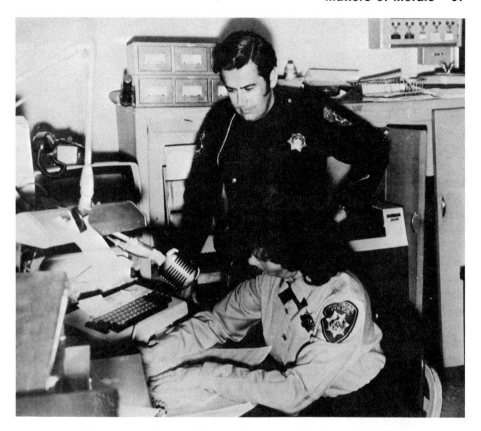

Photograph courtesy of Livermore, California, Police Department.

What to Know and Do
About Morale

Perhaps the best, most primitive, and purest manifestation of morale may be found in the attitude of an enthusiastic high school freshman. When he starts that first beautiful fall semester, everything that is wonderful about the new life will be embodied in the exploits of the varsity football squad. The youth will be caught in the wave of that nebulous something he learns to call school spirit. He is not on the team and perhaps never will be. But this is of no consequence. As each game is played, his excitement will run higher and higher. If his team wins, he will ecstatically proclaim triumph by riding in some wildly horn-honking car in the victory parade. If the squad ends its season with a dismal 0–9 win record, the reality of that inspirational school spirit still will cushion his disappointment.

Most representative of true morale will be what happens in the rooting section when his heroes are on the opposition's ten-yard line. As if in church, he will join in the prayer-like chant, "We want a touchdown!" Note that it will always be "we" who want the score—never the "I." Morale in its pure form implies that the "I" is absorbed in the "we" of the group. The satisfaction found is in what the group is, and in what the group does. The individual shares in the rewards of group accomplishment, and in turn is driven to contribute enthusiastically to that accomplishment.

Similar to the high school novice in attitude is the rookie patrolman assigned to the police academy at the start of his career. How he sits enthralled as the chief of police, glittering in all his gold, addresses the class. It's a great job, in a great outfit, he tells himself! That evening, when a friend recites one of those inevitable tales about having called the police and getting only the worst service, he blindly and passionately will leap to his department's defense. On reading about that shoot-out and arrest the next morning, he will beam with pride over what other officers have done, because he is part of this grand organization.

Time may temper this almost fanatical enthusiasm. Soon he may be startled by the awareness of organizational weaknesses and how these disappointing failings affect him and his job. In place of his earlier conception of unselfish team effort, now he sees patrolmen and detectives working inefficiently as individuals, customarily concealing information to make sure that his rival does not come out ahead. For the first time the disillusioned novice sees a foreign motivation in much of his associates' extended efforts: their actions are seen as governed by the probabilities of personal aggrandizement, or even material gain. It is a painful realization to learn that what hitherto had been perceived as the enthusiasm of group effort was only an all-out effort to take care of one's self.

At the same time, the superior officers whom he once beheld with reverence are now found to be riddled with incompetency. What is more, he sees himself as relegated to being a kind of pawn in their inept hands. In contrast to what he earlier had thought, they are not at all interested in what he is doing and accomplishing. The naive rookie becomes the cynical veteran, engulfed in a tide of bad morale formerly obscured by the deceptive glamour of a bright new world.

Thus, if the idea of morale has to be put into a definition of words, it might be called the pure enthusiasm of the individual for his group, which inspires him to accomplish the organization's objectives with proficient and efficient endeavor. Morale is school spirit carried over into adult organizational life. Morale is the driving force that conditions one to willing persistency in attaining the group's goal. Morale is an elementary attitude of being glad to belong to a group, because there is great satisfaction built into the state of belonging.

The Distinctiveness of Police Morale

The factors that make up morale in a factory come from inside the organization. The satisfactions the company provides the workers during their 8 hours on the assembly line or warehouse wholly determine their degree of morale. What the public thinks about the firm and employee, if the public cares to think of them at all, can hardly have any effect on the morale of the workers.

But the morale of a police agency is most likely to be influenced jointly by both administrative forces from within, and by public attitudes from without. The complaint from patrolman and superior that there is insufficient public support is commonplace. Men resign from police service decrying the fact that court decisions have made good police work most difficult. What is called a "lack of respect" is continuously deplored. Being caught in the middle of social strife not of their making is branded as an unfair burden.

The new group militancy also has a telling effect on police attitudes. In some places the patrolman must make each arrest under the fear of touching off a mass disturbance, or of being the subject of attack. Also, most of the hackneyed, vague, and repetitious charges of brutality hurled at the police are most certainly undeserved.

The police agency remains vulnerable as a whipping boy for political ills on the local front. A police department represents the most powerful agency of municipal government. Accordingly, it is most subject to attack at times when city hall is under fire. Because the police are visible and tangible, they are singled out for the onslaught when the actual grievance is with government, not the police. This vulnerability is an unjust penalty that follows from the prominent role a police organization plays in the American system.

All of these forces have a potential bearing on police morale, although to what extent, is not entirely clear. Wilson suggests that the police may be becoming less dependent on outside opinion. One of his studies indicates that fewer officers feel it is important to be liked by civilians. He suggests that there has been a start of a police withdrawal from a dependency on civilian opinion.°

It might be conjectured that real or fancied assault from the outside may lead to higher morale. This upswing will result from the increased cohesiveness in the organization that comes from being under attack. Consequently, traditional pressures to which a police agency is exposed actually may raise the level of morale that ordinarily would be quite low. The hostile forces on the social front may actually be compensating for archaic and ineffectual management policies. Accordingly, when considering morale, administrative weaknesses are just as worthy of attention as the social militancy and judicial restrictions directed at the police.

The Making of Good Morale

There appears to be no invariable correlation between production and morale, although research does seem to indicate they go along hand in hand up to a point.°° Consequently, it may not follow that the technically efficient police department is inevitably one of high morale. If high quality of operation is not necessarily the mark of correspondingly superior morale, what then are its ingredients?

Consider the example of City "A" and its famous police tactical squad. The unit is as spirited as it is competent. Carefully handpicked from an ever available reservoir of eager applicants, the members of the special team are strong, bright, and personable. The commander insists that there be a clear channel of com-

°James Q. Wilson, "Police Morale, Reform, and Citizen Respect: The Chicago Case," in *The Police*, pp. 159, 160.
°°Norman R.F. Maier, *Psychology in Industry*, 3rd ed. (Boston: Houghton Mifflin, 1965), p. 121.

munication with the chief, and the lines are used continuously and effectively. When a good piece of work is performed, word of the success is relayed above immediately. Then there is instant playback to the ranks, carrying a warm message of praise and appreciation.

Similarly, the men are kept well apprised of what is happening in their department. No one in the unit ever has heard of a grapevine, for none is needed. Administration eloquently passes word down the line on the conditions of the policing scene as they should be known. Little information is considered classified for tactical squad personnel. Any proposal a man may have for operations or policy change is sent to the top by his supervisor without delay. What counts most is that there is early return comment on the idea offered, including thorough reasons for acceptance or rejection. Blossoming suggestions never die on the bureaucratic vine while their maker waits and wonders.

There is continuous communication between the members and their supervisors. Information, data and plain speculation are passed back and forth eagerly and freely. To withhold information on a lead for personal use would be unthinkable. The supervisors talk teamwork to a point just short of monotony. If a sergeant has to make a decision, it is done cooly, well thought out, and strongly to the point.

If a tactical squad patrolman wants some personal consideration, as some particular duty tour or time-off, his superiors do all possible to grant what he desires. Consequently, there is no hesitancy to ask a favor, and there is no abuse of privilege when it has been received. The member enjoys a strong sense of security. He knows his removal from the squad will not be arbitrary, or made to provide room for a more favored subject. If he does foul up, he is certain the breach will be handled in a way proportional to its magnitude. Conversely, the good work he performs will be recorded in detail, included in his service ratings, and made to count towards promotion.

The equipment placed at his disposal is the best. It is readily available when needed, and always well maintained. The car in which he rides is new, in top performance shape, and always clean and polished. His training is relevant, complete, and continuous.

With his working environment so well ordered, it is incomprehensible that he would appear for duty with spots on his jacket, beard stubble on his face, and unshined shoes on his feet. A sergeant never has to correct him for his grooming, bearing, or appearance. Actually, few overt orders have to be directed at him by a superior. He always knows what is expected of him, and responds spontaneously without prodding. His initiative is strong. His sense of cooperation is excellent. All of this adds up to a model of police morale.

Factors of Bad Morale

At the other end of the scale, the archaic traffic squad of City "B" is the horrible example of morale at its worst. Traditionally, assignment to the unit has been random, although sometimes punitive. Its function is steeped in ineffectual strategies and tactics. A member of its congestion unit stands at curbside, waiting for traffic to come to a halt, and then steps out in an attempt to untangle a mess he passively allowed to form. The motorcycle men work on a quota system of tags, with little rhyme or reason in the selective enforcement dictated by vague policy.

Its commander is a politician at heart, spending the bulk of his duty time making contacts from which he can reap personal benefit. He makes no effort to know his men, hardly even recognizing their names. His incompetency is glaring, but his political strength makes him invulnerable.

The lieutenants confine themselves to the protective seclusion of their offices, seeing and hearing a minimum of evil. The sergeants offer purely token field supervision. Their subordinates know that their primary activity is to hide out in quiet, hidden spots, and pour over books in preparation for the next examination. There is little communication with the squad members. The automated visits to the men in the field consist of little more than a sloppy exchange of salutes. If an incident of magnitude is encountered, it is usual for the supervisor to be the last to arrive at the scene.

No attention is paid to administration. Top management virtually ignores their commander, who takes little time from his private enterprise to confer with his lieutenants and sergeants. There is no ear to which the men may carry a grievance. There is no interest in any suggestion or criticism that may come from the lower ranks. Assignments are badly planned and irrationally made. The patrolmen have little sense of anything being accomplished.

There is no recognition of a man's good work, and zeal goes completely unnoticed. Initiative and imagination are discouraged. Complaints from the citizenry on the actions of patrolmen are met either with supervisorial indifference or panic, depending on the prestige of the complainant. Discipline is erratic, with a quickness to pounce on the errant member who can boast of little political strength, and virtual immunity conferred upon the officer having the proper ties.

Equipment is in horrendous condition. The cars and bikes are old. The headquarters offices are untidy and dirty. The bulletin board is strewn with overlapping ancient, discolored announcements. The squad is as unkempt as the squad room. No supervisorial voice is ever raised to correct the disheveled appearance of the patrolmen.

The expressed attitudes of squad members are as negative as the environment of their work. Rumors run rampant. Suspicions are intense. The continued tendency for supervisors to huddle among themselves gives rise to almost paranoid feelings among the men that a lot of plotting against their interests is taking place. No one knows exactly what the policy is that should govern his work. No explanation is ever given for why an assignment has been made. The men see no goal, no purpose, no objective for their efforts. Each member is almost completely on his own, yet, paradoxically, without any stated right of autonomous, decisive, or imaginative action. Morale in the traffic squad of City "B" is bad, bad, bad!

Measuring the Team's
Morale Quotient

In the happy and sad tales narrated, extremes are deliberately depicted to give emphasis to the factors that make up police morale. In actuality, the line between good and bad morale is ordinarily not so graphically drawn. It may not be evident whether morale is improving or worsening.

Jucius points out that there are four major measures of the morale of employees: observation, interviewing, questionnaires, and record keeping.° These devices may be adapted easily to determine morale levels in a police agency.

Observation represents the most elementary method of assessing the spirit of a police group. For instance, when the training officer watches the veteran patrolmen return to the academy for an in-service session, he may get indications of morale in the field. To find them huddling beforehand on the building steps, and then reluctantly shuffling into the classroom as if for the start of an ordeal, there is fair reason to suspect departmental spirits are down. When they begin taking seats from the rear forward, with the last man being forced into a state of quiet panic when forced to sit in the front row, it is reaffirmed that things are not looking up for the rank and file.

Similarly, the field supervisor does not have to be too skilled to diagnose dread signs of plummeting morale. An increase in cynicism, growing suspicions, loss of humor, a paranoia of forces from outside as well as within are symptoms of sagging morale. Or there may be a new irritability towards peers as well as citizens and a decrease in spontaneous response to duty. If the supervisor looks and listens carefully, the evidence will be unmistakable.

Interviewing is an extension of that age-old journalistic mechanism for getting a feel of grass-roots sentiment. There are opportunities for a team supervisor to conduct regular interviews with his men. While these talks should be somewhat structured to ferret out significant information, they can be conducted while on patrol almost as well as in headquarters office. It may not be sufficient for a superior to enunciate a "my door is always open" policy, and then wait for the men to come to him. The first-line supervisor must go to his patrolmen and record the reactions that will indicate present levels of morale.

The very act of seeking out the feelings of personnel about working conditions, department policies, and operational deficiencies will in itself be a boost to morale. It will imply an administrative eagerness to uncover weakness and initiate remedy. This initiative taken by supervision to define trouble areas will remove any feeling on the part of the men that they must stick their necks out in order to carry grievances to a superior.

The questions asked should elicit information on the quality of morale. Accordingly, the interviews should be structured, at least in an elementary sort of way. However, there should be a willingness to talk in other pertinent directions once the flow has begun. New channels for effective diagnosis may be uncovered by the interviewee's concern with areas not singled out for exploration by the interviewing police supervisor.

While written questionnaires at first may appear impractical for a unit the size of a squad, they can still be used as gracefully as with a larger complement of men. Particularly if the patrolmen get used to their team leader passing out

°Michael J., Jucius, *Personnel Management*, 6th ed. (Homewood, Ill.: Richard D. Irwin, 1967), p. 275.

short questionnaires for completion, they will not be inclined to look on the practice as some gimmick. Inasmuch as formal morale measurement should be expanded from the team to the entire organization, the first-line supervisor may find that he had started something that top management will adopt. The men may be expected to welcome the opportunity to put their views in writing—particularly if their comments are submitted anonymously.

The questions may be formed in a way that specific answers will be obtained, or more comprehensive open-end responses received. Jucius points out that the "always; usually; sometimes; seldom; never" choice makes it easy to compare answers for the group.° But the supervisor would then exclude indepth elaboration, or unanticipated answers which would shed better light on the problem under consideration. Consequently, open-end questions may be preferable for obtaining information.

Finally, record-keeping affords a workable device for measuring morale. Well-kept service ratings obviously will have the built-in property of quantifying relevant attitudes. Three-dimensional crime statistics, refined to relate to actual team performance, may present a vivid picture of intensification or relaxation of effort. Time study analysis of dispatched calls can be indicative of the speed and snap with which both response and return to service are accomplished. Citizens' complaints about the actions or attitudes of personnel may indicate inefficiency or abrasiveness that could represent ailing morale.

These simple and effective methods for a police supervisor to test the morale of his unit will be of particular value if pursued frequently and regularly, for then they may be used for comparison purposes. In endeavoring to appraise morale in a definite and concrete way, it will remove the subject from its vague and nebulous setting, and present it as a realistic and tangible factor of supervision.

The Team Leader as Morale Therapist

While it may be conceived, quite correctly, that the determination of morale is at the top of the organization instead of bottom, supervision can be as much involved in its enhancement as management. Actually, morale can be quite high in a unit, while being simultaneously low in the parent organization—and vice versa. A police agency is structurally well-adapted to maintaining high morale because the basic operational units are usually of relatively small size. Maier points out that small groups generally are better suited to maintaining good morale among employees than larger ones.°° Consequently, the sergeant or his equivalent, being the leader of the smaller-sized squad, is the key man to measure, preserve, and, if necessary, restore morale in a police department.

The primary prescription for the morale therapist to dispense is that of absolute fairness in dealing with personnel. In general, it is not uncommon for an employee to be vocal in his repetitious refrain that employers are unfair.°°° This is equally

°Jucius, p. 276.
°°Maier, p. 127.
°°°Maier, p. 135.

true in a police agency. Particularly because of the strong political ties nurtured by police members, they frequently are separated by their peers into the "in-boys" and the "out-boys" of the team. In their cynicism, the men are especially prone to see a good deal of supervisorial treatment of personnel as gauged largely on the patrolmen's political strengths. To neutralize this expectancy, the first-line supervisor must go well out of his way to avoid the accusation of playing favorites.

The supervisor has a duty to drive home an important perspective for his patrolman: he must convince him he is part of what really constitutes a *team*. If the supervisor engenders good communications habits in the squad, the interchange of information will be automatic. The customary covering on calls will enhance an ongoing spirit of cooperation. Carrying down news from above, conveying all aspects of policy clearly, and leaving no unanswered questions on the purpose of plans and practice comprise a key to making every man feel like an insider.

Also, no one is in a better position than the immediate supervisor to stimulate in the patrolman a sense of personal prestige that comes from recognition of work well done. Acknowledging a man's achievement should be frequent and warm. There is nothing incompatible with a supervisor's role in expressing appreciation even for the performance of routine tasks. It is perfectly proper for him to say "thank you" after a simple detail has been accomplished. If the assignment has been a particularly undesirable one, indication that the supervisor was aware of its difficulty carries a special morale-stimulating warmth.

One of the best antidotes for sagging morale is a bit of relaxed supervisorial smiling and friendliness. This is particularly important because of a tendency for subordinates to read cold sternness into a superior's demeanor. What should be recognized is that being a "nice guy" can be quite contagious, and the immediate supervisor is in a good position to spread around this delightful form of contagion.

While not always thought of as such, good housekeeping is as important in a man's world as it is in the feminine realm. A sloppy police business office can pull down morale. Headquarters should be kept immaculate. Patrol cars should be kept spotless and shining. Personal grooming should be impeccable. While good morale is not only dependent on order, cleanliness, and neatness in the policeman's working environment, it can hardly thrive in an atmosphere of filth and disorder. An important role of a first-line supervisor is that of head housekeeper.

Because morale is an attitude directed to the effectiveness of the team, the men should have a clear idea of how well their agency is meeting its objectives. *Uniform Crime Reports* may provide data which in a sense add up to achievement, but only in a two-dimensional way. A better profile of actual criminal activity, showing the degree of increase or decrease should be available as relevant to the particular areas of individual assignment. The breakdown should not only take the form of numbers, but also of gravity, method, time, and place of customary crimes. Thus the current pattern of burglaries may be more significant than their volume. The modus operandi and customary haunts of the thieves should go hand-in-hand when data on auto thefts are presented. Even while the overall incidence of robberies is down, it is well to know there are still locations where distances are measured not in blocks, but in "two muggings from here, three muggings from here," etc. Clearly perceiving police team effectiveness in a full picture of local crime will provide a setting for improved morale.

There is morale therapy in providing a police team with the opportunity to exercise professional discretion in getting the job done. To keep the men in a strait jacket of inflexible rules and formulae on how to respond to the wide potential of situations is to make good morale unlikely. When there are many restrictions on judgement and action, it may be justifiably implied that there is an administrative recognition of a widespread incompetence in the ranks. Curtailing the right to make decisions and to evoke personal discretion will stultify enthusiasm, kill creativity and imagination, and drag morale to the depths. When the police supervisor insists on wide latitude for the patrolman in performing his tasks, he will be eliminating an inherent frustration that otherwise may point inward as well as outward. Restrictions on initiative produce intolerance and suspicions between unit members; inevitable products of the poorest morale.

The Significance of Grievances

Once upon a time there was a built-in formula for handling employee grievances. It was a simple, "If he doesn't like it here, let him get out!"

The world of work is quite different today. The labor union has replaced heaven in protecting the working girl and even in some instances, the harried policeman. If not actually a union, it may be that institution of growing power called "the police association" that extends its protective wings. This organization may offer a grievance committee which can right the wrongs felt by the membership. Or the officers of the organization have access to the offices of management with the complaints of the downtrodden. This particularly will be the case if the internal hierarchy is so unwise as to be indifferent to the gripes and groans emanating from below. No longer can the police supervisor—or his superiors—ignore with impunity the grievances which may undermine the stature and structure of command.

Grievances of the patrolmen should not be of concern only because new intimidating forces have come to bear on management in the police agency. Good operational principles and a sense of what is human and fair alone will demand that the grievance be recognized, studied and resolved. In the interest of efficiency as well as morale, the supervisor should provide a willing ear and an administrative will to right what is wrong. The first-line supervisor represents the level at which grievances are received, analyzed and processed. He should see this function as a duty built into his supervisorial status.

The Reservoir of Human Grievances

The supervisor is relating to real, complicated, and sensitive beings who make up his team. Each man is endowed with a self-image easily subject to hurt. Each has a sense of dignity, a somewhat fragile entity that a calloused superior is not always conscious of injuring. Additionally, a desire for equity will feel thwarted if the men find performance is not being rewarded adequately.

Whenever two opposing people come together, or a single person finds himself at the mercy of the corporate monster known as an organization, sparks may fly from the interaction. Sometimes these confrontations are real and concrete, founded in a reality which has become cold and painful. At other times they may be either totally imaginary or considerably blown out of proportion. Sometimes they may be largely symbolic, standing for something other than what they seem to represent. It is then that they serve as "pegs to hang the hat on," while below the surface there is the painful reality that gnaws away at image, dignity, or a sense of right.

The supervisor must see the grievance as a phenomenon which is to be expected in his team, no matter how well the unit may be run or constituted. He has to perceive the grievance as a message either saying something as it really is, or telling it in a kind of code calling for skilled deciphering. The grievance should be understood as a painful reality for the aggrieved, even though a superior may be incapable of entering into the agonies of those personally affected.

There are certain common sources of grievances in a police unit which must be understood. First there is the system. In an age of bigness, it is not hard to find deficiency here. The police concept had its origin in a less complicated age. The world has become complex, while principles of law enforcement may have remained somewhat simplistic and dated. In certain agencies the system has become deficient to some policemen who look for exacting efficiency. They sense blockage to the innovation and creativity which they may offer. But sometimes this dissatisfaction may amount to a substitution. The establishment outside the individual may often serve as a symbolic scapegoat for the inadequacy of the individual. It is easy to blame the world, or the organization of which one is a part, for the inner pain of experienced failure.

Or it may be the superiors—particularly the first-line supervisor—with whom the policeman is really aggrieved. There is an acute awareness of being trapped when one has nowhere to turn except to supervisors who lack empathy and ability. Nowhere does a sense of indignity develop faster than in having to accept direction from persons who are incapable of offering direction.

For example, a supervisor may be crude and discourteous in dealing with his subordinates. He may jeopardize them legally or physically with his poor judgement or outright stupidity. Perhaps he totally fails to appreciate effort. Maybe it is impossible to communicate with this superior, to exchange thoughts in a way indispensable to the process of supervising and being supervised.

There are sometimes members of one's working group who can be a source of trial and tribulation to their fellows. Here again incompetency can be glaring, with the inadequacy of individuals remaining almost ignored by insensitive superiors. There is that pervasive fear that the trouble-prone policeman suddenly may fall over the brink, and drag his innocent partner with him. Or one's co-worker may simply be obnoxious—rude, unfeeling, abrasive. With so much of one's life spent in the working environment, it can be painful to have to spend 8 hours a day in the company of an undesirable associate.

The expressed grievance usually does not take the form of disliking a way of doing something, a superior, or another policeman. The grievance ordinarily is directed to a condition that chronically weighs on the man. At times it may assume a complex form that obscures the underlying reality. Thus what may be more important is the supervisor's recognition that there is a grievance, rather than necessarily focusing on what the grievance is about. Consequently, in looking for a solution it may be necessary to dig deeply, thereby uncovering heavily concealed roots.

The Grievance Mechanism

While the notion of an ombudsman for citizens' complaints against the policeman may not be accepted in respectable police circles, an internal ombudsman for handling the grievances of the policemen themselves may be quite acceptable. A grievance procedure may be set up and focused on a skilled internal trouble-shooter to prod for sources of irritations and solutions. Perhaps in a police agency the logical grievance processor is the personnel officer. But a problem may arise when this staff official is the one about whom most grievances are centered.

Most departments do not have a grievance officer per se. Perhaps adequate police management and supervision as presently exists can substitute fairly well in place of a formally designated official. Yet even if there is a specialist for handling the various gripes and groans, a good supervisor will be the one who processes the team's complaints anyway. The men will turn to the person in which they have the most confidence. The superior nearest to them who demonstrates the ability to do his job will be their natural grievance processor.

The first-line supervisor should let it be known that there is a grievance receiving mechanism built into his official role. It is not enough to indicate there is an ever-receptive ear, he must also insist that the complaint be brought to him when it has been generated.

He must assure confidentiality in accepting the grievance, where confidentiality is possible and not a barrier to a solution. He must not overlook the reality that there is always a fear of retaliation, possibly by disciplinary action at a later time. He will find that even though an investigation of a widespread grievance has been begun, and it is clear that the administration actually is seeking solution, many of the men still will display a reluctance to talk openly on it. The attitude of a representative sample will always be, "You can't get hurt for what you don't say!"

While the men may be enlightened as to the supervisor's role in grievance processing, they must additionally be convinced of his ability to do something about a more highly placed injustice or deficiency. If they see him as impotent or, worse, unwilling to represent them before management, they will not bring him their troubles. He must show that he has sympathy with the man who is unhappy over what he sees as a concrete wrong. The supervisor has to give assurance that there will be an analysis and referral directed to specific resolution. He must prove his function as something more than one of appeasement. The grievance mechanism is one of problem solving, and should be understood within this active, dynamic framework.

The policeman should be aware that the first-line supervisor's decision need not be a final one. He should be led to understand that there will be channels of appeal if his superior's proposed solution is considered unsatisfactory. The man with a grievance must be kept from seeing himself as trapped in a dead-end street of one person's whim.

The Process of Solution

Perhaps the best environment to receive a grievance is the relaxed atmosphere of lunch. The midday meal should always be seen as a primarily social interlude, rather than a purely nutritional institution. Or maybe sitting at home—in the quiet living room of either supervisor or officer—will provide the best place for initiating complaint processing.

The team leader should convey the attitude of being sincerely anxious to hear the details of the grievance. When the man begins to express his tale of injustice or dissatisfaction, the police supervisor should listen without interruption or distraction. After the first version is given, he should ask that highlights be repeated. At this point he should zero in on significant details, asking the clarifying questions that will put specific elements in proper focus.

Listening should be sympathetic. This does not mean there has to be official agreement with the complaining policeman's allegation. Even if the receiving supervisor does not find it possible to accept the grievance as valid, his rejection of it should not be pointed. It should not be forgotten that the man always believes he has a legitimate complaint. When necessary, he should be led gently to the recognition that it is illegitimate, and not beaten over the head to force acceptance.

When input has been completed, the police supervisor may have to examine all facets of what has been put forth. In some cases he may have to observe certain persons at work. He may have to talk to individuals. Or it may be necessary for him to do homework on the actual workings of a policy or process that is at the bottom of the grievance.

It may become necessary to carry the grievance upstairs to accomplish a solution. When it is clear that topside referral is what is needed, communication should be undertaken immediately and deliberately. If the actual source of complaint is on the command or administrative level, the grievance should be transmitted through the proper channels in ascending order.

But what if middle management receives the patrolman's legitimate grievance from the supervisor, but then is unwilling to convey it to command? The sergeant now has to make a decision whether he should bypass his lieutenant in conveying the matter above. If there are rules against sidetracking his immediate superior, he obviously must respect the policy. In this case, conveyance of the grievance laterally to his fellow supervisors may help to establish a momentum of upward communication that will reach the top by its own force. Thus a kind of back-door approach will be used successfully to attain a solution to the grievance when regular bureaucratic passages are blocked. Meanwhile, the policeman with the complaint should be made familiar with the actual steps in processing. He always must be told of its ultimate outcome.

When a supervisor attracts a free flow of grievances from his men, he will learn graphically how to avoid them in the first place. What the grievances will teach him may be shared profitably with his immediate superiors and fellow supervisors.

The Grievance Procedure and Morale

The supervisor should never hesitate, and should consider it one of his primary responsibilities, to convey when necessary, dissatisfaction or unhappiness in the ranks to the higher echelons of the agency. Morale is enhanced when the men realize their supervisor is a true bridge between them and management. Lower ranking personnel feel strongly about the frequent communications void separating them from administration. They may look on their supervisor as powerless to obtain the job satisfactions they seek. At the same time, there appears to be a growing tendency for police officers' associations to be the sole intermediaries with high command. While the role of communicating grievances to management is a natural one for employee groups, when this becomes their exclusive right it may indicate supervision has failed to establish its own adequate liaison with the level of command. The association's officers may be converted into the de facto leaders in the formal hierarchy simply because of the supervisor's default.

It is an obligation of office for the team leader to be the intermediary for his men to command. He is the one to accept the role of counsel who pleads their case above. If he is rebuffed in the process, he should enlist the help of his fellow supervisors and middle management in opening the vertical communications channels. There is no reason why these officials in the formal organization cannot develop the same voice that is listened to so intently when used by those of the informal structure, the employee representatives. If the first-line supervisor cannot deal with a morale break at his own level, he has the duty to seek remedial attention from the higher plane.

The supervisor should guide command into recognizing that if it does not respond to his plea to cope with the difficulty, administration may be confronted with a problem of morale breakdown which will not be remedied easily. Morale problems are too persistent to disappear by being foolishly ignored.

How to Supervise the Non-sworn Member

The inroad is now a reality. The policeman has truly been put on the street. Even on that street others have taken over a police officer's traditional jobs. Within ten years the 1–2 percent of civilian personnel in the typical department has become a whopping 10–20 percent. At the typewriter, on the "three-wheeler," at the laboratory desk—people who are not policemen have replaced the people who are. The more highly paid police officer now is doing the work it takes a police officer to perform. The lower salaried civilian is taking over the tasks that do not need the skills of a highly qualified officer.

With few exceptions, the supervisors of these civilians continue to be the sworn sergeants or their equivalents, with the result that frequently the police supervisor has a team made up of two classes of personnel, the sworn and the nonsworn. Two new factors in exercising the police supervisory function may have followed the change. In the first place, supervising the civilian is different from supervising sworn personnel. Secondly, having these two classes of personnel to direct in the same unit has the potential of a built-in complication. This is particularly likely when police officer and civilian are at least partially doing the same tasks. Thus the supervisor will find that new demands will be made upon him when he supervises the nonsworn department employee. The importance of good supervision for these new members of the team should not be overlooked. Their morale and efficiency are as important to the functioning of the unit as the performance of the sworn officers. A drop in morale in any segment of the team will have an adverse effect on the group as a whole.

The Question of Differential Treatment

Policemen in some organizations have offered a kind of elitist resistance to the full acceptance of the nonsworn member. There was the early fear that the officer would actually be replaced by the civilian, cutting down on the agency's sworn strength, and, consequently, the opportunity to advance. Even introducing school-crossing guards may have been looked on with suspicion in some departments. While the early uncertainties have not been realized, there may still be a tendency for the policeman to look down on the civilian aide. The nonsworn employee is without the career qualifications that are his own, and usually makes half the pay of a regular officer.

Civilian members may soon be inclined to show a balancing resentment for their policeman counterparts. First of all, the nonsworn employee may justifiably see himself in possession of abilities superior to those of his policeman associate. A skilled secretary or an accomplished identification technician may be aware that his or her qualifications are of higher value to the organization than those of the patrolman who is working alongside. When both are performing the same chore, the civilian's own superior output at half the salary of the sworn member will account for an understandable dissatisfaction.

This rift may widen when the patrolman becomes the supervisor of the nonsworn. When both are working together in the same unit, authority commonly will be conferred on the patrolman over the civilian. Thus there will be a somewhat untenable administrative inequity when an officer, less able to perform than his nonsworn counterpart, will be given control over the superior effort of the civilian.

The nonsworn member expects that the sworn superior will tender favoritism to the policeman. More often than not, the prophesy will be self-fulfilling. The "blood brotherhood" reference frame of policemen may sometimes dictate that the officer be given preferential treatment. Thus tardiness will be condoned for the sworn member, while the civilian is called to task for being only infrequently a few minutes late. The policeman's inferior production will be tolerated. His disciplinary breaches may be gracefully ignored. Yet strict demands will be imposed on the nonsworn aide, stirring up quiet dissatisfaction among the employees who lack peace officer status.

The rule for the supervisor to follow is that where sworn and nonsworn work side by side, the supervisor should go out of his way to make it known that the same treatment will be given both parties. He must strive to avoid the accusation of favoring his police officer peers. If the civilian is accomplishing more, the supervisor should let it be clearly shown that he appreciates the effort of higher quality. His relationship with the civilian should be at least as warm as it is with sworn personnel. He should not just preach equality of treatment—he should demonstrate his concern for sworn and nonsworn alike.

The Profile of the Nonsworn

It is obvious that the policeman and civilian in a law enforcement agency are set apart as far as the permanence of their jobs. Short term employment is more generally the rule in nonsworn categories than police officer ranks. Yet many older civilian employees have the same intention of remaining on the job until retirement as the sworn members. The career aspiration and quest for security in the aging clerk or traffic controlman are very similar to those of sworn personnel.

But perhaps for most, civilian employment in the organization may be seen as a temporary interlude. It is likely to be a form of "treading water" while waiting for the big job to present itself. Or it may be just a post to which the nonsworn accidentally falls heir. It could have been an incidental placement from a civil service eligible list, that instead might have sent the successful applicant to the public health, works, or park department. A particular young female employee may have been attracted to police employment by the fertile reservoir of potential romance in the ranks of the youthful sworn, and her tenure is at least partially guaged on this practical and worthy consideration.

The police officer may see the civilian's position as an easily acquired one. As for himself, he had to meet rigid specifications, go through boot-camp training, and adjust to a semimilitary environment in order to achieve his position. Now he has to face danger, take responsibility, and fill grueling assignments. Yet the civilian enjoys the ease of a routine. He, the sworn member, is on a higher level of career calling, he tells himself. His role is to police, while the nonsworn civil servant is only a recent adjunct to the police. This sense of status may express itself by looking down on the civilian employee.

Then the question of loyalty comes into focus. The policeman sees himself as the bona fide member of the agency. He is the defender of the organization, and the champion of his fellow officer. It is his duty to expound institutional virtues and ward off attack. He prides himself in being an exemplar of that nebulous something known as loyalty.

The civilian owes little allegiance to the agency, he tells himself. Less career oriented, he is not as likely to see himself identified with the job. The shorter term of employment he anticipates does not carry with it the firm bonds that bind the career patrolman to the agency. His civil service status usually provides for a mobility that will permit transfer to another department of the same jurisdiction if dissatisfaction sets in. What is lacking is the cohesiveness of fellowship that binds officers in the ranks of the sworn.

It is incorrect and unfair to look on the nonsworn member as a necessary drag on the police function. Customarily, there is high efficiency in the civilian camp. The nonsworn usually provide the real pivot of a department's auxiliary operations. In assuming their new place on the line, they are able to perform the traffic task with amazing effectiveness, by way of example. In many agencies the civilians are able to provide an admirable output, despite deficient supervision and management provided by the sworn segment. Thus there are instances when the "second class citizens" in an organization are able to produce despite the floundering system of which they are captives. They still are more apt to be silent sufferers than protesters in the frustrating environment imposed upon them.

The Woman Employee

When the sergeant said he did not believe in introducing equality for women—that it would bring them down too many notches—he really was not speaking a traditional police theme. Women are relative newcomers to police work. Only the expansion of auxiliary services in recent years has provided a sizeable number of feminine employees in the police agency. On the line, except for the usual small component of policewomen, traffic alone presents a usual place for the woman employee. In making a careful analysis of police activities, it is hard to escape the finding that many of the line services still provided by the sworn officer could be performed well by the civilian.

The comparatively recent arrival of women in police roles may be responsible for the line-oriented sworn supervisor's ignorance on how to supervise her. Inadequate supervision may stem from a hidden resentment of women being brought into the police world. The weakness of supervision may for the most part represent male insensitivity to feminine sensitivity. This may be the real barrier to exercising the supervisory role effectively when the female nonsworn member is part of the team.

The office supervisor in particular must understand that woman is a "different kind of creature." He must be aware of a different structure of emotion in her makeup, one not found in the male on his team.

By way of example, when Christmas comes to an office, the sworn males will not think of decorations. It will be the woman employee who will make certain there is a tree and wreath and holly—and a bit of mistletoe over the door, as well. When the noontime party is planned on Christmas Eve, it will not be the policeman who will do the planning. The office girls will put the emotional energy of weeks into enthusiastic and careful preparation. There will be nervous anticipation that all will go well, in what is truly a thoughtful "big deal!"

Nothing can be more painful for the female than to find thoughtless male participants "dropping the ball," by missing the opportunity to show they are having a good time. The uneasy stiffness that an almost embarrassed policeman may display as he sips his punch and nibbles at the cake will be a fulfillment of her worst fears that the party will be a flop.

Thus the police supervisor has to make it an official duty to show warmth when he supervises the woman employee. He must show his appreciation for some good work or a special bit of thoughtfulness coming from her. He must carefully avoid the impatient tone or look of dissatisfaction—even if they are justified on the singular occasion. If harshness and sarcasm are taboo in dealing with any employee, they may be seen as particularly intolerable when directed against women. The male supervisor must see women employees as a multitude of sensitivities to be handled with care!

Despite the rule of treading lightly in the world of feminine work endeavor, there are factors in supervising the female that may be trying to the supervisor. Many women employees are accustomed to keeping their sick leave reserve to an absolute minimum. If she has children, one may suspect that the sick day claimed is due to a young one having to be kept home from school. Her more frequent absence from the duty lineup must be expected by the supervisor. If he is inclined to generalize by condemning the entire sex for this kind of subterfuge, let him remember that malingering is not foreign to the sworn male member.

To add to the burden of supervising a mixed team, once in a while there may be romance on the job that becomes a matter of supervisorial concern. A supervisor may be unrealistically worried about sex in the office, even to the point of wanting to erect a wall between male and female employees. He may be unnecessarily obsessed with the possibilities of an illicit relationship between a man and a woman in his unit.

While not suggesting that police headquarters be converted into a romantic boudoir or lonely-hearts clubroom, a police supervisor should recognize that mutual attraction and admiration may be expected wherever male and female paths cross. He must understand that this anticipated interaction does not have to be steeped in the erotic. The inclination to stay on the lookout for the remotest signs of potential closeness, and then to act by transferring or otherwise separating the suspects, is a primitive and misguided response. If a relationship approaches the point where a genuine breach of morals with extended implications becomes evident, where social tragedy looms on the horizon, or where there is a threat of interference with work, then the supervisor may become involved in what otherwise should be a personal concern. He should determine his sound footing first, if this kind of interference seems predicated.

A supervisor must consistently be aware that there may be suffering and sorrow brought to work from an unhappy home. With a woman, whose center of gravity is rooted in a world of people, there are more likely to be tensions arising out of interpersonal relationships. It may be the marriage which is not working out. That son or daughter might be heading for difficulties which are of obsessive concern for her. Or it could just be that last big chance for romance which is threatening to slide away. Unlike the sworn member with the outdoors to offer distraction during the 8 hours of duty, the woman tied to both office and the monotony of the routine may be left to brood inwardly and alone during the entire working day.

Loneliness is likely to pervade the life of the aging civilian. The widow who has passed into her declining years may be very much alone. It is natural that feelings of rejection may be present in the older woman. Oddities of temperament that creep into her personality may have the effect of separating her farther and farther from her peers. When she leaves her working environment at a day's end, there may be only an impersonal studio apartment to offer solace. Here her chronic sadness is not relieved by memories of days when she had a husband, when there were children and friends to make up the world she now finds empty.

The most hard-bitten police supervisor must consider these emotional components when he is supervising the woman employee. He must recognize that every deficiency and each breach of the female worker may have its roots in some personal problem. He has to keep in focus her sensitivity, even though he might be calloused from a life spent in a rough and tough environment of trouble. If it becomes necessary to call attention to a deficiency, the proper approach should be an easy one of planned action, not the spontaneous word which is designed to hurt. His discipline should never be harsher than that directed at the sworn member.

There is a close identity between the world of one's work and the personal world of life itself. One does not leave home at home, or work at work. A woman's characteristic all-or-nothing response particularly results in this identification of the environment of her work with that of personal living. So the work setting should be made one of warmth and satisfaction. It should be steeped in personal overtones, and must provide the opportunity for emotional growth and well-being. It will be good for the supervisor to look at his woman subordinates as making up a kind of family. Attention to their welfare, adding a personal quality to the words that make up his communication, and a continuously expressed attitude that he really cares, constitute the summary rule for supervising the female non-sworn member. He will find that this positive and pleasant attitude will work pretty well in supervising his sworn personnel too.

SUMMARY

What Morale is. • Morale has many definitions, each based on a singular point of view. • Morale most properly refers to a perspective of the group. • The makeup of police morale is more complex than that of other kinds. • Morale in its purest form implies the "I" is absorbed in the "we.". • The person finds satisfaction in what the group is and the group does. • Morale is school spirit carried over into adult endeavor. • Morale is the driving force in pursuing the group goal.

How Police Morale Differs. • Morale of a police agency is influenced by factors from within and without the organization. • A police force may be attacked when city hall is the real target. • The extent to which external forces affect police morale is unclear. • The police may be becoming less dependent on outside opinion. • Higher morale may result from the cohesiveness caused by outside attack.

Measuring Morale. • Observation is the most elementary method of assessing police morale. • An increase in cynicism, suspicions, and scowling may mean a loss of morale. • Irritability, hostility and lack of spontaneous effort mean morale is low. • Interviews may be used to determine morale levels. • While interviews should be structured, they can be conducted informally. • The very act of seeking out feelings can produce a morale boost. • Questionnaires can be used as a morale assessment device. • The men will welcome the opportunity to "put it in writing" anonymously. • Questions asked may be of check list or open-end variety. • Records may be used to find out the quality of morale. • Service records have value in quantifying attitudes which depict morale. • Citizens' complaints on actions and attitudes may give clues to morale. • Morale measurement will be most effective if performed regularly and often.

Improving Morale. • The determination of morale is at the organizational top rather than bottom. • Morale can be high in the unit and low in the organization, and vice versa. • The small unit size in a police agency is conducive to maintaining morale. • A primary prescription for morale is absolute fairness in dealing with the men. • A supervisor should go out of his way to avoid the stigma of playing favorites. • The men must be convinced they are really part of a team. • Policy, plans, and practice must be made clear to personnel. • The recognition of work well-done builds up the morale of the men. • It is proper for a supervisor to extend thanks for a detail performed. • Relaxed supervisorial smiling and friendliness prop up sagging morale. • There is a contagion in being a "nice guy." • Good housekeeping is as important to a man's world as to a woman's. • A clear idea should be provided on how well the agency is meeting objectives. • Being permitted professional discretion is a moral stimulant. • Frustration is lowered by allowing latitude in task performance.

Place of the Grievance. • At one time the employee who revealed a grievance was told to quit. • Unions and associations have changed attitudes towards the grievance. • Employee satisfaction is necessary for the smooth functioning organization. • Workers need an ear for the grievance, and a medium to right wrongs.

Dynamics of the Grievance. • The team member should be thought of as a complex person, not a machine. • Whenever two persons come together, a problem may arise from their interaction. • Grievances either may be very real or totally imaginary. • Often grievances are symbolic, rather than being what they seemingly indicate. • The supervisor should hear the grievance as trying to tell him something. • Even the grievance without merit is a painful reality for the aggrieved.

Sources of the Grievance. • Deficiency of the system may be a primary cause for grievance. • Dissatisfaction with supervision is a prominent cause for men quitting. • One's fellow patrolmen can provide a source of grievance.

Handling the Grievance. • The grievance itself is more important than what makes up the grievance. • It may be necessary to ferret out painstakingly the real roots of a grievance. • Good management and supervision may make the grievance specialist unnecessary. • A supervisor will be the grievance processor even though there may be a specialist. • The supervisor should let it be known there is a grievance processing mechanism. • Where possible, a supervisor should assure confidentiality to the aggrieved. • It may be necessary to dig out a grievance from the close-mouthed aggrieved.

Grievance Processing. • The processing of grievances must be seen as having several steps. • A supervisor must indicate there will be channels of appeal from his findings. • The proper setting for receiving the grievance should be arranged. • Lunch or a home visit may be ideal for setting the stage for grievance receipt. • A supervisor should convey the attitude of welcoming the grievance. • A grievance should be heard first as a whole, then in detail. • Listening to the grievance should be sympathetic. • Blunt denial of validity may merely reinforce the grievance in the member. • It may become necessary to carry the grievance to command for solution. • The supervisor may have to decide to bypass his superior to convey it above. • Fellow supervisors may assist in communicating the grievance up the line. • A policeman should be made aware of the steps grievance processing will take.

Grievances and Morale. • Grievances do not necessarily mean morale is low. • Personnel grievances may be turned into an asset for the organization. • Frustration builds up when the men have nowhere to turn with grievances. • Morale is built up when the men see the supervisor as a true bridge to command. • The team leader should get the other supervisors to help open communication lines. • Morale problems will not disappear by being ignored.

Novelty of the Nonsworn. • The policeman has been released by civilian employees for street duty. • Large components of nonsworn workers have been added to personnel rosters. • The sergeants continue to be the supervisors of the civilian employees. • The morale of the nonsworn member must be considered along with the rest of the team.

Mixed Personnel Differences. • Having the two classes of personnel in the same unit may lead to difficulty. • Sometimes sworn personnel have resisted introduction of the nonsworn. • Occasionally the civilians may show resentment of their sworn co-workers. • When the nonsworn are more skilled than the sworn, friction may develop. • The civilians may believe a supervisor is inclined to favor the sworn personnel. • Where sworn and nonsworn work together, the supervisor should stress impartiality. • Short-time employment is more general in civilian than in policeman ranks. • The police officer may see the civilian attaining his agency place too easily. • A sworn member may perceive himself extending greater loyalty than the nonsworn. • High efficiency should be recognized in the ranks of the nonsworn. • Often the civilians function well in spite of inadequate supervision.

The Female Employee. • Women are relative newcomers to the police ranks. • Inadequate supervision of women may stem from resenting their inclusion. • A supervisor must be aware of the female's essential structure of emotion. • The supervisor must consider it a duty to show warmth to the female employee. • A supervisor may have to be tolerant of sick-leave abuse by the woman worker. • Too much concern with the way male and female employees relate should be avoided. • The female employee does not have the escape of the outdoors enjoyed by policemen. • Loneliness should be seen as pervading the life of the aging civilian employee. • The roots of female breach or deficiency often should be seen as personal. • A woman should be reprimanded only through planned action. • The work setting of the female employee should be one of warm satisfaction. • A supervisor should display the attitude of caring for the employee's welfare.

CHAPTER 6

Behavioral Disorders

Handling the Problem Drinker

He used to keep the bottle in his locker. He called the high proof solution "pineapple juice." Each duty tour, he would make a few trips from the office counter to quench his thirst. Then one day the precinct jokers got access to the container. They emptied the contents, and replaced them with—real pineapple juice. The next time he put the bottle to his lips, he lowered it quickly. "Hey, who put the pineapple juice in—er, my pineapple juice?" he demanded indignantly.

The Disease of Alcoholism

This little tale about a policeman and his problem is just fiction. Fact would have him a lot more wary about sneaking a drink. Also, he would see nothing funny about his habit. The portrayal is typical, however, of the attitude the rest of the team is likely to take to his misfortune. The men ordinarily respond to the drinker's problem as being funny. But their sense of humor does not make heart disease or cancer funny. They seem to overlook the reality that alcoholism is a disease. However, unlike many heart ailments and malignancies, it can be controlled, providing there is a willingness to control it.

The police do not talk much about their drinking members. But what vocation does? Doctors rarely bring up the subject of drunken doctors. A lawyer does not often challenge another lawyer for being a lush. An acknowledgement of a man's drinking habits might indict his superior. For every department has a rule against drinking to excess, and a supervisor should not let it happen. So probably because the problem of drinking too much is swept under the rug, it is not met squarely. How extensive it is is not well known. Accordingly, a solution has not evolved.

The Incidence of Alcoholism

If a police organization does not really know how many problem drinkers it has in its ranks, it might extrapolate a figure from overall counts. Even these, however, are not definite. The usual estimate today holds that in the United States ten percent of those who drink may be alcoholics. More important, four times that number have their lives intimately affected by the person close to them who drinks. By all the rules of probability, a police department should not consider itself open to censure because a small proportion of its members may be problem drinkers. Indictment will only follow the failure to do something about it.

Alcohol has been used throughout the history of mankind. It is a drug which quite usefully can lower anxiety. It has social value in facilitating interpersonal contacts. It is a recognized food, particularly in Italy—a country, incidentally, which has an extremely low rate of alcoholism. The United States is one of the places where alcohol is looked upon especially as a beverage, and this nation has an extraordinarily high alcoholic rate. But a person who drinks a lot is not necessarily an alcoholic, nor does the route of heavy drinking invariably lead to alcoholism. Consequently, the old simple explanation heard in police circles that "a guy gets that way from all the free booze available" may not be scientifically accurate.

How the Alcoholic Develops

While the disease of alcoholism does not necessarily come from the quantity one drinks, there still is an interplay between the need of drink and the satisfaction of that need that pushes one down the path to sickness. Today the business executive's "happy hour" has started appreciably earlier each afternoon, and reaches further into the evening. When the promising person begins to feature a dependence characterized by mental disturbance, health interference, or a breakdown in interpersonal relations, then the World Health Organization's criteria for defining the alcoholic have been met.

Attempts to categorize a personality type vulnerable to alcoholism have failed. Similarly, no particular design of life experience marks the disease. However, there are cultural and situational factors involved in alcohol abuse. It is generally conceded that the abuser suffers from some sort of personality disorder.

The experience of drinking can be similar for the predinner Martini habitué and the quart-a-day lush. For both persons drinking produces some degree of euphoria, that oceanic feeling where one is identified with his universe. This is why drinking has been referred to as the poor-man's mysticism. There is a satisfying glow of self-esteem, a kind of reassuring carefree omnipotence. Worries and concerns become less acute as the sedating and tranquillizing properties of the drug take over. But while the ounce-a-day and quart-a-day consumers both equally enjoy these classic benefits of the cocktail or shot, the alcoholic has developed a pathological need for the sensations produced. His different psyche makes him particularly vulnerable to the impact of alcohol's effects.

Identifying the Alcoholic

It may not always be easy to spot immediately the liquor abuser. For example, there was the wife who said she didn't realize her husband was a drunk until he came home sober one night! Indeed, alcoholics look very much like other people, and even those dilated facial blood vessels might be found in the teetotaler. Painful though the deprivation may be for him, the problem drinker who is a policeman might not drink during his eight-hour duty tour. Perhaps it is the omnipresent breath cleansers rather than the grain spirits' aromatics which are the giveaway. Or his supervisor may become aware of noticeably contrasting periods of gaiety and moodiness. There may be evidence of a new kind of suspicion and hostility in his attitudes. Then there are the increasing episodes of the red eyes, the flushed face, and the sloppy appearance that indicate the throes of a hangover.

Of course, in most cases the problem of detection may be less difficult. The breath properties may not always be concealed. Early morning odors of liquor are detectable, these being especially significant. Most important, reputation has a way of becoming well known, particularly if it is not a good one. The drunk will become known as a drunk, despite the coverup tactics undertaken by his protective buddies.

Confronting the Problem

An immediate supervisor will not always stand up to the impending peril. He might consider the easy way out of ignoring the problem. Or he may join the subject's well-meaning peers in trying to conceal the disease. Then there is a rerun of the familiar story of a misguided superior assuming the role of condoning parent. The signs and symptoms of sickness become more obvious. Overtones of developing troubles in the man's personal relations, most frequently at home, are heard. He either may do his work with careless disregard, or with a poorly chosen overly officious ardour. Either of these styles may lead to the irrational, perhaps criminal, incident that cannot be concealed.

The police first-line supervisor should not wait for his team member's sickness to force itself on his awareness. He should constantly be on the watch for the classical symptoms of problem drinking. For instance, when the suspicion of a hangover is first prompted, he might look for supporting evidence of possibly incipient alcoholism. It might be considered a somewhat obsolete and low-grade practice to seek out telltale breath indicators occasionally. However, this somewhat crude supervisory technique may still be of value even in an age of sophisticated management. When the supervisor has become certain his suspicions are well founded, he should confront the policeman on the situation.

He should bring up the subject quietly, and without punitive threat. He should get the officer to talk about his difficulty. It can be expected that denial, excuse, protest, and promise will be poured out with emphasis. It must be remembered that there is sickness present. It will be naive for the supervisor to believe confrontation will cause the party to discard his habit at once. This preliminary talking through is merely the start to formulating a solution.

Referral of the Alcoholic

Mindful of his own limitations as a therapist, the supervisor should obviously consider professional referral the best approach. Merely advising, admonishing or warning the drinking member holds little promise. As to the help of a clergyman, the ancient "pledge" administered by the parish pastor is of questionable value, but the cleric's new perspectives of psychological counseling may be put to use. The family doctor probably knows of the condition, but a doctor may be too busy to handle this kind of problem. However, he might make a psychiatric referral. But treatment from a psychiatrist calls for the patient's sincere cooperation, and this is not always forthcoming.

Most successful is the celebrated system of mutual aid—the kind of group therapy known as Alcoholics Anonymous. Its twelve steps for conquering the disease have provided sobriety and tranquility for countless alcoholics. It is an inspiring experience for an outsider to attend the organization's annual banquet. A large urban affair might include a thousand persons, most wearing the identifying ribbon of membership.

The nonmember invited to participate will respectfully neglect having his evening Scotch beforehand. He will caution himself against alluding in any way to the subject of liquor during the conversation with his dinner partner. When the master of ceremonies greets his confreres with, "Hello, all you old drunks!", and they respond with a roar of hilarity, the guest will be surprised. However, surprise will be followed by an early and delightful case. Through an evening listening to recounted memories of terrible drinking days, testimonials to dramatic victories, and never-ending reference to the status "I *am* an alcoholic," the observer gets living insight into how amazingly therapeutic Alcoholics Anonymous really is.

So when the police supervisor tackles the problem of his member by proposing AA, he does not have to go far for help. Someone has said that the magnificent group's designation should not be "AA," but "AAA," the third letter standing for "Apostles." The man who once has been helped thereafter lives to help others. This is the spirit of the organization. Consequently, a telephone call will bring all the help the supervisor needs to get his sick member into therapy. It is not unknown for a large enough police department to have its own Alcoholics Anonymous chapter, a commendatory bit of realism.

The assumption here has been that the alcoholic will accept help. However, it cannot be overlooked that a "join-or-else" ultimatum might have to be given. This may be necessary notwithstanding receipt of that famous tongue-in-cheek assurance, "I'll straighten out, Sarg." It might have to be recognized finally that there is no other course than to drop the unredeemable problem drinker from department rolls. One thing is certain. If there is any hope for the alcoholic, the place it is most likely to be found will be Alcoholics Anonymous.

Confronting Mental Disturbance

The scene is the patrol car on a quiet midnight watch. He had always been odd, but the fellows traditionally found his grotesque suspicions amusing, and they would cruelly ride him on them. But it can shake you up a bit when your partner suddenly goes way-out into left field with, "You know, the FBI has a tail on me. Those lousy Commies have been dropping word that I'm one of them. I'd like to have my apartment checked for a bug, but I don't want to kick up a stir by asking our lab to do it."

Then there was the old-timer who said they would carry him off the job in a box before he would retire. It embarrassed you to hear the ragtime he talked to the public. And sloppy! The gutless bosses would not say a word about that soup stained tie he always wore. Now his memory of things that just happened was shot, too. And they will not do a thing about it!

Or take the young patrolman who did not seem to have anything to worry about, but would he get low! His wife was becoming pretty concerned, and dropped word at the station about him. But the whole thing just did not make sense. And, anyway, he kept on doing his job. There was no way of knowing he was going to shoot himself in the head in the locker room that night.

The Forms of Emotional Illness

Psychiatric labels can be tagged on these three unfortunate policemen whose stories are told above. The first one fits the profile of the classical paranoid. Even the layman can recognize the signs and symptoms of the second case as senile dementia. The depression of the third would be classified "affective disorder" or "situational," depending on what we learned of his background. On-the-job cases that may arise are not only matters of medical concern, but involve the strong need of early constructive attention from the first-line supervisor.

Despite the growing trend away from institutionalizing the mentally sick, the hospital population of these persons still runs fairly high. The classical psychiatric approach has been to categorize emotional disorders in the way one classifies physical ills. The "psychotic" is defined as one who has lost touch with reality. The "neurotic" is in contact with what is real, but is plagued by hysteria, compulsions, depressions, and the like. The "sociopath," formerly known as the "psychopath," is in regular touch with reality, may not be particularly unhappy himself, but usually causes society to suffer by his irresponsible activities. Many criminals fall in the latter group.

The contemporary trend in psychiatry no longer pays as much attention to labels. Now we find a perspective of mental illness that takes into account physical, psychological, and environmental factors and therapy that involves forces outside the patient too. The man who is emotionally sick is no longer one who is feared and ostracized by the community. Mental illness is accepted as a common reality of life, not to be denied and concealed by the families and social groups that find it in their midst.

Incidence in the Ranks

Perhaps police departments have not been sufficiently concerned with the sick emotions of their personnel. At least in the exceptional case, there may have been a reluctance to admit that some policemen are in need of psychiatric help. After all, so the distorted reasoning may go, it might jeopardize a supervisor to recognize formally that one of his men is disturbed. Policemen carry guns, a timid supervisor may tell himself, and if he did something crazy that you could have seen coming— well, picture the spot a boss would be in! Maybe it was public pressure that was more responsible for psychological testing and psychiatric screening in a police department. This may be accepted. However, suggesting therapy for a member who is in the organization, one tells oneself, might amount to an admission which could be held against you as a supervisor if something happened later.

This occasional variety of administrative timidity is usually shoved aside when a veteran gets so bad he is forced into treatment. There ordinarily may be a strong reluctance to file charges that might result in job termination. Consequently, when the physician suggests his patient is ready again for duty, the man may be returned to his post and officialdom hopes for the best. But with all the worry about self-indictment, it seems to be overlooked in the unenlightened organization that a supervisor could still be held responsible for not taking referral action when an emotional disorder was in clear evidence.

Detection of Emotional Disorder

First-line supervisors should be on the lookout for incipient psychosis, indications of severe neurosis, and even the dread symptoms of sociopathy among their members. It is not suggested that the supervisor assume the role of a professional diagnostician, for he is not qualified for this. It would not only be wrong, but dangerous for him to see himself as a sort of psychiatrist-without-a-couch. But even where the question of abnormality is not acute, it is perfectly proper for him to make medical referral. A sizeable incidence of disciplinary breaches by a policeman raises the issue of sickness. In everyday supervisory practice, a questionable change in attitude, appearance, and work habits might call for professional review.

Consequently, it should be accepted department policy for a supervisor to impute to any member the possibility of emotional disturbance. An organization with a regularly assigned physician is best suited for easy referral. It may not be necessary to send the officer to the doctor first. The superior himself may consult the police doctor and merely recount his observations. The medic might suggest what to look for and how to proceed in a way to acquire the data needed for a later diagnosis.

The supervisor should know the signs of mental illness for application both in his regular patrol and administrative functions. The signs of psychosis are varied.

The person may simply be starting to act differently. His memory failures become noticeable. He expresses ideas about himself that are ridiculously grandiose. His judgement is markedly poor, and many of his actions lack sense. His speech shows confused thought, and his sudden changes in mood are without evident cause. He may be unreasonably overtalkative or undertalkative. Perhaps he is growing suspicious, and sees himself as the victim of diabolical plotters. He hears voices and sees visions. He talks to himself. He may complain of bodily ailments that are nonsensical.

Because the neurotic is in contact with reality, he may cover up his symptoms to the point where they are undetectable. However, certain psychic mechanisms may show through. Strange compulsions may take the form of senseless rituals. He gives indications of unreasonable anxieties, phobias, and obsessions. His physical complaints are clearly exaggerated. There may be an unaccountable stammering and learning blocks that cannot be explained.

Sociopaths, the group from which many criminals come, are not expected to be found in a police organization. It is fortunate that the sociopathic personality usually does not fit into the pattern of police aspiration. However, when the policeman-burglar or policeman-rapist makes the headlines, it might mean a true sociopath has slipped past initial screening or subsequent supervisory attention. This kind of individual may be considered well-adjusted to his own drives, but not to his environment. He is vigorously self-centered, has a wild fantasy life, and is irresponsible. He is an impulsive nonconformist, and his tolerance of tension is low. His sex life is active, but not his love life, the latter calling for a give and take of which he is incapable. Psychotics and neurotics in many instances can be expected to respond well to therapy. There has been little success in reaching the sociopath.

Confronting Mental Disorder

When an emotional disorder is suspected in a member of the team, the supervisor should start the process which will lead to diagnosis and disposition. First, he should observe the man intensively. Next, he should consult with the man's earlier supervisors. Then he should tactfully determine what he can learn from the member's working associates. Now he should report his suspicions to the commanding officer. Finally, he should consult the department physician for a possible diagnosis and advice on how to proceed.

Now the crucial step has to be taken. The initial confrontation of the apparently sick policeman should involve informal, hopefully revealing, conversation. The discussions might have to be sufficiently structured to ferret out facts that will confirm or contradict the loose hypothesis. More delicate, a visit to selectively chosen close family members might have to be made. The investigating supervisor may find they have been sharing his own concerns. They may sincerely welcome his intervention in face of their own reluctance to bring the matter to official attention. In some instances, the investigation may take a new turn by a visit disclosing that there is a wife at home who is mentally sick. In light of the new total-environment concept of mental disorder, she will be a necessary factor in the policeman-patient's ultimate therapy.

Final confrontation of the member on his condition might be the most difficult phase. A primary goal should be to get the man to seek help on his own. If it becomes evident there will be no cooperation, he might have to be ordered to go to the department doctor or to a psychiatrist. Less difficulty in this regard may be expected in the case of the neurotic, whose suffering may prod him into seeking out help.

Because the sociopath represents a character deficiency without true recognized pathology, his detection and examination might have strong disciplinary significance, and treatment of his case cannot be expected to be solely medical. Termination of employment may have to be considered. However, in the absence of wrongdoing there may have to be extensive study and observation, with final psychiatric referral the outcome.

Concern with Emotional Illness

There are several reasons why the emotional difficulties of police personnel have to be resolved. First, the man needs help. Second, the department has to be helped, inasmuch as the sick member will represent a drag on its efforts. Third, the working associates must be relieved of the pressure of having a mentally ill officer in their midst. Finally, the public is strongly involved, because the disorder may precipitate an incident where many lives will be drastically and irrevocably affected.

The public has become gradually enlightened about mental disturbances. A police department that calls for public education should be the first to face up to the problem of emotional disorders among its own people. When a member seeks psychiatric help it should be looked upon in the same way as if he were to go to any physician. There should be no automatic stigma or question regarding his job suitability. Even when his difficulty appears to be far short of psychotic, he should be encouraged to look for professional assistance. Psychiatry does not claim to be an exact science. It does not invariably promise a cure. Nevertheless, during its brief history it has done much to alleviate the suffering of the mentally sick and of others whose lives are affected by emotional derangement.

It is not intended that supervisory concern extend to the point of identifying every unusual act or attitude on the part of a member as sickness. Emotional illness is not as clearcut as most physical disorders. We are neither black nor white relative to being mentally sick or well. Most of us reflect the grays.

SUMMARY

Alcoholism as a Sickness. • A policeman's drinking problem may be looked on as funny by the other officers. • Alcoholism can be controlled if the patient is willing to control it. • The police speak little of the alcoholics in the ranks. • Acknowledging the drunk may be seen as making the superior responsible. • In the United States, ten percent of those who drink may be alcoholics. • Lives of many others are affected by a man's drinking. • A police organization must accept blame for doing nothing about its drinkers.

Defining an Alcoholic. • No particular personality type has been identified as the alcoholic's. • When health, mind, or affairs are affected by drinking a man is an alcoholic. • Alcohol is a sedating and tranquillizing drug producing euphoria. • It is not easy to spot immediately the one who abuses liquor. • An alcoholic policeman may not drink during his duty tour. • Breath cleansers, change in moods, suspicion, and hostility may mark the alcoholic. • Hangovers may be indicated by flushed face, red eyes, and sloppy appearance. • Drinking in the morning may be a sign of incipient alcoholism. • Reputation for drinking to excess will develop readily.

Handling the Alcoholic. • A supervisor may find it easiest to ignore a man's problem. • There should be observation to detect the signs of alcoholism. • No time should be lost confronting the identified alcoholic. • The drinker should be led to talk out his difficulty. • Advising, admonishing, or warning the alcoholic may have little effect. • Professional referral of the drinker should be made early. • The family doctor may have little time to deal with the problem. • Alcoholics Anonymous provides effective group therapy for the drinker. • It is easy for a supervisor to get help for his man from Alcoholics Anonymous. • The problem drinker may have to be ordered to accept help. • If all else fails an alcoholic policeman may have to face dismissal.

Categories of Mental Disturbance. • The psychotic has lost touch with reality. • The neurotic features hysteria, compulsions, and depressions. • The sociopath may cause society to suffer for his irresponsibility.

New Views of Mental Disorder. • Less attention is being paid to identifying tags. • Mental disorder is seen as relating to the total environment. • It now is accepted as a common reality of life.

Mental Disturbance in Police Ranks. • Not enough attention may have been paid the problem. • A supervisor may feel jeopardized in recognizing disturbance. • A supervisor may be liable if he fails to act in behalf of a disturbed man.

Detecting Mental Illness. • Supervisors should watch for signs of disorder. • Frequent disciplinary breaches may indicate disturbance. • Changes in attitude and appearance may be telltale signs. • A supervisor should relate his observations to a doctor.

Detecting Psychosis. • The signs of psychosis are varied. • Acting differently, memory failures, grandiose ideas may be signs. • Poor judgement and unreasoned actions may be signs. • Suspicions, voices, and visions may also be indicators.

Detecting Neurosis. • Compulsions, anxieties, phobias, obsessions are signs, • Exaggeration of physical complaints may be signs. • Unaccountable stammering and learning blocks may be signs.

The Sociopath. • He is not expected to be found in a police organization. • The policeman who commits criminal acts may be a sociopath. • He is adjusted to his drives, but not to his environment. • He is self-centered, has a wild fantasy life, and is irresponsible. • He has low tolerance of tension and is a nonconformist. • He has an active sex life, but no love life. • Therapy for him has not been successful.

Confronting Emotional Disturbance. • The first step is keeping the subject under observation. • Then the supervisor should learn about him from superiors and fellow workers. • Finally, he should consult the department physician. • He should engage the man in conversation. • The supervisor should visit the man's family. • A primary goal is to get a man to seek help on his own. • A sociopath may have to be handled disciplinarily.

Need to Cope with Disorder. • The man, his associates, and the department are affected. • The public is involved because of the incident he may cause. • There should be no automatic stigma because a man seeks psychiatric help. • Psychiatry can do much to help the victim of mental sickness. • Tragedy may be averted by making psychiatric referral.

SECTION III

CHAPTER 7

Basic Skills in Supervision

How to Give a Talk Without Making a Speech

Who would think of the police officer as one whose duties entail speaking in public? A look at the work of the policeman, particularly if he is in the supervisory bracket, will reveal that talking to a willing audience is more than just an incidental activity.

First, there are the public-speaking assignments which go along with the notion of police-community relations. No longer is it the chief alone who is called on to take his place at the rostrum. Now there are appearances in school classes ranging from kindergarten to college sociology. There are women's clubs of every variety, and the businessmen's service organizations. Neighborhood associations have also been traditional subscribers to police oratorical talent.

Television has opened new vistas for the policeman aspiring to stardom in the world of communications. The investigating officer is an increasingly common figure on the six o'clock news, as he tells thousands of viewers about the drama of that afternoon. The comments and opinions of higher ranking members are sought in interpreting the tumult, turmoil, and troubles on the local urban scene.

From the perspective of the police supervisor, an era of continuing education in law enforcement has placed new demands on him for the exercise of speaking skills. Training being elaborate for all personnel, from nonsworn up through top management, the occasions for a sergeant to stand at the podium of the police academy have become frequent. With increased staff meetings on the department agenda, there are more and more occasions for him to discourse from his seat at the conference table.

Most important is the need for a team leader to talk to his men as a group. There is built into the supervisor's function the role of everyday speaker. Accordingly, it cannot be looked on as a frill to include in his training as a supervisor, some instruction in talking effectively to team and public. He must be convinced that it is easy to talk providing he does not try to make a speech.

Talking Without Fear

There are two elements that cause an otherwise brave person to shy away from doing something new. Fear stems from being confronted by the unknown; and fear comes from reflecting too intensively on one's internal mechanics while doing it. Most of the fear of speaking in public comes from not having spoken in public. Any training officer knows the pangs of inadequacy and uncertainty suffered by the department specialist who is brought to the academy for the first time to talk. The same training officer also knows how fast this fear disappears after the novice's initial appearance, when growing self-confidence becomes a dominant force.

Much of our emotional response, whether it be love or hate or fear, is not gauged on reality itself, but on what we believe reality to be. Thus the veteran patrol sergeant who is called on to talk to a recruit class on the patrol he knows so well is afraid of what he believes the ordeal of speaking to a group to be, not of what it in fact is. After taking the first plunge, the fledgling orator will find that the water is not nearly as cold as he had imagined. He will find that giving a talk can be fun. Instead of being a terrifying experience, he now sees it as a delightful one he wants to repeat. So, another public speaker has been created in one easy lesson!

It is unneeded self-reflection that contaminates outward-directed action. The would-be public speaker can develop a virtual paralysis of speech when he reflects on the act of speech, rather than on what he is saying. The same short-circuiting occurs when he tries to remember several things simultaneously, instead of relying on his memory's own automatic retrieval system. Consequently, the speaker should confine all his attention to the content of what he is saying and avoid reflecting neurotically on the act of memory and whatever else goes into the process of speech.

Thus the first step in learning how to talk in public is just to do some talking in public. Advice and verbal reassurance will not necessarily curb the innate fear of facing an audience. What will be of value in talking to a group is to realize that talking to a group is easy. No theoretical instruction will replace actual speaking as an effective form of learning. Consequently, the aspiring speaker should not wait for an opportunity to speak; he should make his own opportunities to talk.

Having Something to Say and Getting it Said

If a budding speaker has to be concerned with any pitfall, he should be wary of having nothing to say in the first place. If he is told to talk on a subject of no substance; if the topic is outside his experience; if the theme is completely beyond his sphere of interest, then it may be almost impossible to give a talk. There has to be a reason for speaking to the group. Someone has to derive benefit from listening, even if the only gain is in having his curiosity satisfied.

If a person knows his subject, and is interested in that subject, he should be able to pass on his knowledge and interest to another. But just because one is familiar with a topic does not mean he can convey it in a way to bring satisfaction and pleasure to someone else. The lawyer may be horribly dull when he discusses the law. A nuclear physicist may cultivate boredom and slumber in his audience when he talks learnedly about the atom. A policeman can fail to move his audience with a discussion of police theory. The reason for the failure lies in the expert not seeing the glamour and fascination of his field from the viewpoint of an observer who is not a technician.

The speaker has to be convinced that what he is going to say is worthy of being heard. If he has any choice of subject, he should make a selection that appeals to him. If he is given a topic, he may modify it to fit his own area of interest. If he is going to convey a feeling he must have that feeling himself. Before he can transmit something to another he must experience it as a part of himself.

This is why a supervisor should never memorize a talk. It will detract from all that would otherwise personalize it. It will deprive every word and every thought of any life they would otherwise contain. Then what will happen to the man who memorized his talk when he forgets the first sentence of the next paragraph?

Only if one's high office demands avoiding the danger of even the slightest misquote, should he ever read a talk. True, there are masterful readers. But the usual public speaker is ordinarily not one of these. As in memorization, there is a flat depersonalization that comes when one works from a prepared script. No one ever would think of reading his part of a conversation he is having with a friend. The effective talk made to a group should be as natural as a quiet chat with another person.

When a police supervisor is called on to give a talk—to his team or to a civilian group, he should first determine whether there is something worthy of being said. Then he must become emotionally involved in what he is going to say. Finally, the other fellow should get something out of having it said to him. If he is not going to meet these requirements, then the supervisor should wait for another day, or let someone else do the talking.

Getting Ready

After a subject has been assigned or selected, the first thing for the speaker to do is to find a moment to think through what he is going to say. Initially he should do this without looking for sources of information outside himself. He should tap his own experience for the thoughts and ideas to relate. A good time for this working introspection is while he is walking. Both the speaker and writer who walk know the high incidence of inspiration that comes while "toe and heeling it" along sidewalk or path.

After the subject has been thought through on the basis of what is already known about it, the rough and random ideas should be jotted down on a piece of paper. The speaker may find that there are sufficient points here for a completely adequate address. Or he may decide the key thought will have to be expanded. Now he can turn to the sources of data others have prepared. An amazing amount of information may be readily available as his resource.

If his subject is one related to police activity, there are many men in the organization who will be ready to help him in his preparation. The police service is full of specialists; each of these has a wealth of experience and know-how to offer him. Not only will he be able to get factual data from the experts; a single anecdote or vignette can be worth the lengthy lecture that alone would leave the listener cold.

It should be easy to find material on a subject if one has even minimal knowledge of how to use a library. The card catalogue, along with the guides and indices found on reference shelves, will usually provide plenty of fascinating ideas on his subject. Two-dimensional facts should be avoided if the intent is to keep an audience in fascination and anticipation. Nothing can be as lacklustre as to enumerate bare principles and cite empty statistics. In looking for more material, the speaker should gather interesting details and illustrative elaboration that can be used to expand what he already knows. There will be a temptation to pick up someone else's formulated facts, and construct the talk around them. But the best nucleus is what comes from the top of one's head. If the pivotal material is borrowed and used without becoming a real part of oneself, the address is almost sure to be forced, artificial, and dull!

After the basic points have been jotted down on a sheet of paper, two sets of index cards should be prepared. A single point should be put on each card of the first set, with brief modifiers inscribed underneath. When the set has been completed, the cards should be arranged in an order that would be suited to presentation. Then they should be studied to make sure the material is complete.

When the substance of an entire address is found to be in the first set of cards, a second set may be prepared. This is the set that will actually be used as needed for reference on the rostrum. Each card should contain a main thought and its modifiers, as in the first set. But now all is coalesced in the fewest possible words, designed for a single glance of the eye as prompting is required. A number should be placed at an upper corner of each card indicating its place in the sequence. Now a single master card is prepared, containing a highly abbreviated version of each of the main points of the address. Preceding each point listed here will be the number of the card in the second set which gives it elaboration.

When the talk is being delivered, the speaker need only refer to the points set down on the single master card. If he needs a crutch, he can go to the proper card of the set and use it for developing the thought. All of this can be done quite inconspicuously.

The Way It Is Said

There is a right way to give a talk. There is a correct form for using mind, vocal cords, and gestures in the process. After he has gotten over the preliminary fright of addressing an audience, the speaker should begin to give some attention to tone and mannerisms. If they are faulty they will detract from his effectiveness.

The voice should be used properly. There may be too much volume. Today the microphone is commonly at the disposal of a speaker; thus it is rarely necessary for him to shout to be heard. It may be that the emotional pressure under which he is working may find relief in unconsciously talking loudly. But this boiler-factory style of delivery will bring early pain to his audience and certainly will detract from the conversational naturalness that is needed to make a talk effective.

Then, too, the excitement of the occasion may cause a rapid-fire delivery that leaves the listener blocks behind. The fear of not having enough time will unconsciously spur the speaker to speeds that make the sharpest minds in the audience dizzy, while it will not seem that fast to the sprinter at the lectern.

Related to pouring on the volume is the exaggerated placement of too frequent emphasis. This is done either by voice or demeanor. It is tantamount to putting an old legal adage into play: When you have the law on your side, pound the law; when you have the facts on your side, pound the facts; when you don't have either on your side, pound the table! This form of dramatics can not only exhaust the audience in short order; if used consistently it will amount to shouting "wolf" too often. With everything bearing emphasis, nothing gets emphasized.

The opposite too can prevail. A monotonous delivery can be an excellent cure for insomnia, but it has no place in the classroom or auditorium. The too soft voice will elicit nothing but work from the audience: work in trying to hear what is being said. Meanwhile, with all effort being directed to hearing, no energy is left in the listener for comprehension and absorption.

Sometimes a speaker will attempt either to induce or give the impression of nonchalant ease, and do it by moving around the platform. Soon the one-man parade will take on a regular cadence which will not only be quite distracting, but will call for so much neck movement in the listener he will think he is at a tennis match.

As most extremes are equally undesirable, the opposite of violent mobility on the speaker's platform can be similarly distracting. Remaining motionless at the podium, or swaying to-and-fro while using it for support, can all but hypnotize an audience. Ideally, there ought to be no barrier between speaker and listener, as the obstruction may symbolically block good communication. Standing in front of an audience without benefit of furniture, with notes in hand if needed, can best personalize a speaker's remarks.

The most frequently used word in many fledgling orator's vocabulary is the fill-in sound of "uh," with its more complex variation of "ah-uh." This is a nervous vocal gesture indicative of an unconscious assumption that there must be an uninterrupted flow of verbiage. Its intonation is a way of spending the time while deciding on the next thought, because even momentary dead time is intolerable in a talk. The way to overcome this annoying mannerism is simply to drop "uh" from the speaking vocabulary. Conscious effort should be made to pause whenever pause is needed. The speaker has to convince himself that it is perfectly proper to stop, look, and listen as often as required. An audience will prefer the occasional gaps in delivery to being slowly "uh'd" to death.

Finally, there is the hand pocketer, who either is striving for an easy demeanor, or just feels neurotically emburdened by a couple of hands which are constantly getting in the way. When a speaker keeps his hands in his pockets for long periods, or alternately inserts and removes them, the attention of the audience will certainly be drawn to the habit. Thus the listener will be distracted by the gesture. A good way to overcome this distasteful compulsion would simply be to sew up the pockets.

If a speaker becomes aware that he is falling prey to any of these distracting mannerisms, he might add another word to that card of advice on the rostrum. "Natural!" is an important admonition to keep always within his gaze. The bad habits he should want to avoid are there because ease is absent. They are crutches to compensate for feelings of inadequacy. If instead, he directs all his attention to what he is saying, and none to the self who is communicating, there should be a beautiful ease in his delivery. A speaker at ease will put an audience at ease. It all adds up to listening without pain—better, to listening with positive pleasure.

The Framework of a Good Talk

There has always been an unchangeable pattern for any good talk. Call it "introduction, body, conclusion"; or "start, stretch, finish"; or just "beginning, middle, end"—it all amounts to the same thing. An audience has to know what it is going to hear; it has to hear it; and, as final icing on the cake, it should hear again what it has heard. Anything less than that will leave the listener distressingly suspended in the air. A lot of air has been improfitably tossed to the winds by a talk's poor arrangement.

Perhaps in any talk the opening and the close are the most important. A good start can get the listener into a state of anticipation; he is going to hear something really good. A spectacular conclusion can even make up for weaknesses that were found in between start and finish. But a good body of the talk can fall flat on its face because of an inadequate ending. Accordingly, an effective talk should have a strong start and a strong close, regardless how satisfactory the middle may be.

A good introduction must accomplish two things: it should tell the listener what he is going to hear; and it should make him anxious to listen. He must not be kept wondering far into the talk what it is going to be all about. He should not have to watch the roadway so carefully for curves and dips that he misses the scenery along the way. The proper introduction provides him with a roadmap of sorts and will keep him in readiness for every feature of the trip.

Curiosity should be elicited by the opening remarks. Sometimes the audience can be shocked into anticipation by being confronted with what is unusual and curious about what he is going to hear. The introduction should serve the purpose of making the listener glad to be in the room. He must be made anxious to stay there, for if he leaves he may miss something very important.

If any rule of good speaking should be singled out as most important, it is: say it simply! Simple does not mean the audience has to be insulted by an approach so elementary it borders on the trite. Certainly the level of understanding does not have to be gauged on the lowest I.Q. among the listeners. But thoughts can be in words that call for the least effort in comprehension. The listeners should not be made to work too hard, as this would interfere with their full enjoyment. The flow of words should be easy, and their sequence should add up to getting the idea across clearly. The points should be developed in an orderly, self-evolving sequence, with the theme unfolded in neat, logical steps.

Nothing can be worse than presenting some dry, abstract principles, and letting it go at that. Everything said should be made real. If abstractions will assist in understanding, the listener should be helped to construct his own abstract principles after he absorbs the realities presented. Illustrations should be used freely; stories may be told wherever a point has to be made vivid; examples should be cited giving each principle full dimensions. If this is not done, the address is likely to be flat, incomprehensible, and unreal.

A speaker will sometimes resort to venom and sarcasm, attacking this and attacking that, simply to be sensational. He perceives sensationalism as a sure way of putting himself over. While part of an audience may always be expected to give "boy, did he tell 'em!" approval, most of those present may show dissatisfaction, and even bristle at an attack they see somehow directed at them. The best attitude for a speaker to take is that of a nice fellow, with a receptive mind. He should avoid every semblance of the authoritarian and dogmatic. Alternatives in thinking should be presented whenever possible. Almost any challenge from the audience can be met well with a "You may be right in a sense, however" reply, rather than openly rejecting the assertion. The voice should be smiling, and the words should be smiling. Remember, a smiling customer is more apt to buy than one whose fur has been made to bristle by the salesman.

Visual aids are not something designed for exclusive use in the classroom. The speaker can add to his presentation with well-selected props and materials. A film can give living motion and color to an otherwise dull theme. Slides are excellent for a background that makes words stand in sharp relief. If there is a bit of the artist in the speaker, charts, and even three-dimensional aids in the form of models and mock-ups can be readily improvised. There is also that poor-man's visual aid, the chalkboard. This primitive tool can be as valuable as the most sophisticated device for making a complex idea highly understandable.

The conclusion must be carefully planned. It should be ready for insertion at any time it is decided things should be brought to a close. Here is where the would-be orator becomes disgustingly corny. Here is where the tear-jerking appeal may be made.

Poorly chosen dramatics will not add to the conclusion; they will only detract from the impact of what has been a fairly good address. The effective close will be one where there is a summation of what has been heard, and its significance is made clear. This is what it all adds up to, says the speaker. This is what it should mean to us. This is what can be done about it. If the poetic and philosophical can be incorporated to add a touch of final beauty or inspiration, fine! But the speaker should be genuinely inspired by what is poetic and philosophical himself in order to tap the reservoirs of great thought validly.

How to Make Speaking Even Easier

When a supervisor is called for the first time to give his talk at the police academy, his concern may be that he will not have enough to say. This fear will be readily assuaged after he finds himself only one-third through his outline when the alloted hour has ended. What he may not realize as a novice is that a long talk is not necessarily a good talk. The shortest talk is usually the most effective, with Lincoln's Gettysburg Address often being pointed to as the finest embodiment of this principle.

While the speaker should have at his disposal five times the material he will actually need to make the presentation, it does not mean he should use it all. A common fault of the speaker who has too much to say is that he tries to get too much of it said. Accordingly, important material becomes diluted by quantity, and the impact of the message may become lost in a volume of facts. It will mean more to the listener if he gets a few salient points across, and then rests with that accomplishment.

Most prominent among a speaker's considerations is to know how long it will be before fatigue causes the listener's attention to taper off. In most cases one-half to three-quarters of an hour is enough for an outside-the-classroom address. But the period may be lengthened appreciably if time for audience participation is provided.

A speaker may be inclined to look upon calling for questions as a gesture to fill the alloted time. The truth is that if the subject interests the audience, there will be more than plain willingness to participate in the discussion; its members will insist upon doing so. If questions are entertained during the body of the address rather than at the end, the real problem will be to limit them, and keep them from interrupting the planned train of thought. If they are confined to a period at the end of the address, there may be so many, it will be difficult to call a halt to the session when the time has expired.

Depending on the nature of the subject, an opportunity for asking questions and expressing personal views may be offered early in the talk. Participation may be invited by a well-timed, "Does everyone agree with this premise?" or "Who has something to say on this point?" However, it should always be kept in mind that things get out of hand, particularly if the topic is highly controversial. Therefore, calling others into the arena by no means entails sitting back, and letting the show run itself. Discussion leading is an art, and it is work. But it can be delightful work, made so by the delight of an audience being allowed to participate.

It may be that it will be better to restrict questions to a portion of the period set aside for the purpose. There ordinarily will be complete compliance if the speaker asks that all questions be held until the end, with most audience members rather having it this way. Then when a question is asked by one person, the speaker can skillfully use it to promote in-depth participation by many. Often a question can be tossed back to the interrogator with a, "Well, what do you personally think about it?" and await the almost certain response of others to the answer he receives. Or it may be directed to the group as asked, with "I wonder if anyone here has a thought on what the answer should be?" This will have the effect of getting a group to think through a subject actively. It also will provide an opportunity for the listener to express himself after interest has been aroused, a very satisfying personal experience. Control will have to be exercised to stay close to the actual subject; otherwise there may be a tendency to become enmeshed in confusing irrelevancy.

Thus the job of speaking can be easy by allowing the listeners to share the burden of the work. The novice speaker will feel far less pressure if he is aware others are anxious to get into the act. In patterning the alloted time for his address, he should set aside an adequate portion for audience involvement. It may not be overdoing it in some instances to allow half the total time for this purpose. But there should be strict adherence to a final deadline. Time is more likely to race by for the speaker than to drag. While he is speaking, he will have to improvise, curtail, and abbreviate to meet time demands. But he must restrict himself to a final gun, regardless of the temptation to go on just a little bit longer.

Decision-making without a Computer

A computer to make all of a field supervisor's decisions has not as yet been developed—at least in a size to fit the inner jacket-pocket. Perhaps both patrolman and superior officer will always have to decide on a course of action on the spot and not subscribe to the complex processes of programming and retrieval that constitute automated decision-making. But they can still learn from the computer, if not have the device actually do their work for them. They can be taught to make computerlike decisions in the field, and these will be scientific, efficient, and valid. They can realize that it is not enough merely to play-it-by-ear, make an educated guess, and rely on something vaguely called "intuition" to decide how to meet a problem. There is an art to the do-it-yourself decision-making process.

Photograph courtesy of San Joaquin County, California, Sheriff's Office.

The Agony of Decision-making

When there is only one chance, there is an understandable timidity in making a choice. Turning down a one-way street to the unknown can be frightening even to the brave. Many people go through life sidetracking decisions. If a fellow had risked making that small investment five years ago, he might be a wealthy man today. If he had not ignored thinking about that other job, a management post could now be his. In each case of the "if," he had comfortably selected to do nothing, choosing inaction over action.

However, in each instance there really was action in choosing inaction. There was a decision in not deciding. On each occasion there had been a decision to ignore the possibilities of choice: a decision was made by default.

Then there is the "administrative no." This is a form of supervisorial or managerial escapism which holds it is easier to say "no" than "yes" to a citizen or policeman making a proposal or request. Because of a reluctance to adopt or permit any course of action where the outcome is in the slightest degree unpredictable, management and supervision become frozen in inaction.

If the reluctance to make a decision had no effect except on the reneging decision-maker, there would be no adverse results to the rest of the men. But the failure will reach out to the mass of victimized personnel. An example may be found in the policy of "robotism" which governs the operation of a particular police radio-room.

Here dispatchers receive calls for service and subject them to only superficial filtering. They could spend a moment longer getting the telephoned story, and then analyze it to determine what resources should be dispatched and how. Instead, receipt and processing is regularly sketchy and superficial. It takes too much, the policy-maker tells himself, to make a decision on the basis of a telephone call from an excited citizen. The easy thing is to go to the microphone with a nondescript "interview a man," "investigate a disturbance," or an unelaborated "man with a gun" dispatch. Little attempt is made to ascertain whether the manpower sent to the scene is adequate, or to give the dispatched officers an account of what they may expect to find on their arrival. Thus the dispatchers are not the decision-makers they should be. They are robots who spew forth street addresses and simply codified guesses about what an incident may involve.

Thus the men are jeopardized by the failure of a command or supervisory officer to enter into adequate decision-making. In a rush to make a call, a man may wreck his squad car and land in the hospital, never arriving at a scene which turns out to involve no emergency. Or if he does get there, the patrolman may walk blindly into a danger of which he could have been warned had the dispatcher seen his job as one of a decision-maker and news reporter. But the man in the radio room perceives his role as that of a mechanical announcer of location with stock phrases that vaguely identify the assignment. So the policeman of the example is the victim of administrative decision by default.

The Decisions Made by the Supervisor

It is the supervisor's strategic decision that is most closely related to police planning. Planning still may be considered a sort of frill in much of police service. The predominant play-it-by-ear approach in law enforcement is still the primary rule of most agencies.

While planning is a function of high command, it has to be implemented on the line. In most cases, the decision-making involved in handling a situation for the unit is exercised at the bottom, without master guidelines from above. It will be the supervisor of the unit who designs the plans and makes the decisions for handling the incident in his area.

Take as an example a weekend youth fair in a lower class neighborhood. It is not a simple matter of assigning a car to make random calls to the location, or detailing one or two men to be present during the festivities. Based upon experience, it is expected that rough play may occur, since there are a couple of outside gangs who will be looking for trouble. The supervisor must ask himself, should a special detail be made to cover the function? If so, how many men should be used? Should there be only plainclothes officers in attendance, or ought they too be in uniform? Would it be wise to assign only juvenile specialists, or police-community relations members? Should the tactical squad be alerted? The first-line supervisor is probably responsible for the decision on how the fair will be policed. This will be the kind of strategic decision he is called upon to make. The strategic decision is made relative to a situation that is expected to occur, and for which there is the opportunity to plan in advance.

The tactical decision differs from the strategic in that it relates to a given circumstance that has arisen unexpectedly, and presents alternatives for solution. A tactical decision will ordinarily be made after a patrolman presents a problem to his supervisor to solve. While most will be resolved by talking through the alternatives with the subordinate, occasionally a critical one will arise for the supervisor and he will have to make the decision alone.

An example of a situation that calls for a tactical decision may involve a young girl who is a possible runaway, but a team member is not certain she is. Another person has pointed her out as a fifteen-year old who ran away from home in another state. The informant is sure of this, and has called the patrolman. But the subject identifies herself as someone else, twenty-two, and employed. She looks twenty-two, carries identification of sorts, and vehemently protests being questioned and detained. The party who called the police is equally adamant in insisting she is a runaway. The patrolman calls his sergeant to resolve the dilemma. The supervisor's erroneous tactical decision may bring a $100.000 lawsuit. There is no time for long and elaborate study, for the detention is illegal if her claim is correct. The first-line supervisor must decide now. His decision will be tactical.

Unlike the strategic and tactical, the supervisorial decision will pertain to his own individual role of superior officer. Take the circumstance where one of his better men is getting involved in what appears to be an extramarital affair. Yet the significance of the relationship is not clearcut. Can it be called an "affair?" Can it be looked upon as work-related if it is? Is it any of the supervisor's business in the first place? Finally, what can and should the supervisor do about it anyway? After he has weighed all the facts and applied the alternatives, the solution he comes up with will be a form of a supervisorial decision.

Lastly, there is the administrative decision that a supervisor will be called upon to make. This one will relate to the role of a higher ranking officer in the decision-making process. In being made, the decision will directly or indirectly involve higher echelons or another unit.

For example, there seems to be some weak evidence that a vice condition is developing. Whether those flashy young women in that certain apartment can be called girls or call girls is at least open to question. Their observed comings and goings are must unusual. Word has been dropped that they may be involved in an enterprise not considered legal and proper for respectable ladies.

The department has a vice detail which should be apprised when a suspected condition takes on fairly definite shape. Should the supervisor make the notification at this point or endeavor to collect a little more evidence first? If he delays getting word to the specialists, is there a likelihood they will come up with an arrest in the interim, perhaps in the apartment itself? This will make him appear negligent. If he does pass on information regarding his suspicions now, because they are so fragmentary, will it be considered premature? The decision he makes may be classified as administrative.

Thus the supervisor will be called on to make many decisions in the course of duty. Relative to his function, a decision may be thought of as strategic, tactical, supervisorial, or administrative. It may actually involve a secondary decision on whether to refer the matter elsewhere. Or it might pertain to a decision to withhold decision.

The Decision to Decide

The supervisor's decision-making frequently calls for higher command's assignment of authority or approval of action. The degree of authority held by a supervisor cannot be defined exactly. Often management avoids spelling out authority too finely. Then the only way of determining the right to make a decision with finality is to ask a superior.

The intangibles of situations on the police scene make it quite difficult, or even impossible in some instances, for higher echelons to spell out the exact times they want to become involved. This means that the police supervisor is constantly facing a secondary decision whether he should refer a matter to a higher authority for primary decision, or make it himself. To beat a path incessantly to the captain's door will draw down silent displeasure, if not out-and-out wrath. To fail to go knocking on the commander's door with a tale of trouble may leave the supervisor open to censure for having acted outside his authority.

Thus the supervisor has to be constantly aware that command may be concerned with matters calling for decision on the line. He has to remember management's constructive, if not active, interest in every problem he faces. So he must often make a decision as to whether a situation is worthy of or proper for referral to higher echelons.

Allied to the considerations regarding referral, is the matter of disagreement with a superior's decision. An example might be a judgment of unfair disciplinary action taken against a team member. Old-fashioned tenets of traditional discipline seem to dictate that the subordinate is at a definite disadvantage when he challenges the decision of a superior.

Modern commanding officers usually will listen, and even respond to, a reasonable objection directed at their decisions. A tactful, "I certainly understand the basis of your order, Sir; however . . ." might still result in being struck with a broom, but now only with the soft end.

When appeal is useless in the face of resistance, the questioning supervisor may have to choose one of three alternatives. Either he can surrender and forget about his challenge; or he can withhold further protest until the consequences of the seemingly bad decision backfire, causing the decision-maker to see the deficiency for himself. Or he can look for the help of his fellow supervisors and nearest superiors in a joint plea to revoke the ruling. The latter is a perfectly proper way of disputing a decision. In an era when police leaders have largely discarded the absolutism of bygone years, a group voice against a higher decision may be quite effective if reasonably made.

The Blind Decision

Just as unproductive inaction may be used when a choice of alternatives is difficult, so may inefficient blind action be undertaken when a decision cannot be avoided. Because the circumstances of police work present themselves in a sequential fashion, each incident unrelated to the preceding, the men usually see their decisions as simple judgements made after sizing up individual situations.

While anyone who has worked a beat for a single day knows good sense is indispensable to getting the job done, it is not valid to hold good judgement is the sole requirement for effective decision-making. Playing it by ear is ineffective in the face of incomplete information. However, the human tendency to feel one's information is sufficient prompts this deep down feeling of total adequacy. The sense of right and wrong one embraces is usually clear-cut. Thus easy solutions are looked for in every problem.

A police supervisor may fall victim to the wishful thinking that the dimensions of most things are definite and self-evident. He may be drawn into feelings of self-sufficiency that preclude the need for facts. He may look upon data and statistics as worthless in making a choice of alternatives. Then the supervisor may stumble into the trap of believing the things he wants to believe, simply because he wants to believe them. The educated guess and snap decision will take precedence over the scientific selection of offered alternatives.

The tension felt in the face of having to select a single path may result in unthinking impetuosity, and he will improvise a hasty decision. Emotions make it difficult to tolerate uncertainty. The desire for the definite, and the rejection of the indefinite, will drive one to make a choice without setting up an adequate basis for decision. The tension of the occasion may force a supervisor into getting it over with, blindly hoping his choice is a good one. Then another badly-made decision, founded on emotional response rather than logical induction, takes its place in the graveyard of administrative blunders.

The Ingredients of a Good Decision

When a supervisor sets out to make a decision, he should try to see what he is doing as a kind of game. He should engage in role-playing of sorts, but the role he now plays is that of a machine—a computer. The computer is an infinitely better decision-maker than man. It displays no individual caprice in making a choice of alternatives. Its mechanical brain can think of many more things at one time than the man who created it. It can store and retrieve and analyze and compare in the shortest possible time. It can untangle the problems of a complex game and it can fight wars. It may be taught to tell how many policemen should be where in order to discourage crime. It can be programmed to predict where the next police incident will occur. It can be made to locate the places and amounts of traffic congestion during the late afternoon rush-hour.

The police supervisor, turned decision-making computer, will first set out to define the problem. Take the matter of assigning his men to cover that youth fair. Trouble is a fairly broad concept. What kind of trouble may be expected to occur? Is trouble possible or probable? Will particular persons or groups be involved in causing it? Can trouble be expected to confine itself to a certain location, or will it spread into the adjacent neighborhood, or actually away from the environs? Why is trouble anticipated in the first place?

After delineating the dimensions of a problem, the supervisor should construct models of the possible actions he might take. He may keep policemen away from the site altogether, considering their presence to be potentially inflammatory. Or he may have passing visits made by adjacent patrols, to view the goings-on from their vehicles. Or he may have the men leave their cars, and periodically pass through the fair site on foot. Or he may detail a couple of uniformed men to police the function. Or he may have select officers in plainclothes stand around inconspicuously on location. Or he may assign a complete team under his supervision to perform the policing task in a visible, active way. Or he can choose any of the alternatives and request the tactical squad to stand by as a resource besides. And so on, and on, and on . . .

After enumerating the possible decisions which may be made, the supervisor can begin to gather data. What has been the experience when anything similar was held here or in a comparable neighborhood? Was there trouble? What form did it take? What were the precipitating incidents? What persons contributed to it? What was the extent of trouble? How long did it last? What kind of policing had been in effect at the time trouble broke out? What were the resources used to control it? How was the trouble brought under control? What was right about the police action used to suppress it? What mistakes did the police make?

When all the details of previous experience have been arranged in an order conducive to analysis, they may be applied to what is known about the fair which will be held. How comparable are conditions today? Are the same kind of persons and circumstances involved? How good is the intelligence on what may be expected? Is the attitude of the youth to the police any different now? Is there reason to believe there will be a repetition of what happened previously?

Having defined the problem, enumerated the alternatives, considered what has been learned about solving similar problems, applied that which was previously learned to the present situation; the supervisor is now ready to test the alternatives from which he must make a choice. He can do this by theoretically applying each course of action to his data. He may consult with command, other supervisors, and the men. He may talk it over with juvenile and police-community relations division personnel. He can confer with the youth and their leaders.

When all this has been accomplished, the supervisor will be able to make a choice. He will present his decision clearly to the men who will implement it. He will explain how it has been reached, and why each other alternative was rejected. He will explain how his decision will be subjected to test under field conditions, and he will suggest the nature of potential circumstances which may call for contingency actions. He will outline the alternatives that may have to be invoked on short notice, and tell how they will be executed.

One factor makes this decision easier to effect than others. Its provisions are revocable: unless the unexpected happens without enough warning to make any change. Then a tactical decision will have to be made in a hurry to meet the new circumstance. But lack of time will call for a shortcut to problem formulation, description of possibilities, gathering of data, application of alternatives, and the final selection of one of these. Then there will be a determination of whether the new choice will stand the test. If not—then so on ad infinitum.

The Decision and the Men

A good leader is aware of the talent pooled in the team. He knows how to get his men to do a job for him—or a better way of putting it—with him. He knows that many hands do make light work. He also knows that many minds used in the process may be expected to come up with better decisions.

There is nothing which says a police decision has to be made by a single superior. Group participation is ideally suited to the decision-making process. First, the combined group experience may be far more extensive than that of a single supervisor. Second, the several perspectives of the members are invaluable to create a composite viewpoint that gives final shape to the decision. Finally, the supervisor's tension at having to make a choice of alternatives is lowered in direct proportion to the number of others with whom his pressure is shared.

As the decision will affect the action of the subordinates, the patrolman's participation will influence the way the patrolmen respond to it. A decision which is the creation of the men will enjoy a spirited acceptance. Thus when a decision has to be made, the team members should be considered an essential resource for designing it. They should be apprised of what is being done; they should be told of the process by which the decision will be reached; they should be asked to make their contributions to that process.

They will play a primary part in testing the alternatives and should be asked to apply their experiences to hypothetical courses of action that have been formulated. Their opinions on the choices should be sought. They should be directed to think through the implications of putting the alternatives into practice. If they can offer new facts; if a new proposal for an alternative can be made; if a new form of programming can be suggested—then their contribution should be accepted and put to work.

A common administrative failing in decision-making, and typical of the timorous supervisor, is to include an equivocal element in its substance. The decision-maker leaves himself an out—a loophole. There is room for an alternate interpretation. If something goes wrong, he can slide gracefully away from blame. Possible contingencies may be left uncovered, again providing an escape from censure in case of foulup.

There must be an unmistaken clarity built into any decision which affects the group. Whether it is ironclad or subject to change must be made known to the men. In principle it should cover every contingency. The supervisor who has made the decision should hold himself personally responsible for its implementation. This acceptance of responsibility should be clearly made known to the team.

Finally, wherever possible the rationale of a decision should be presented to the man who must implement it. His better understanding of what went into the decision will help him put it into play more effectively. Any questions concerning the reason and purpose of a decision should be answered adequately. It is unacceptable, reprehensible, and intolerable that a supervisor would answer a subordinate who asks why something has been ordered with "Because I say so, that's why!" That pseudo-explanation is probably the only reason for the bad decision.

Self-conditioning for Decision-making

If the basic deterrent to decision-making is fear of making decisions, then that fear must be overcome. Fear is largely conquered by a self-conditioning that blocks it out. Some kind of activity is the best antidote to fear. Whistling while walking through the graveyard at midnight is an example of an age-old remedy for fear. Doing that which one fears is an excellent neutralizer.

Thus, if fear discourages one from entering into situations where he will have to make a decision, a man should seek out circumstances where he will have to decide. The best conditioner is to force oneself frequently to do what is undesirable or difficult, rather than succumbing to its avoidance. If difficulty is regularly encountered rather than avoided, its confrontation has to become easier.

If a police supervisor is resolved to master the fine art of decision-making, he at least should play the game mentally. It will be helpful to design theoretical situations that might call for a decision. He should mentally select input data and place them in storage (to use the analogy of a computer), and concentrate on the process he has adopted. He should come up with fancied alternatives, and play the game of evaluating and comparing them. He should make an imaginary decision and ponder the likelihood that it will work or fail.

The discipline that should govern all decision-making must be strong when the important decision of the moment has to be made. There must be self-conditioning to control the impulsiveness which may take over the tactical decision. There must be a conscious restraint on the drive to come up with an unreasoned snap decision. There has to be coolness under pressure; there can be no blackout of the reasoning powers brought on by the panic of being confronted by conflicting alternatives and highly uncertain results. This means that the emotional components of decision-making must be kept in a state of perfect, conscious check. A disciplined, practiced self-conditioning can prepare the supervisor for controlling his impulsive and unreasoned drives that will interfere with the intelligent selection of a course of action.

Finally, the gymnastics of decision-making self-conditioning should extend to putting the decision into effect. Inasmuch as a process of communication is involved, something of the person must be passed on with his decision. A determined stance in announcing a decision is an essential feature in leading to its ready acceptance. A sense of self-assurance will instill confidence in those who will implement it. An attitude of determination particularly must be shown in a crisis situation. Signs of uncertainty and hesitancy will have no place in the emergency decision. Consequently, the self-training in making decisions should result in a mental set that provides for announcing a decision without an unsure or vacillating attitude.

Regardless of how well conceived a decision may be; regardless of the computer-like approach which may have produced it—if a supervisor moves with uncertainty

Photograph courtesy of San Francisco, California, Police Department.

in its enunciation; if he displays a wavering attitude indicating he has not really made up his mind; and if he makes an early and arbitrary withdrawal or substitution after it has been announced, then there may be faulty operational consequences. An old principle of military science concisely sums up the anticipated results of the vacillating decision: Order—Counterorder—Disorder.

How to Relate to Management

Whenever there is organization, crude or developed, there are social hierarchies. To be able to perform or produce within a group, one must understand how he relates to those above and below in the hierarchy. The sergeant, or his equivalent, in a police agency has an organizational problem to solve—one of identification as head of the squad or team. Is he part of management, or is he part of supervision? As to task performance, is he an executive, or is he a worker?

There is the problem of communication. If his perch is somewhere in the middle, if he is a kind of bridge, what is the proper form of transmitting thoughts from topside to below, and from lower levels to high? Does he communicate purely as an inanimate electronic circuit, merely transmitting impulses? Or does he put part of himself into what is communicated, thereby identifying with the message itself? The supervisor must first determine where he stands in relation to management, and what is the most effective way to relate to management.

A Word on Police Administration

A proper perspective of what a police agency is will help the supervisor make his all-important role determination. The understanding should not be just one of static organizational charts, of solemnly defined duties, and of sterile notions concerning responsibilities and coordination. A supervisor should see his agency in an existential sort of way. He should perceive his department as a living organism, a strongly influential and strongly influenced part of government. The concept of police is not fixed but evolving, and it must subject itself to crucial alteration in the years ahead.

The police organization has always represented local government's strongest arm. It enforces the standards of society as society is able to define them by law. It presents the form of service and function that the tax-paying populace dictates. It accurately reflects the strengths and weaknesses of city hall. The populace get the kind of police organization they want.

Influential forces have traditionally been directed from outside the agency. The political powers have been able to regulate policy and procedure and control activity or restraint. Business and real estate, the major tax producers, have usually set the tone of function because they have held the purse strings. When local government was corrupt, the police were usually the agents of corruption, filtering the divided spoils into illicit coffers.

More recently, law enforcement has become the scapegoat for society's ills. As the most tangible representative of the body politic and given their role as the enforcement arm of the established authority, the police have been transformed into the target of the dissident's wrath. In the new urban strife, the police have been identified as the hated enemy. Since the tumultuous Sixties began, the sometimes militant and negativistic voice of both disadvantaged and nonconformist has had a dynamic impact on police administration.

While these external influences on the police agency have been well recognized, less comment has been attracted by the newer internal forces that have come into play. There has been a growing politicization of the police.° In some instances the police association has taken on the characteristics of a strong labor union. The members have sometimes become loud in their partisan endorsement or comdemnation of particular elective officials. Meanwhile, a public, frightened by the threatening urban jungles; obsessed by the rising incidence of crimes against person and property alike; have been supportive of the police in a way not known in the past.

All the while, the agency head, the chief, has found himself in an increasingly precarious position. Always vulnerable to outside forces, he is now subject to assaults from within. Besides, he has to live in fear of a publicized major breach of his personnel that could be his demise.

There are sensitivities in a police agency that will be the real determinants of its operations. Policy may be a product of panicky pressure of the moment, rather than of long-studied considerations. Perspectives may be shaped by recognition of political weight rather than realistic evaluations. Superior officers may be timid in the face of condemnation by the men, if not outright mutiny itself. This is the organization of which a supervisor is part; an organization he must understand when he performs his duties of supervising the men who make it up.

The Supervisor As Middleman

In a police organization, there are the patrolmen or deputies, and there are the superior officers. The first-line supervisor is a ranking officer of the lowest level, yet he is the executive of his team. While the semantics of his role makes definition difficult, one thing is quite clear: he is right in the middle. He is the representative of the men, and he is the representative of management. He is the link between administration and the operational level. He wears more than two hats—he literally wears two heads!

When management passes down policy, an order, or regulation, the team leader transmits it to the line. When the patrolman has information, a proposal, or grievance to project above, the first-line supervisor is the voice that transmits them. He is not a static, inanimate communications device for passing signals up and relaying signals down. He must interpret; he must emphasize; he must

°Jerome H. Skolnick (Task Force on Violent Aspects of Protest and Confrontation of the National Commission on the Causes and Prevention of Violence), *The Politics of Protest* (New York: Ballantine, 1969), pp 268–272.

defend. It is he who gives full dimension to the words that pass from rung to rung of the hierarchical ladder.

Labor law has recognized that the foreman is management's representative. Thus the police supervisor may be seen technically as management's representative. While he is a superior officer, removed from the rank of patrolman, he is an integral part of the team made up of patrolmen. He is with them on the line. He shares his authority with them, he joins them in decision-making, and he helps them do their work. He can be seen as part of the management team, but extending two-way supervisory sensors that pick up signals from the deepest recesses of the squad. He is the man in the middle of the middle!

That Elusive Something Called Loyalty

The patrolman may be expected to spend his lifetime working in the police organization. Recognizing that there is an identification, or at least an intended one, which will extend through the entire span of one's laboring years, what are the ties of loyalty that will keep organization and man together? What should be the supervisor's role in promoting that nebulous notion of loyalty to administration?

In the days of the more military orientation of the police, when there was more of a subscription to standards and tradition, there was unquestionably a mental set which led the individual to believe he owed a kind of debt to the organization. He had to stand behind it, to endorse its tenets. Right or wrong, he had to accept and defend attitudes and policies which emanated from it and were part of it.

The dimensions of relationships between individual and group have become blurred in the light of today's redefinitions. Not only has the policeman assumed the right to be openly critical of his agency, but through his employee organization he may be exercising the prerogative to challenge official attitudes and policies. It appears that the loyalty once tendered to management as its exclusive due has been transferred to the peer group.

Thus the supervisor may be faced with what on the surface appears to be a need to take sides in the growing strife between the men and administration. There may be a dilemma as to how far the supervisor should go to defend or contest the polarized stands being taken by management and personnel. Without sidestepping issues, a tactic which appears to be the most political course in bureaucratic exchanges, the supervisor can put the conflicting perspectives into focus. It is not being disloyal to admit inadequacy; inadequacy is ordinarily not monopolized by a single aide. The only disloyalty will be to himself if he denies the deficiency of either adversary when it is there. This will be the case regardless of whether he is championing the cause of police administration or police association.

The way in which a supervisor may ride the fence honestly and professionally is to be specific with his responding appraisals of "yes," "no," and particularly "yes, however." It is dishonest and unprofessional to shut off fair communication on the subject of agency weakness. There is no obligation for patrolman or superior to be defensive when an organizational defect is demonstrated. His sole responsibility lies in placing deficiency in proper context. His primary focus should be the possibilities of correction and improvement.

The rule of loyalty is to be fair and honest about what affects the larger group, or subgroup. A police supervisor can concretely promote loyalty by proclaiming both to the men in his team, and to the staffers above him, that loyalty is a reciprocal relationship. To be real, loyalty must be a two-way street. If the organization is loyal to the men, it is more than likely that the men will be loyal to the organization. So now the question of a nebulous loyalty to management and group itself becomes nebulous and evanescent.

The Spokesman for and to Management

The best way to give a police team that trapped feeling is to encase it in a communications vacuum. If the men are unable to get the message up the ladder to the policy- and decision-makers, the result will be stagnant personnel, shattered morale, and neurotic workers. There have to be rules controlling upward communications. If every patrolman were to knock on the chief's door each minute of the day with a welter of reports, proposals, rumors, and gripes, chaos would result. There should be a structured channelling of communication to management from the field and the obvious link between levels is the first-line supervisor.

There has always been a pronounced reluctance of men in the bureaucratic middle to communicate adequately to those on the higher rungs. Even staff conferences have failed to produce communication, and the men with the heavier weight of gold on their sleeves and shoulders do all the talking. Many supervisors will not risk their future well-being by taking an administratively unpopular stance on behalf of their aggrieved subordinates.

The growing strength of the employee organization in a police agency may often have been a product of supervision's and middle management's reluctance to provide a line of communication to the upper levels of command. The police association must not be a substitute for the voice of supervisors.

The supervisor should be obliged to get communication moving. When something is wrong at the bottom because management is doing something wrong at the top, he should go to his immediate superior with word management might do well to hear. If this fails to have impact, the supervisor must consider bypassing this level closest to him. If he needs support, he should enlist his supervisor-peers to combine voices. Then a volume level may be attained to cause insensitive ears to hear. If enough of the supervisors approach their next levels of communication to force word through, something has to happen.

The men should see their supervisor as one who will communicate what is in their interest to be communicated. They must recognize him as one who is not too timid to tell middle or top management that all is not well below. If a supervisor is afraid to offend managerial ears, the men will be readily aware of his timidity.

The supervisor has to face up to the prerogatives of his place in the organization. He has to see himself as a superior officer, not just as a patrolman with rank. He has to realize his responsibility to the policeman below, but not by ignoring his responsibility to management above. When he is called on to speak for the patrolman, he should do so as the natural representative of the patrolman. His voice should always be that of a supervisor who is part of administration, if he is to add impact to the message he is transmitting. His confidence in getting communication through to upper levels should be bolstered by knowing that in any police organization the line between supervision and management is paper thin.

SUMMARY

The Occasions for Talks. • Speaking to a group is a frequent activity of the police supervisor. • A supervisor should regularly speak to his men as a group.

The Ease of Speaking. • Another's fear of giving talks is incomprehensible to the able speaker. • Fear of doing stems from the unknown and exaggerated self-reflection. • Fear is not based on reality, but on what we believe reality to be. • The speaker will soon learn talking can be fun. • It is wrong to reflect on the act of speech instead of on what one says. • The first lesson in public speaking is to do some speaking in public. • The concern one should have is with whether there is something to say at all.

Having Something to Say. • In being addressed, the group must derive some benefit from listening. • Familiarity with a subject does not mean ability to inspire interest in it. • The nonexpert may be able to convey enthusiasm better than the expert. • What is said must be worthy of being heard.

Speaking with Feeling. • To convey feeling, the speaker must have the feeling himself. • A talk never should be memorized, as this will depersonalize it. • Only when there is a danger of misquote should a talk be read.

Preparing the Talk. • Initial preparation should be made without the help of outside sources. • A good time to start planning an address is while taking a walk. • Rough ideas should first be jotted down on a piece of paper. • Outside data then should be sought to expand one's own points. • The experience of associates should be tapped for material. • The illustration can give life to what is otherwise lifeless. • The library catalogue, guides, and indices will lead to many ideas. • The nucleus of an address should be what comes from the top of one's head. • One set of cards should be used for the first expansion of the points. • A second set should include abbreviated elaboration for use at the rostrum. • A single master card will carry the outline of the address.

Mannerisms in Speaking. • After overcoming his fears, the new speaker should turn to his mannerisms. • It is seldom necessary to use much volume to be heard. • Too loud a delivery will bring early pain to the audience. • Excitement and lack of self-assurance will cause a speedup in delivery. • A speaker may not realize the excessive speed of his delivery. • The speaker will quickly learn from others of his undue loudness or speed. • A card at the rostrum may remind him to speak more quietly and slowly. • Too consistent emphasis will detract from its use when really needed. • Too little volume will call for all the listener's energy directed to hearing. • Pacing back and forth will be distracting to the audience. • Remaining motionless at the rostrum, or swaying back and forth, can be annoying. • Ideally there should be no furniture between speaker and audience. • The intonation "uh" should be dropped from the speaker's vocabulary. • Keeping hands in pockets, or alternately placing and removing them, will be distracting. • A key to a good delivery is to keep it natural. • Bad habits in speaking come from trying to compensate for something.

The Plan of the Talk. • The only basic pattern of a talk is that of introduction, body, and conclusion. • A good introduction and conclusion can make up for a weakness in the middle. • An introduction should put the listener in a state of anticipation. • The opening remarks should elicit curiosity.

Making Listening Easy. • First in importance is the rule of keeping it simple. • Minimal effort should have to be used in understanding the thoughts expressed. • Making the listener work too hard will detract from his enjoyment. • The flow of words should be easy, and the sequence of ideas, logical. • Points should be developed in an orderly, self-evolving sequence. • Everything said should be made real for the hearer. • To add reality, illustrations should be used freely.

Winning the Audience. • If venom and sarcasm are used, it is probably to be sensational. • An audience may bristle at an attack it sees directed to it. • The best attitude in speaking is that of being a nice fellow. • A speaker should be nonauthoritarian, and display an open, receptive mind. • Alternatives to expressed opinions should be offered when possible.

Speaking Aids. • Well-selected props and materials should be used as aids. • Slides and film are excellent for accompanying talks. • The chalkboard is a poor-man's visual aid that is ideal for use.

Ending the Talk. • The conclusion should be strong and carefully planned. • Poorly chosen dramatics will detract from a conclusion. • An effective close should sum up what has been heard. • A good conclusion should make the significance of the remarks clear. • To quote a great thought, a speaker should be honestly inspired by what is quoted. • The first misgiving of the novice speaker is that there is not enough to say. • A long talk is not necessarily a good talk. • A speaker should have five times the material that will be used. • A speaker who has too much to say may mistakingly try to get it all said. • It is better to get a few salient points across and rest with that accomplishment. • Outside the classroom, 30–45 minutes may be enough for the talk.

Audience Participation. • The audience usually will insist on participating with questions or comments. • Allowing the audience to participate does not mean the speaker may relax. • Questions may sometimes be invited early during the address. • Uncontrolled questions during the body of the talk can annoy the rest of the audience. • A speaker can use a question asked to promote in-depth audience participation. • The work of speaking may be relieved by having the audience share the burden. • Adequate time should be planned for the listeners' participation. • It may be better to provide a question period at the end of the address. • In some cases half the total time allowed may be for group discussion. • Flexibility of coverage must prevail in order to meet actual time demands. • There should be strict adherence to a deadline for ending the address.

Computer in Decisions. • The computer has replaced man in the making of many of his decisions. • The police may be far behind other enterprises in computerizing their decisions. • Police supervisors can be taught to make scientifically valid decisions. • There is more than "playing it by ear" and educated guesses in deciding. • A supervisor may think of himself as processing decisions computer-style.

Fear of Decisions. • Realizing there is but one chance may make the decision-maker timid. • The fear of making a decision can become an emotional anchor. • Not to make a choice may amount to making a decision by default. • Management may discourage decision by its failure to spell out policy. • The "administrative no" is a manner of defaulting in decision-making. • There may be an organizational timidity toward making decisions. • The agency's reluctance to decide may victimize personnel.

Decisions through Planning. • The supervisor's strategic decision is a form of organization planning. • Many agencies still subscribe to a play-it-by-ear form of decision-making. • While planning is a function of top management, it has to be implemented on the line. • In most cases police decision-making has to be done in the lower echelons.

Kinds of Decisions. • The strategic decision relates to a situation that is known to be about to occur. • The tactical decision relates to a condition that arises unexpectedly. • A supervisorial decision relates to the exercise of the supervisor's function. • An administrative decision will involve a higher echelon directly or indirectly.

Approval of Decisions. • Often a supervisor's decision must be concurred in by command. • The degree of autonomy held by the supervisor cannot be defined exactly. • Often management avoids spelling out authority delegation explicitly. • No commanding officer wants uninterrupted referral of problems from below. • The supervisor must always decide whether a matter should be referred above. • A subordinate is at a disadvantage when he challenges a superior's decision. • Commanding officers usually respect a tactful challenge to their decisions. • A group voice, if reasonable, challenging a command decision may be expected to be heard.

Inadequate Decisions. • Good judgement is not the only requirement for effective decision-making. • Playing-by-ear will be ineffective if little information underlies the decision. • The formulation of easy solutions is commonplace in everyday affairs. • Data may be blindly ignored in choosing an alternative. • The supervisor may fall into the trap of believing only what he wants to believe. • Tension may lead to an invalid impetuous decision. • The desire for the definite may force one to an unstudied decision. • Tension may produce a get-it-over-quick attitude in decision-making.

Decisional Process. • In a sense, the computer is an infinitely better decision-maker than man. • The first step in decision-making is to define the problem. • The supervisor should next construct a model of the possibilities of choice. • After this, the supervisor should begin to gather his data for decision-making. • The details of another experience then should be fitted to the present problem. • After this, the alternatives of choice should be subjected to test.

Announcing the Decision. • The decision should be presented clearly to those who will implement it. • It should be explained to the men how the decision was reached. • The alternatives which may still have to be invoked should be presented.

Group Decisions. • A supervisor should elicit the help of his men in making the decision. • Group participation is ideally suited to the decision-making process. • A composite viewpoint will give better shape to the final decision. • Tension is lowered in having others share the decision-making task. • Acceptance of a decision is spirited when one has assisted in making it.

Completeness of Decisions. • Sometimes the decision-maker leaves himself an escape route from responsibility. • The maker of the decision should hold himself responsible for proper implementation. • Where possible, the rationale of the decision should be made known to the men. • A supervisor should never respond with the dictatorial "because I say so."

Conditions for Decision-making. • If fear is the basic deterrent to decision-making, fear must be overcome. • To overcome fear of decision-making one should make many decisions. • To become proficient in decision-making one should practice it mentally. • The decision requiring quick resolution must be particularly disciplined. • Conditioning will overcome the impulsiveness common to tactical conditions. • The panic of facing conflicting alternatives should not black-out reasoning. • Only disciplined self-conditioning can prepare one for decision-making. • Self-conditioning for making decisions should extend to putting them in effect. • Something of the person should be passed on with the effective decision. • Self-assurance will instill confidence in the men who receive the decision. • Self-training in decision-making should lead to this sense of confidence. • As self-conditioning, the supervisor should mentally present decisions to the men. • A principle of military science warns of "order, counterorder, disorder."

The Supervisor's Place. • A supervisor should know his place in the whole before relating to the parts. • A supervisor must know whether his role is supervision or management. • A supervisor's communication may or may not incorporate himself in it. • The supervisor must know the agency before making his own role determination. • A supervisor should see his agency as acting, and as acted upon.

Police Administration. • The police agency has always been local government's strongest arm. • Forces have traditionally been exerted by the outside on the police agency. • More recently, law enforcement has become scapegoat for society's ills. • Lately, there has been a growing politicization of the police. • The police have support today they did not know in earlier times. • Always vulnerable from without, the chief is now vulnerable from within. • Sensitivities in the agency will determine operations and policies. • Policy may follow panicky pressures of the moment rather than cool study. • Political weight rather than objective evaluation may shape perspectives.

Supervisory Liaison. • The supervisor is the representative of the men and management alike. • The supervisor has to interpret, emphasize, and defend communications from above. • Technically management's representative, the supervisor is still part of the team. • As part of management's team, he has to pick up signals from the team.

Agency Loyalty. • At one time there was more of a feeling one owed a debt to his organization. • The relationship between man and agency has been blurred by redefinitions. • Policemen now exercise the right to be critical of their administrations. • The loyalty once tendered management now may be directed to the peer group. • A supervisor may see a need to take sides in the strife between men and hierarchy. • It is not disloyal for a supervisor to admit organizational inadequacy. • The rule of loyalty is to be fair and honest about what affects the group. • A supervisor should proclaim the reality that loyalty is a reciprocal relationship.

Supervisory Communication. • The team has a trapped feeling when it senses itself in a communications vacuum. • Communications, up and down, should be channelled through the supervisor. • Men in the bureaucratic middle have been reluctant to communicate above. • The growing strength of associations followed this reluctance to communicate above. • The association should not be a substitute for the supervisorial voice. • A supervisor should get communication moving in an upward direction. • Combining the voices of all supervisors strengthens upward communication. • The men should see their supervisor as one willing to communicate above. • A supervisor's unwillingness to speak for the men will soon be noted. • Loyalty to management will call for enlightening threatened management. • A supervisor must see himself as a superior with rank, not as a patrolman. • A supervisor should know the line between supervision and management is thin.

CHAPTER 8

Special Skills in Supervision

How to Assign and Deploy Policemen

The occurrence calling for police attention cannot always be anticipated, and the contingencies in any incident are infinite. All too often the haphazard approach to getting the job done represents a reluctance to plan because of laziness and lack of know-how. Beat patterns may follow twenty-year-old crime maps or population densities. The major incident is allowed to happen because little concern is paid to past experience. The potential availability of manpower at any particular time receives little attention in anticipating a given emergency.

Fixed assignments may be made with little regard for the competence or desire of the men filling them. No attention is paid to personal preference and qualifications in naming specialists to do particular jobs. While a planning and research unit may officially assign and deploy personnel, in the long run the task of assignment and deployment falls to the supervisor. In the unanticipated emergency, it is he and his team who are the ones on the street to restore normalcy. For the ongoing assignments between emergencies, he is the logical one to refer men to command for assignment, or to confirm the propriety of the selections made by staff. Thus the supervisor should have knowledge of the key factors to be considered in assigning and deploying personnel.

The Question of Permanent Assignments

While the overall specialization of the department is an administrative consideration, the supervisor has a certain number of posts in his team to fill. There is always the car beat that must be manned, and in the larger cities there may be foot patrol to consider. Then there is the fixed post, and sometimes the specialty detail. If the supervisor is given a free hand in placing men in the established niches, he will first have to consider which assignments should be permanent, and which should be temporary.

The criterion for making assignments permanent is obviously the degree of specialization required. If the patrolman will be able to do his job better through intimate knowledge of the neighborhood, then assignments should be made with a degree of permanence. This particularly will apply to foot patrols, where persons and places should be known in detail. It will also be the rule in auto patrols throughout trouble neighborhoods, where there is much personal contact requiring familiarity with individuals and groups. But in districts where the demand for service is more generalized, where there is less advantage to intimate and personalized knowledge of the physical setting and the clientele, there may be little or no concrete benefit in assigning an individual patrolman to ongoing coverage of a specific beat. A consideration in favor of fixed assignments for the officer is the pride of ownership that encourages motivation and efficiency in doing the work. The familiarity with persons gives satisfaction in the wake of friendships that develop. Inasmuch as what is new and novel is ordinarily accomplished only with painful uncertainty, the officer knowing he is in familiar surroundings on each duty tour removes some of the trauma that goes with work performance.

Revolving assignments also has its satisfactions for the patrolman. The more desirable and less desirable beats are spread around for all to sample. Responding to calls outside a well-known area may be made easier because of the familiarity that has been gained from floating. The acquaintance with persons and places that comes from a roving assignment is wider and potentially more advantageous because of its extensive origins.

Picking the Man
to Fit the Job

If assignments are permanent, how much consideration should be given to special requests for established posts? There may have been a time when a superior would respond to a request for a particular job with an unenlightened "And who is he to ask?" reaction. At the same time, he would acquiesce smilingly to the urging of a political heavyweight that a favored detail be granted to a favorite. Today it is well recognized that motivation to do a particular job will not have to be instilled in the man who is motivated enough to ask for it. Also, if a patrolman gets the assignment he wants, it is fairly certain he will work to keep it.

It may be asked whether assignments should be made punitively. This is the oldest disciplinary device in police administration: exiling a man to Siberia for having been in trouble. What this crudely disguised disciplinary action amounts to is simply putting one superior's problem in the hands of another. These isolation cells for errant policemen, which the less desirable districts and beats have been turned into, still have some dedicated and good officers. Thus these men who are not there for punishment will unjustifiably become categorized as trouble-prone. This practice penalizes the neighborhood as well. Because it is a less desirable assignment, it has probably a greater need for dedicated and able policemen.

If an area becomes overburdened with less efficient personnel, then the supervisors there will have a nasty task set out for themselves in terms of administering rehabilitation and dragging work out of individuals who are not accustomed to producing. So, setting up special assignments for the offenders and incompetents as a form of sentencing should be avoided. However, this is not to imply that a supervisor should avoid giving less favored posts to those who deserve no better. The less welcome assignment individually made may jar the growing disciplinary case to his senses.

There arises the question of seniority preference in making assignments. Should the better spots go to the senior men as a reward for service only determined by a dimension of time? One theory is embodied in the druggist's response to his beat patrolman's query, "What do you have for graying hair, Doc?" "Only the greatest respect, Officer." It is just respect for seniority that matters in assigning the men of longer service to the attractive posts.

Another rationale suggests that policemen of longer years have grown a bit spoiled, and will not produce when placed on the less sought-after assignments. The veterans may be expected to do better when put in the better places. Then some see it as elementary that longer experience is automatically beneficial in getting any police job done.

Administrative theory holds that seniority should not be a consideration in making assignments at all. Ability does not necessarily run parallel to experience. It may be argued that automatic preference on the basis of seniority will remove the incentive that leads to superior effort.

A supervisor may assign the new academy graduate to an unwanted team task. He feels that newness implies less claim to the nicer job. An old ex-Marine in the police ranks may say giving the fledglings harder assignments will have a toughening effect, preparing them for the worst police work has to offer. While the rookies should not be made immune from assignments to arduous jobs, there should be enough flexibility to give them a taste of many tasks. The supervisor should offer no permanent assignment to the team recruit until the newcomer's indoctrination is complete.

Desire and ability are the primary criteria a supervisor should use in assigning his men. If a given task is undesirable, assignments to it should be revolved as much as possible. While length of service may be recognized as a secondary consideration, to be applied when all other factors are equal, years of faithful service should not blindly provide a ticket to all of the best details.

The Use of Manpower Waste

The perennial cry voiced at every administrative level of a police agency, down to and including the supervisor has been, "Give me more men!" In the past, little consideration had been paid to the economical use of manpower in the police agency. With the cost of running an organization spiralling and the taxpayer reluctant to pay more for services, administrators and supervisor alike have to give more concern to the way their manpower is assigned and deployed.

When taking over a team, the supervisor should look at all standing assignments from the perspective of productivity and need. Statistical studies and computerized analysis ought to be used to determine adequacy. Even without these technical aids, at least crude workload studies can be easily made. If he can introduce flexibility into the assignment structure, all the better. Beats should be set up so that they provide the best patrol coverage and response to service requests. The more traditional planning norm of following the status quo should not be the automatically accepted criterion of deployment.

When special crime problems arise—for example, a sudden upswing in the residence burglary rate—regular patrol resources may have to be tapped to provide for the special assignment. If this is done, however, there should be a structured operation designed to resolve the problem. Too often the establishment of crime prevention teams, saturation patrols, and even tactical squads represent a mere substitute for inadequate patrol. Beefing up regular patrols can often be more profitable than creating special units. If a supervisor is going to design a special task force, the formulation of a special plan on how it will operate is the important thing.

Then there will be the tactical emergency that presents itself—the siege, the stakeout, the roadblock, by way of example. When this happens, deployment will have to be rapid, yet planned. The supervisor should be thinking through hypothetical situations in advance, giving emphasis to the deployment of his men in a fictional incident. Many manuals define adequate emergency procedures that need only be implemented by supervisorial know-how. The competency of each man should be the rationale of his assignment to a specific emergency post. Wherever possible there should be backup for each man. Maximum safety under the circumstances must be a primary consideration.

When the occurrence covers a long time span, all too often proper relief for the man is not considered. The fatigue factor is of an importance that has been somewhat ignored in the past. Men cannot function efficiently for an unlimited period of time. There is a relevant theory that a toxicity may develop from long periods of being awake, and that this systemic disturbance results in a distortion of judgement. Deprivation of food, drink, and the privilege of elimination over a long time will have a telling effect on the sense of well-being and temperament.

In any deployment, relief for the men must be of primary concern to the supervisor. As soon as possible after the emergency arises, relief should be planned and the schedules publicized for the men. The team should know the exact times, subject to changes in the given situation, when they may expect their reprieve. Being kept in the dark will represent a vacuum, and this in itself will induce fatigue. Fatigue will affect alertness, spirits, and efficiency.

Finally, the difficulty of each specific assignment should be considered in determining its duration. The more demanding posts should have their personnel switched at frequent intervals. When the supervisor is giving thought to the welfare of the men in their arduous assignment, he is accomplishing more than a mere mechanical effort to lower fatigue and promote efficiency. He is adding the magic touch that comes from knowing that a superior really is concerned with their well-being.

How to Supervise at Demonstrations, Disorders, and Disasters

When disaster strikes or a riot is triggered, the policeman is the first one on the line; it is his job to restore order. When a mass emergency occurs, police work is transformed from an individual effort into a mass operation. There must be detailed planning, a careful formulation of tactics, and on-the-spot decision making. Massive team effort will require a specialized form of supervision. The supervisor will be responsible for developing proper frames of reference for his team members, which are indispensable in times of abnormality.

When Catastrophe Occurs

Disaster strikes where it is most unexpected and, at times, when it is totally unanticipated. When a catastrophe occurs, the policeman is the one who plunges into the immediate job of rescuing and lifesaving. He must control the movement of people and safeguard their welfare. He must protect the disaster-striken from those who would prey on their misfortune. In other words, the police officer must restore the social order that was wrecked when the natural order was violently disrupted.

Here the supervision needed to shunt individual effort into the channels of group purpose must be performed with great skill. Police work no longer consists mainly of individual activity. Now, more than ever, the activity of the policeman must be coordinated with that of the group.

In considering the role of the police sergeant on duty during a natural disaster, the degree of supervision called for on the streets of Texas City after an explosion in 1947 was about the same as that required on the streets of Detroit during the riot of 1967. The basic supervisory task of planning, coordinating, directing, and controlling the police function is common to each form of mass emergency, but with a difference in magnitude. In the social disorder there is an added ingredient of emotion and will, intangibles that are harder to cope with than the forces of natural energy. In preparing for the police handling of a disorder

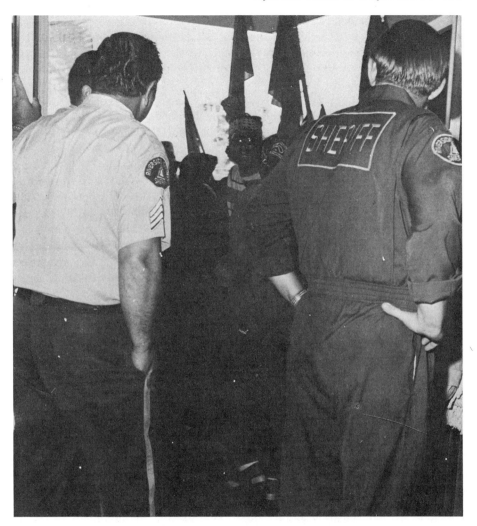

Photograph courtesy of Riverside County, California, Sheriff's Office.

that involves people, emphasis must be given to the dynamics of the individual and the group. Supervision of the policing of a disorder is like supervision at the scene of a disaster, but with an added dimension of difficulty and sensitivity.

Police Versus Protestors

The policeman should understand the dynamics of protest before he takes his place before the assaultive protestors. It is not enough to decry the breakdown of respect, or to point to an intangible Communist conspiracy as the cause of modern upheaval. He must consider government as being suspect to a sizeable segment of the populace. The political entity's authority figure, the policeman, is no longer merely passively resented—he is now subject to active attack. It is the spirit of rejecting traditional ways, which are viewed as oppressive and unjust, that has unleashed a positively purposed protest. Too frequently this protest evolves into negative criminality.

The supervisor is in a position to help his team comprehend its role in a confrontation. He can explain to his men that the police are not just a third party interjected into a strife in which they have no stake. Policemen should be aware that they are the symbolic targets of political wrath vented by people who look on themselves as outside the system. The police officer must learn the lesson of self-identity if he becomes puzzled and angry at the forces that have formed the modern world of his work. And his first-line supervisor is the appropriate teacher.

The policeman standing on the line of a mass disturbance should realize that the disorder may be politically motivated. The police officer may remember nostalgically the days when sit-ins and peace marches were the manifestations of turmoil. Yet he should not forget that these somewhat innocuous forms of protest were considered at the time as being major assaults on the orderly processes of society.

Among the pioneers of protest were people who were sincere in their belief that the ways of the establishment were not American ways. They acutely perceived injustice in the system and because of this, were loud in their demands for change. Furthermore, they succeeded with demonstrations where traditional legal processes had failed. Many who had been looked upon as subversives have now been transformed into heroes through the processes of social redefinition.

Although the aforementioned zealots may make up a sizeable component on the protest line today, the new militants are prominent at their sides. These groups have foresworn the design of bending the establishment by passive protest and a less destructive disorder. The new order bandies about such words as "Now!" and "Nonnegotiable." Their goals, unlike earlier ones, are vague and generalized.

Closely allied to the unreasoning militant is the protestor who needs a cause. The cause may be any cause, and he seems to be tremendously chagrined when the cause is removed by solution. These "causists" are the exemplars of an age of negativism—when being against is much easier than being for. Perhaps having a cause gives them status and identification in an era of anonymity. The low achievers and persons of low intellect fit well into this category of dissenters, because a potential of accomplishment is hardly required.

Then there are the mentally disordered and the borderline disturbed personalities (dangerously close to the psychotic) who find something that is needed by their psyches in the excitement of protest. Also severe neurotics may find satisfaction in the opportunity to belong. The policeman must remember that there are many in the mass disturbance who are sick and who may be stimulated to act out their warped fantasies in the ensuing confrontation.

Finally there are persons who are chemically stimulated, predominantly the speed-freaks whose paranoidal symptomatology is well adapted to the conflict. Aggressive manifestations in a mass disorder may stem mainly from amphetamine use. The hostility and suspicions that characterize persons who resort to methedrine pointedly characterize the modern protest group.

The supervisor should convince his patrolman that the cast of the drama represents a hodgepodge of participants. There are multiple motivations and purposes. There is health; also sickness. There is a complete range of intelligence quotients and a comprehensive spectrum of human propensities. This awareness of complexity will prevent the policeman from oversimplifying the danger and also the possible reactions.

That Elusive Attitude of Neutrality

The policeman is basically conservative in his perspective. He is not apt to be oversympathetic with protest and nonconformity. He will probably resent odd attire and appearance and, perhaps with some merit, will suggest to an associate that he cannot see how people who do not change their clothes can expect to change the world. Therefore, we cannot expect that his basic attitude at the scene of confrontation, no matter how peaceful it may be, will engender complete neutrality.

Consequently the supervisor may find it necessary to remind a somewhat embittered team member that when a crime does occur at the scene, not everyone in the group is responsible for it. In other words, a rock thrown from the rear of the crowd does not justify the retaliatory act of punitively seizing someone at the front. Nor should the policeman ever be permitted to berate or ridicule a participant because of his ideology, looks, or dress. For example, to tell a demonstrating mother carrying a baby that she should be home with the child is completely outside the patrolman's prerogative, regardless how foreign her act may be to his own concept of propriety.

It must be emphasized that the supervisor has a duty to promote an attitude of neutrality among his men. In conversation and in more formal briefings, he must insist that they avoid any form of condemnation or punishment. Their sole task is to protect people and property from harm—and the public to be protected by them is on both sides of the line of confrontation.

The reason for a proper attitude of neutrality toward the person and the cause is twofold: if the policeman's attitude is not neutral, his judgment and action is bound to be affected and injustice might result; there is an expectation that the establishment's agent is biased against the protestor. This self-fulfilling prophesy will be realized by his prejudiced demeanor and activity; a point in the protestor's favor. Traditionally, police boast of their impartiality in the exercise of their duty. Above all, in times of a mass demonstration, this boast should not be an empty one.

Leadership on the Confrontation Front

Everyday police work differs from work at the scene of a mass disorder in a most important aspect: in everyday work, the policeman ordinarily is not pitted against an active adversary. Situational equilibrium is to be restored; a service is to be rendered; a violator is to be sought or pursued. On the other hand, at the confrontation front there is an active aggressor pitting his wits (and, perhaps physical effort) against the police. Anyone who has been hit by a rock, or by a bag of human refuse, or who has been victimized by taunts, has become acutely aware of the difference in work settings.

Normally police endeavor is proactive; that is, a move is made in anticipation or prevention. However, at the site of a disorder it is purely reactive. There is a complete dependency on the opponent's action. The feint must be separated from the directed blow. The strategy and tactic of the adversary must be hypothesized. Uncertainty and doubt exist, with a resulting tense expectation. This breeds fear—not the nervous, panicky variety, but a fully reasoned kind. In describing the Detroit riot of 1967, the Kerner Commission included the comment: "The city at this time was saturated with fear. The National Guardsmen were afraid, the residents were afraid, and the police were afraid."°

This form of fear is one that nature has instilled in us to promote our survival in danger. It is hazardous to fly in an aircraft with a pilot who does not know fear. But while this fear serves an indispensable purpose, when it is without control it becomes debilitating and paralyzing. Its antidote is leadership. In other words, one is less afraid when his action is being directed by another who has mastered a situation. At the line of confrontation, the supervisor is looked to for guidance of the team and for relief from the emotional pressure that a touch-and-go situation has invoked.

In the role of leader in the emergency, the team leader must show that he has a plan of action. Also, he should indicate that he knows the unit's more embracive plan of action, or that of the department itself. Furthermore, he should apprise the policemen of these plans insofar as he can. If he is left in the dark, and does not know what his superiors intend to do, he must seek out the information and pass it along to the team.

The welfare of the men should be fully considered. Too often, they go into action during emergencies without knowing what provisions for food and drink have been made. These personal matters should be settled as early as possible. Although uncertainties may make it difficult to forecast material needs with exactitude, the needs should be approximated. The men will be satisfied to learn the rough plans for their welfare, even though circumstances might subject them to change.

It is most important for a team leader to determine the amount of sleep that his men must have. While a man's efficiency understandably falls radically over prolonged periods of being awake, psychological testing has revealed that long periods without sleep may cause him to hallucinate. The dangers of making delicate decisions when the mental processes have been distorted by fatigue are obvious.

Consequently the supervisor should establish duty spans soon after the emergency has developed. If the changing situation makes it impossible to establish working

°*Report of The National Advisory Commission on Civil Disorders* (Washington, D.C.: United States Government Printing Office, 1968), p. 56.

periods, he should keep in touch with his superiors in order to make at least tentative determinations of duty tours. If individual assignments at the scene are hazardous, arduous, or monotonous, they should be revolved to permit all men to share the burden equally. As a universal tenet of leadership, the supervisor should not direct a policeman to perform a duty that he himself is unwilling to perform. When a police chief, after a major confrontation, was accused by his men of not being behind them, his simple answer was, "Of course I wasn't behind you. I was in front of you the whole time."

The primary factor in exercising leadership of policemen at a demonstration or mass disorder is the making of decisions that will not fan smouldering embers into an all-out conflagration. The adversary will be looking for an incident that will promote his cause. The experience of a decade of disorders should cause the police to realize that they are constantly being baited into taking action that will provide a cause in itself.

The team leader should constantly be on the lookout for propaganda traps. For instance, there may be an order to allow no one to stand on a particular window sill near the ground outside a public building that is the object of a demonstration. Someone climbs onto the sill with a camera in order to take a picture. Should he be removed by force if he insists on getting the photo? Of course, you may say. But this may trigger the crowd into some kind of aggressive action. Nevertheless, the orders are to keep the sill clear. What should be done? A supervisor may have to make a decision—one that takes into consideration practicality, possibility, and contingency.

While there is restricted entry to the same building, a woman may be arguing with the policeman at the door about the validity of her credentials. He refuses to admit her. "Let her in! Let her in!" shouts the cause-seeking crowd, without any knowledge of what the incident is all about. What should be done? Refusal to admit this woman may cause a new confrontation. A possible solution is: the sergeant lets her in—and promptly has her ejected through the rear door, which is outside the vision of the crowd.

This does not mean that the supervisor and his team should adopt a weak and apologetic stance. Far from it! The earmarks of policing at a confrontation should be decisiveness and determination. But the set jaw is not incompatible with the smile. And determination is not the same as an inflexibility that conflicts with reasonableness and good timing.

The Intelligent Appraisal of Intelligence

Police plans for the handling of mass emergencies should include provisions for the establishment of "rumor clinics." In the 1943 Harlem riot and the 1965 Watts disturbance, early stories ran rampant that the police "had beaten a pregnant woman." This falsehood provided tangible cause where there was actually no cause in the lackluster precipitating incidents. Thus, there was a practical reason for fabricating the low grade myth.

But there are more hidden motivations for concocting the simplistic tale under stress. In natural disasters, particularly, there is the desire to have one's fears contradicted. Posing them as facts offers this possibility.

Then, too, there is the need of a scapegoat; a mechanism that often makes the welfare agency that accomplishes the most for the refugees the victim of slander directed by the refugees themselves. And finally there is the simple assumption of status by professing to know something the other fellow does not know—typified by the child's "I know something you don't know!" The rumor clinic has the function of analyzing a circulated story and disseminating the confirmatory or contradictory findings.

However, the setting up of a rumor clinic for the internal use of the police department never seems to be a part of planning. The intelligence unit, of course, theoretically serves this purpose, but sometimes it exaggerates during an emergency. The magnitude of crowds and incidents are more likely to be distorted by exaggeration than to be evaluated accurately. Tales of the adversary arming himself and planning operations with military precision are commonplace. Imaginative reports of intended sabotage are circulated. And anyone who has served on the line of confrontation knows that the internally disseminated reports are subjected to little skepticism by policemen who should know better; the reports are passed along almost enthusiastically.

Despite the credibility bestowed on an agency's intelligence, there generally was not the slightest indication that disorder would occur. The insignificant arrest of a Los Angeles driver for drunkenness, the early morning raid of a drinking establishment in Detroit, and the Newark row with a taxicab driver were the precipitating incidents to violence that came unexpectedly. Similarly, the stages of the riots that followed developed with the same unanticipated spontaneity. Despite this natural limitation on intelligence, undue credence is ordinarily bestowed on the accounts that pass down the line. Sniping in the ghetto riots of the 1960s was not substantiated to the extent of reports. The regularly predicted mass movement of hostile supporting forces almost invariably proved false. The gathering of arms and ammunition, when it did occur, seemed to be at an unexpected place.

The supervisor on the line is in a key position to establish adequate and accurate communication with the team. He should strive to keep lines open to high command to get accurate information for the men. When a questionable horror story comes to his attention, he should seek out its substantiation or invalidation. The team should be apprised of situations and circumstances that are accurately portrayed in order to function intelligently, efficiently, and with a minimum of stress. But the team leader, in his earliest unit briefings, can help to build up a healthy skepticism of the information to which they are likely to be exposed.

Losing Points Through Overkill

Reaction to the police handling of demonstrations and mass disorders has been far from uniform. In some instances, law enforcement agencies scored highly in the evaluations made by the press, public, and participants. In other cases, they were criticized and condemned. Most significantly, sometimes the organization that drew fire from all sides for its handling of an earlier confrontation now drew praise for its handling of a new disturbance.

Were all of the brickbats thrown by subversives, the conquered, and people who just plainly hated cops? Of course, dissidents will be omnipresent with their assault on the police. But it would be naive to argue that the peace-keeping units acted at all times with restraint and propriety. The frequency with which praise replaced criticism, for the same agency, on a repeat performance indicates that some organizations learned from their inadequacies during their first confrontation.

When a department is berated for its policing of a disorder, it may have fallen victim to its own support and success on the line of confrontation. A police organization goes into action during a mass disturbance with public support. Except for a small minority, people are opposed to violence; rioters are viewed as a criminal mob. The job of the police is to suppress conflict and restore order, and polls show that the majority will even endorse punitive counterviolence in accomplishing this mission.

Although policemen are popularly supported, they are exposed to verbal abuse from participants in the disorder. Physical violence or the threat of physical violence is directed at the uniform. Furthermore, there is uncertainty about the adversary's next move and the possibility of terrorist activity. Also, the men's lives have been disrupted by the emergency, and long hours of duty have brought about ill humor.

If the police come out on top in a particular incident, there is a danger of what is commonly called "overreaction" or "emotional follow-through." This danger may cause the officer to take one more punitive punch for good measure after the subject has been subdued. In other words, when a person is fired up there is an emotional relief in not putting on the brakes too abruptly.

At a mass confrontation, overkill may express itself in the reckless wielding of nightsticks. There may be indescriminate arrests, regardless of whether the subjects had performed criminal acts. ("Well, what was he doin' there, anyway?") There may even be property damage such as smashing a camera. Retaliatory name-calling and other forms of verbal abuse by the police are not uncommon. This tactic is sure to neutralize the support that the "good guys" have been receiving.

If one suggests that this is no Sunday-school picnic and that if anyone wants to be there he must suffer the consequences, he should be reminded of the phenomenon called "self-fulfilling prophesy." In other words, this is the way the opposition expects the police to act. An image takes shape in the exact form that the adversary has portrayed it. Word of a new police riot is going to be disseminated, particularly if the press falls victim to a policeman who follows-through emotionally.

Inevitably, the police will have things going their way at a confrontation. Coming out ahead, they will take bows and accept the accolades of the public. But now they have let the opportunity for acclaim slip through their fingers. In the vernacular, "They have loused up a good thing."

The responsibility for averting this overkill rests with the supervisor. Wherever the police have unnecessarily and destructively given way to their emotions, there has been strong evidence of weak supervision. In an official police report of the handling of a particular disorder, a law-enforcement observer from an outside department stated:

> There is no question but that many officers acted without restraint and exerted force beyond that necessary under the circumstances. The leadership at the point of conflict did little to prevent such conduct and the direct control of officers by first-line supervisors was virtually nonexistent.°

The inclination for a supervisor to look the other way when his team member is meting out a little punishment is natural. After all, he tells himself, this is the way the people would rather have it. And the men have been putting up with a lot, so why shouldn't they be allowed to get it off their chests? Furthermore, if I try to clamp down on it, what kind of a heel will I be made out to be?

On the other hand, the police supervisor should not only keep a tight rein on team emotions that are likely to run wild, but steps should be taken at the earliest possible time to indicate there will be no tolerance of overreaction or counterviolence. Permitting a unit member to remove his nameplate and identifying badge should be looked upon for what it is: the granting of license to overkill, regardless of the "danger" that "someone may snatch it off and stab the officer with the pin." There is a duty to prevent the team from walking into a propaganda trap that the enemy has set. The supervisor should impress on his men that they can win the battle but still lose the war.

Finally, sophistication is a word that is insufficiently employed in describing what is proper and improper in police practice and procedure. Sophistication is an operational tool that is in the hands of the police but not the hands of the rioters. The establishment is sophisticated, and the system of the status quo is sophisticated, despite the glaring shortcomings of each. In fact, society as we know it is built upon a system of sophistication.

The police must understand that if they depart from the sophistication demanded of them as society's agents, they too will end up in defeat. The supervisor must pound away at this elementary thesis. He should do all he can to make sophistication a descriptive word in the policeman's vocabulary. Although his own counsel may be effective in implanting a sophisticated attitude in his men, his calculated actions will be the best way of getting across the point of strategic restraint.

Not Striking Out at the Strike

In coping with mass disorders since the 1960s, it has been natural for a police agency to think of college campuses, street people, and racial ghettos as the casts and settings for violence. Organized labor's strike has been overlooked. Even though in recent years labor incidents have not been as violent as they were at the beginning of this century and during the post-depression years, the potential for mass disorder

°*Rights in Conflict,* a report submitted by Daniel Walker, Director of the Chicago Study Team, to the National Commission on the Causes and Prevention of Violence (New York: The New American Library, Inc., 1968), p. 228.

still exists. Consequently, the possibility that labor disputes will get out of hand must not be overlooked by the police when they prepare for potential violence.

In every labor dispute (perhaps as in no other form of disturbance) the police have made an all-out effort to be absolutely neutral. The policeman has been uneasy patrolling picket lines, and has usually tried to look the other way and withhold decisive action as long as possible. Today, when there are particularly close relationships, if not outright alliances, with the unions, law enforcement units may be uncomfortable at the sites of labor confrontation. In view of modern labor's ascendancy, policemen can hardly display the emotional sympathies evoked when the emancipation from sweat shops was at issue. But with the absence of the nonconformist "bad guys" that invoke police hostility, there may be little provocation of police antipathy from the picketing force.

Consequently, the police officer would rather not be on a picket line where he may have to take action against those who might almost be considered his peers. Although there may be few accusations that the police have failed to act when violence occurred at the strike site, management personnel and others who cross picket lines sometimes grumble that a squad car on duty was conveniently facing away from the confrontation or that a foot patrolman was purposely unaware of a flareup that occurred. The supervisor plays the key role of explaining to his team that an attitude of neutrality does not mean a commitment to letting assaults, personal abuse, illegal obstruction of enterprise, and property damage go unseen. While the usual common-sense rule of not fanning a spark into a conflagration applies here, the policeman on duty should not ignore clear-cut law violations.

When people are tense and tempers are touchy, an easy attitude displayed by the authority figures may be contagious. This is particularly true at the strike scene because there is an awareness of the presence of the uniformed police. Furthermore, in the absence of the policeman's image as representative of an enemy establishment, there can still be a traditional respect for his role on the picket line. If his demeanor is one of easy concern, perhaps it will rub off on the strike participants. Building up a good relationship with the pickets may pay off if it becomes necessary to restrain them when circumstances become threatening. After all, rapport may be built up with a friendly word or a friendly smile. The best way to get the men in the team to smile is for the supervisor to smile. The easy smile may be a potent weapon in restoring the emotional equilibrium that has been lost through demonstration, disorder, and disaster.

What Rating Is All About

If there is any mystery about personnel rating, it can be resolved by a simple analogy. Rating is merely a system of making out adult report cards for people who work. There has been much experience with rating since the first formal job report cards came into use. Armies of people have been turned into the "x's" of check lists and the digits of graphic scales. Superiors have spent years of drudgery trying to put square people into the round holes of imperfect systems, in an atmosphere of undefined objectives. All the while, the great debate continued: Is rating worthwhile, or is it just another device for wasting bureaucratic time?

One of the police supervisor's assignments may be officially rating his men. If the department does not rate, he may decide it worthwhile to design his own do-it-yourself rating system. In either case, to do his job well he should know something about the principles of rating.

The Development of Rating

Police organizations have been increasingly engaged in merit rating since World War II. They largely followed private companies and other public agencies in adopting the practice. Often there was a sincere desire to improve personnel efficiency through rating processes. Sometimes it was simply because the city fathers demanded it and there was no choice. Frequently it may have been just pure motion, the objective being to appease press or public when they called for an upgrading of standards: in other words, a matter of empty window dressing.

Neither industrial management nor police administration has produced a final solution on how rating is to be conducted, or, in fact, whether anyone should rate at all. However, private and public endeavors continue to rate their workers, despite the vagaries and imperfections built into the many processes. Growing demands for more output and efficiency for every tax dollar, coupled with the development of improved evaluation systems, the practice of rating will continue to be adopted at an accelerated pace.

What the first-line supervisor should recognize is that rating exists in his department whether or not it is official. As soon as he has passed judgement on one man, or compared him with another, or isolated an individual's particular personality trait, he has in fact rated him. Furthermore, there is nothing strange for a supervisor to design his own system of personnel evaluation, regardless of whether the results become part of official records or his own personal notebook.

Getting the Right Man
for the Right Job

Police agencies could sometimes use a better system for choosing their supervisory and command personnel. Too often the civil service process results in more of a contest than a test to determine job suitability. The criteria for selecting superior officers often date back to the turn of the century. A valid, elaborate rating system may soon replace anachronistic and irrelevant testing. This will have to be administered by trained and fair superiors, with recorded data on personnel being interpreted with a kind of computerized uniformity.

This revolutionary adaptation of rating is still unrealized. But a rating system can still be employed to make assignments within rank, if not to promote one to that rank. For example, a specific temperament, unquestioned reliability, and regularly exercised good judgement may be particularly needed for a certain job.

Thumbing through a packet of rating sheets could produce the man with the desired traits. In other words, an instant profile is available to the sergeant or other superior responsible for making the duty assignment.

In larger departments, a supervisor may not know all of his men equally well. For instance, after a man has been transferred into his team, it will take the supervisor a while to learn enough about him to find his best position. Because he does not know each man in the unit equally well, when a post has to be filled, he will tend to make his selection from the few he does know well, unaware that the less familiar patrolman is endowed with superior qualifications. The profile of the rating sheet makes close personal familiarity less necessary for intelligent assignment.

The Rating System as a Looking Glass

A man may be frustrated because of not knowing what his superior thinks of him. If one is an egotist who sends his mother a congratulatory telegram each time he has a birthday, there may be little concern over what his image is to those above. However, if your's is the more usual kind of personality, there is interest in the regard others pay, particularly the others who hold the occupational reins.

If a rating system is properly administered, it can be used to play back to the rated subject an objective picture another gets of his personality, character, and conduct. If there are deficiencies, these will be reflected back exactly as the shortcomings were perceived by the person outside of himself. If personality strengths predominate, these will be played back for the satisfaction of the well-rated subject. Just as it has been said that the most valid description of a man can be gained by taking what his mother thinks of him, adding what his mother-in-law thinks of him, and then dividing by two, the more accurate appraisal of a patrolman can be the composite of the ratings made by a couple of close superiors.

There is a subsidiary value in getting a mirrored evaluation of personal worth. A policeman is very conscious of being subject to the whims of political forces above him. This sense of subserviency hangs over him despite the security civil service has conferred. He is well aware of the political manipulations that can creep into public employment. Consequently, denial of a select assignment may traumatize him by implanting a profound feeling of injustice. However, this attitude of victimization may not always be well founded. Confronted with a self-portrait etched by a valid and effective personnel rating system, he can be led to see the true, objective rationale behind a fancied injustice.

Warning—Danger Ahead!

Prediction studies are common to correctional science, but as yet have not been sufficiently incorporated into police administrative practice. Perhaps not enough is known about what in an applicant carries the promise of career success. Probably there has not been sufficient formulation of performance factors in a man which could serve as danger signals for his supervisor.

Just as crime prevention methods have not approximated the proficiency of crime suppression, less attention has been paid to avoiding the patrolman's breach than to coping with it when it occurs. Personnel ratings could show a graphic trend which will lead to trouble. Sample upon sample of well-made ratings might indicate a deterioration in job performance that deserves supervisory attention.

When a police supervisor takes official note of a negative course in a man's rating scores, he is not hurting the deficient patrolman. If his interpretation prods him into a bit of close observation and constructive counseling, he in fact will be helping the man. Thus the rating system will be used for warning of, and warding off the incident that could spell the loss of a job, or worse, a jail sentence.

If, on the other hand, a supervisor is confronted by a possible disciplinary breach, examining a sequence of ratings can give shape to an incompletely defined situation. For example, if a complaint of discourtesy is made by a citizen, being able to consult an accurate picture of the subject's temperament can give a preliminary notion of how valid the charge may be. Or if a newly assigned team member has a trace of liquor on his breath as he reports for a midnight watch, a rating form's comment on the unfamiliar man's drinking habits may indicate whether something more than a prior social evening of one or two drinks could be suspected.

Thus, a rating form will give an additional dimension to occurrences involving personnel. This does not mean someone has to be hurt. Ratings can serve just as well as an instrument of exoneration or mitigation as of inculpation. Good ratings might save a job. Acting early on bad ratings also may save a job.

The Supervisor's Camera Eye

The amateur photographer soon will find out that one sees much more when travelling with a camera dangling from his shoulder. Whether driving along the highway, or hiking along a trail, his eye is continuously engaged in framing pictures. Having a shutter to release, he will see things that would be outside the scope of his attention were he to go along in modern man's customary preoccupied way.

The police supervisor who is going to fill out a rating form will be a photographer of sorts. Anticipating his task of rating, he will observe the subject more intensively. He will look for particular traits. Knowing that he will have to collect information to complete a check list or graphic scale, he will be thinking of a form's squares or boxes while he does his work in the field. Particularly after making out rating sheets a few times, he will automatically concentrate on traits that are to be recorded.

Thus what might be a rather general and somewhat blurred mental picture of a team member will now become an image that is sharp in every detail. Through a developing habit, he will look for specific qualities, parts which will make up a multidimensional portrait when put together. The supervisor will actually be completing the standard forms in his mind while he patrols and observes. All that is left will be the clerical task of affixing the information to blanks at a later time when formal ratings are due.

Accordingly, one of the foremost benefits of merit rating is that it forces a supervisor to observe, and evaluate. His working eye literally becomes a camera eye, sensitized to his personnel's adequacy or inadequacy. When the man is aware that a report card will be the product of his supervisor's discerning vision, he automatically will be spurred on to better performance. The policeman will know that the squares and boxes and blanks into which his worth has been translated offer him something which otherwise would be unavailable. Recognition will be given to his ability and personal assets, when it would not have been forthcoming without the rating operation. Now his positive qualities have taken the form of official compilation and become identified with him.

How to Complete a Rating Sheet

When policemen refer to their agency's "rating sheet," but never to the "rating system," the misplaced emphasis is significant. For the superior who does the rating, the faulty perception probably represents painful memories of a distasteful and empty job into which he is forced every six months. For the man who is rated, the misdirected focus may be a factor of the system's poorly defined purpose, nonexistent guidelines, and absence of administrative control. Looked on as sterile and meaningless, the significance of the system is disregarded, and the rating process becomes an aimless clerical task.

Even if the organization goes about its rating with sincere intentions, even though the method may be a good one, the system will be only as productive as the people who are putting it to work. One cannot rate a man with relaxed ease. A police supervisor has to work at his rating, and the effort must be careful and intelligent. There are standard errors that will invalidate the results, and these will have to be purposefully avoided. The rules for performing the rating task with efficiency and fairness are simple.

Some Basic Systems of Rating

The many systems of personnel rating are of widely varying complexity. At one end is the simple device of calling the employee superior in quality and performance to another worker. At the other end is the elaborate method that features combinations of scientifically formulated and tested statements from which one makes his choice. An acquaintance with some of the main types will help the police supervisor appreciate the significance of rating theory and practice.

Free description is simply a brief essay on a man's qualities. In one variation, it may follow a formula designed to assure coverage of all significant traits. Or it may merely call for a general statement of the subject's strengths and weaknesses.

The inadequacies of this loose method of rating will be obvious. There is little opportunity for scoring. Uniformity in evaluation is hard to attain. It takes time to complete. But with conscientious effort it can present one of the most graphic descriptions of the policeman.

More commonly used, and much more workable, is the check list form. A set of statements is offered, each one to be marked as applicable to the person rated. Sometimes there is differential weighting, one trait being scored more heavily than another. To assure objectivity, values may be kept secret from the rater. The check list has prominent advantages. It is easy to use, it is adapted to accommodate more than one rater, and it makes it possible to include a large number of descriptive traits.

The very popular graphic rating scale differs from the check list by presenting a trait description, and the rater indicates the degree of its strength in his subject. Measurement may be expressed numerically, verbally or by percentage, in report card fashion. In some instances the trait in question is well defined. In others it is merely named, and interpretation is left up to the rater. The ability to grade the strength of each quality in the rated subject makes the system particularly attractive.

More complex is the forced-choice form, in which a set of statements is usually arranged in tetrads, two of the four to be selected as "descriptive" and the other two as "nondescriptive" of the officer. The true value of each combination is concealed from the rater. Thus, he may believe he is selecting the pair that will score highly for the subject, but in reality another pair carries more points. While the added complexity in preparing, completing, scoring and interpreting may detract from the forced-choice form's popularity, the ingenious method is ideal for putting the brakes on a superior who specializes in overall high ratings.

The Factors to be Rated

The number of traits to be considered in rating a subject varies widely. Check lists usually include more items than the graphic rating scales, the latter sometimes specifying as few as a dozen characteristics. The selected traits describe the way a policeman does his job, the personal attributes that contribute to, or detract from, task performance, and his attitude towards the organizational framework. Frequently found examples of these three categories are "investigative ability," "courage," and "acceptance of responsibility," respectively.

While it may be difficult to measure exactly job accomplishment in police work, the general way in which a task is performed may be expressed with relative ease. Simple observation ordinarily can assess overall performance. Reports and statistics found in the files sometimes provide the supporting data. On the other hand, the policeman's abstract qualities can be determined less readily, inasmuch as they are revealed by activity which is not always available for observation. Most difficult to discern are the qualities which relate to the organizational role, since these are quite intangible.

A system may incorporate built-in difficulties which cannot be easily resolved. For instance, a trait may not be readily applicable to the subject who is being rated. "Investigative ability" is impossible to evaluate in the man assigned to full-time traffic congestion control. Or the semantics of trait description may obscure what a given quality is supposed to mean. Thus, the commonly found trait "knowledge" may be looked upon as applying well to the policeman with a photographic memory for code and regulatory provisions. But how would one mark the same man who does not know how to relate to his clientele?

Only management can assure the workability of its rating system. It has to select the proper traits to be rated, and then define them adequately. This is necessary to guarantee that the completed rating will amount to a vivid description of the subject. The best way to set up the relevant series of traits is to take a model officer who is close to the ideal, and translate his strengths into a formula. Similarly, the individual rater should mentally select a member to serve as a model for each of the listed qualities. Using this particular image as the norm will add realism to his ratings, as well as a uniform validity.

Knowing the Men Who Are Rated

Police ratings suffer from the false assumption that a rater knows every man he is obliged to rate. A platoon commander may be reluctant to admit that he does not know the patrolman twice-removed in rank well enough to render a fair rating. The lieutenant will not say that he really comes in contact with the subordinate only when the man reports to roll call, submits a written report, or asks to rearrange his days off. Consequently, when rating time arrives, he may copy the markings of the sergeant who is better acquainted with the subject, or simply ask that supervisor to "put one down for me too." Therefore, two sergeants whose proximity leads to intimate knowledge of the man and his work are best suited to formulate his rating.

But even if a supervisor does know the man he is rating, he may be unable to express judgement on a particular trait. Many systems used by police agencies give no opportunity to make a "not observed" comment. Although a sergeant has been most observant in preparing, there may have been no instance from which he could determine the presence or absence of a particular characteristic on which he must rate. It is not neglect to admit uncertainty on attributing a given quality to an individual. This admission of inability to pass judgement should be looked on as an expression of fairness and accuracy.

Obviously it is at the administrative level that the weaknesses experienced on the operational must be corrected. When a supervisor encounters difficulties in the system he has to implement, he should not hesitate to voice his dissatisfaction to command. His fellow supervisors who share his troubles can join him to persuade administration to make the necessary adjustments. To fail to do this will be to penalize the patrolman who ends up getting an invalid evaluation, and this inaction can be looked on as neglect of supervisorial duty.

The Errors of Leniency and Central Tendency

One or more of five principal errors may creep into the supervisor's rating process. These are the common failings of leniency, central tendency, bias, halo and the fear of self-censure. Leniency is the most common deficiency, and it is closely related to the error of central tendency.

There are three reasons why a supervisor may allow leniency to pervade his ratings. First is that pernicious failing rampant in police supervision—he just has to be accepted by his men as a good fellow. Secondly, there is the easy-way-out feeling that ratings do not mean anything anyhow. Finally, he may reason, and sometimes correctly, that if he marks his team somewhat hard, while another supervisor is lenient in his grading, the inequity will penalize his own men.

Leniency will be evident in an inordinately high incidence of superior markings. The potential unjustice to men whose supervisor is rating objectively, while another superior grades his team leniently, should not be ignored. It is not unknown for a supervisor who is rating honestly to find his men with lower scores bypassed for favored assignments because of the differential. He owes it to them to present the case to management. A common balancing action for administration to undertake is to call for written substantiation of each high marking. This extra burden may deter the freewheeling supervisor from continuing his misconceived generosity.

A statistical sophistry holds that if you keep one foot on a red-hot stove, and the other on a cake of ice, you will feel absolutely average. Just as grotesque are the thought processes of a police supervisor who clusters all his ratings about the mean, a practice known in the trade as the error of central tendency. In dealing out these homogeneous markings, he ignores the expected range of trait values that should be found among the members of his team. His prominent adherence to an average may really mean he does not know enough about his men to spell out their differences. Management's review will readily uncover central tendency.

The Errors of Halo and Bias

In rating parlance, "halo" refers to an unreasoned high total assessment of an individual which arises from an admiration of one or a few of his personal traits. It is a kind of snap favorable judgement of the whole man that does not proceed from a careful evaluation made from several perspectives. "He's a good policeman" often is tantamount to rendering halo approval where it may not be really deserved.

Overcoming halo tendencies is a matter of rater training. The supervisor should nurture a self-conditioning where he looks at every subject in dissected parts, rather than as a whole. When rating, he should recall a series of mental images of the man, rather than a single image. It is perfectly proper to find a gradation of values among the various traits of the same individual. It is common to find a highly rated factor standing immediately at the side of a lowly one on the same person's rating sheet. Carefully considering each trait by itself is the way to avoid the halo error.

Bias is that preconceived notion which is not necessarily founded on factual data. A police supervisor's dislike for a particular team member, or his aversion to some group with whom the man identifies, may influence his ratings. In its worst form a person may perceive an individual or group from an on-my-side or on-the-other-side perspective.

Sometimes bias stems from the long memory that characterizes a police department. A singular breach of yesteryear may haunt the one-time errant officer throughout an otherwise very satisfactory career. The incident which lives so vividly in the collective memory may even have been intangible, involving bare suspicion or an unsubstantiated accusation.

Just telling the supervisor to approach his rating task with an open mind will not cause bias to vanish. Part of the self-discipline a rater must develop is consciously to avoid projecting preconceptions of personal worth into his ratings. When assessing the traits of his team member, the supervisor's self-image must be one of the "big man"; too big for the petty animosities and hostilities that customarily are found in human interaction.

The Error of Fearing Self-Censure

When a supervisor talks frankly about his rating practice, he may reveal that fear of himself being called to task will influence his markings. For example, he may ask: "If I say he has the makings of a drunk, won't I be held responsible because I haven't made an issue of it before now?"

This timidity is not completely without foundation. In a police organization where administration panics each time a disclosure of deficiency is threatened, and where there is blind groping for a scapegoat whenever something goes wrong, there may be a defensive tendency to lunge out at the honest rater. An empty sense of corporate self-righteousness is threatened by possible blame, and there is relief in holding a supervisor of a lower echelon responsible.

Alleviation of this fear of self-censure must come from management. Policy must include the positive assurance that there will be no blame for rating factually. Administrative attitudes must imply that it expects occasional deficiency and weakness in the ranks; these will be found in the best of departments. Management must promise that no supervisor will be censured for recording the inadequacy of a member. Censure will only follow the deliberate refusal to reveal a man's shortcomings.

As whenever the rating process is impaired by some built-in obstacle, the supervisor must be quick to call to the attention of the hierarchy his well-grounded fears that the system is being inadequately implemented. Group action of several supervisors will add to the impact of this appeal. The supervisor must under no circumstances crawl into a protective shell, make out the ratings with a minimum of effort, and voice the excuse that no one wants them to work anyway. The victims of an inadequate rating perspective are the men below who end up being badly and unjustly rated.

What the Men Should Know About Rating

The analogy between a rating system and report card would not be completely valid if ratings were concealed from the rated subject. Yet it is quite common in police administrative procedure to file them without disclosure. Permitting a police officer to inspect his ratings serves a dual purpose: first, it affords a self-portrait that can spearhead self-improvement; secondly, it provides the opportunity for redress if he has received a rating he considers unfair. There is no good reason why a man should be denied access to his personal ratings. Where a particular glaring deficiency has been noted, or where his overall assessment is low, the finding should be laid before him by his supervisor in conference.

A man should not be made to feel helpless at the hands of a supervisor, particularly when the rater may be prejudiced or inept. There must be full benefit of appeal. If he is dissatisfied with the justification a rater offers him, his objection should be put in writing. The right to question will afford an instrument of check and balance on the one who holds the power to create an officially recognized image. At the same time, it will elicit greater respect and confidence in the system.

In addition to becoming aware of his marks, the member should have a clear and comprehensive view of what his organization's rating program entails. The department first must have a process which makes sense, and has a clear purpose. At regular intervals, management should delineate its rating standards and objectives. The man must be assured of the fairness and skill with which he will be rated. He should be led into an appreciation of what his ratings will mean to his career. He must understand how the practice contributes to good administration, and how he shares in these benefits. The supervisor has a specific responsibility to sell rating to his men.

A police agency has to make a determination whether it should rate at all. Afterwards, it must decide whether it should continue in the practice it has adopted. Here again, the supervisor should be vocal in conveying to management his opinion on the actual benefits of rating, as contrasted with any possible disadvantages. One question that is vital in this decision-making concerns the legal risks involved. In jurisdictions that subscribe to the legal right of pretrial discovery, will the potential production of rating records in court unjustifiably place either department or member in jeopardy when a suit is brought against either?

Secondly, is rating worth the effort it demands? It is obvious that it is time consuming for the rating supervisor. Additional time and effort go into the administration of the system: tallying scores, following-up of the rater's work. Perhaps this expenditure of time could be used to better advantage? The supervisor's advice on these primary issues should be welcomed by management. Awareness that their supervisors have a voice in formulating rating policy will provide the men with a healthy sense of participation, and this will promote their constructive acceptance.

In passing along a positive perspective of merit rating to the men, it need not be denied that there were good police departments and good police work accomplished before the practice became widespread. There are efficient law enforcement agencies today that do not rate their men. But it should be stressed that there is greater promise of better organization if merit rating is adopted.

Essential to convincing both rater and the rated that an evaluation system is worthwhile, the police agency must sincerely try to make rating work. If the process is going to be sloppy, unfair and uncoordinated; if it is going to be looked on as a big, empty show; then the department will do well to spend its time some other way. If, on the other hand, police chief and police sergeant join together in a resolve to make rating effective, then the practice will hold promise of being worthy of continued pursuit. The men will see it for what it should be: a positive and creative supervisory tool that will contribute to their agency's efficiency, and at the same time add to their own personal job satisfaction.

SUMMARY

Deployment without Plan. • A police weakness has been the play-it-by-ear deployment of manpower. • The availability of policemen for a given emergency receives little thought.

Fixed or Revolving Assignment. • Fixed assignment of manpower may not involve consideration of competence or desire. • The basic task of assignment and deployment ultimately falls on the supervisor. • Required specialization is a principle for making assignments permanent. • Fixed assignment of a man may result in a motivating pride of ownership. • Fixed assignment produces friendships with clientele that are satisfying. • Changing posts regularly will allow undesirable assignments to be shared. • When a man seeks a particular job his motivation may be taken for granted. • Disciplinary transfer only means giving one superior's problem to another.

Assignment Criteria. • Automatic preference for seniority will remove incentive to seek a post. • Desire and ability are the primary criteria for making assignments. • Assignments to less desirable tasks should be revolved. • With the costs going up, more concern must be given to deploying manpower. • Workload studies can be easily made to govern resource distribution.

Emergency Assignments. • A supervisor should think through hypothetical emergencies in advance. • There should be backup for emergency situation posts. • Maximum safety should be the primary consideration in emergency assignment. • The fatigue factor in assignment may have been ignored in the past. • Relief in emergency assignment should be scheduled and publicized for the men. • The difficulty of each assignment should determine its duration. • More demanding posts call for switching personnel frequently in emergencies. • A supervisor is valued who thinks of the welfare of his men on assignment.

Disaster and Disorder. • Disaster and disorder strike when they are least anticipated. • The policeman is first on the line when catastrophe has occurred. • Police work, normally individual, becomes a mass effort in times of abnormality. • Skillful supervision is needed to shunt individual effort into a mass function. • In disorder the supervisor is charged with shaping proper attitudes in the team. • Policing the disorder is more demanding than handling the disaster.

Parties to Conflict. • Policemen should understand that disorder may be politically defined. • Demonstration often has succeeded where other legal means have failed. • Earlier zealots have been replaced by militants on the lines of a disorder. • The protestor who just needs a cause is prominent at the disorder. • The place of the drug-influenced at the disturbance scene should be recognized. • The officer should be prevented from falling into the trap of oversimplification.

Neutral Attitudes. • The policeman is not inclined to sympathize with protest and nonconformity. • He should be prevented from punishing the group for the breach of individuals. • The policeman should never berate a protestor for ideology, looks, or dress. • A supervisor should foster a true sense of neutrality among his men. • An officer's actions will be affected by his biased attitude. • The adversary expects the policeman's actions to be biased.

Leadership in Confrontation. • Police work at a disorder is different because here there is an aggressor. • Normally, police work is proactive; at a disorder scene it is reactive. • Fear arises from uncertainties at the disturbance scene. • The antidote for fear is leadership. • In exercising leadership the sergeant must show that he has a plan of action. • A supervisor should acquaint the men with the plan of action. • The supervisor should indicate he has knowledge of the organization's plan. • The welfare of the team at the disorder site should be prominently considered. • The magnitude of the team's personal needs should be approximated. • Adequate rest and sleep must be provided for the squad. • Spans of duty should be set soon after the emergency develops. • Hazardous, arduous, and monotonous assignments should be revolved. • A supervisor should not order duty he himself would not assume. • The embers of confrontation should not be fanned into a conflagration. • There are smouldering traps in inflexible and unbending operations. • Decisiveness and determination are not incompatible with ease and reasonableness.

Intelligence in Confrontation. • Better police plans for handling mass emergencies call for setting up rumor clinics. • Spreading rumor relieves the author of fear, sets up scapegoats, and gives status. • In disorder rumors are just as likely to arise within the agency as on the outside. • Rumors may be passed along in a police agency with seeming enthusiasm. • Disorders usually arise when there has been no awareness of their probability. • A riot develops with the same unpredictable spontaneity with which it begins. • The team should be apprised accurately of situations and circumstances. • Often there is conflicting reaction as to how the police have handled a disorder.

Overkill Versus Sophistication. • An agency may lose its support and success by giving way to excesses. • After subduing the adversary the police may give way to an emotional follow-through. • An agency's overreaction may be a self-fulfilling prophesy for the adversary. • Inevitably, the police will be in control at the confrontation scene. • There is weak supervision where the police give way to excesses of force. • The supervisor sometimes purposely avoids seeing the team's excesses. • The supervisor should let it be known early that overreaction will not be tolerated. • The removal of identifying badges and nameplates may be seen as aggressive intent. • The supervisor must make the men aware of the danger of losing through excesses. • Sophistication is an operational tool for police use. • The police will lose points by sacrificing sophistication. • Sophistication should be a prominent word in the police vocabulary.

Strikes and Labor Disputes. • The labor strike has the same potential of mass disturbance as the disorder. • The police usually are uneasy on the strike picket line. • Complaints of police neglect to act at the labor disturbance are common. • The supervisor must assure adequate police action at the labor confrontation. • A pleasant police attitude may attract the needed cooperation of the strikers. • The supervisor's own smile may elicit the pleasant demeanor of his team.

The Notion of Rating. • A rating system implies the making of job report cards. • There is drudgery when a system is faulty and objectives are undefined. • A supervisor may design his own do-it-yourself rating system. • It is not difficult to learn the essentials of rating. • Adoption of a system may involve bureaucratic "window dressing." • There may be disagreement on how to rate, or whether to rate at all. • An increasing use of rating may be expected in the police field. • Passing judgement on one man is in fact to rate that man.

Purpose of Rating. • A good rating system may someday replace the promotional test. • The man best suited to a specific job can be identified through rating. • Rating will help assign the new man unfamiliar to a superior. • A man will get a reflected self-image through ratings. • A man's sense of victimized injustice can be corrected through rating. • More attention has been given to handling the breach than to preventing it. • A trend in ratings can forecast impending trouble. • Ratings can be used to evaluate the suspected disciplinary breach. • Good ratings and early concern for bad ones can save a job.

Benefits to the Supervisor. • The rating supervisor performs his task with a photographic eye. • Knowing he will have to fill out a rating form will intensify the supervisor's vision. • The general image of a man will take on a sharp outline through rating. • A rating form will be filled out mentally as the supervisor patrols. • Rating will prod a supervisor into keener observing and evaluating.

Benefits to the Policeman. • A man will be motivated to better performance by knowing he is being rated. • Rating will put in focus a man's good qualities that went unnoticed before. • The man will realize positive ratings may be transformed into career success.

Making the System Work. • The system's effectiveness depends on the men who implement it. • Completing the form calls for careful and intelligent labor. • Committing standard errors will invalidate the findings.

The Methods. • There is a wide range of complexity in rating methods. • Free-description entails a brief essay on the man's qualities. • A check list is a set of statements to match with the subject. • The graphic rating scale allows indication of trait strength. • The forced-choice form calls for checking most and least applicable traits.

Process of Rating. • How well a job is done is easiest to determine. • A man's abstract qualities may be hardest to discern. • It may be impossible to apply a listed trait to a given subject. • Management must make adequate trait selection and definition. • The completed form should provide a word picture of the subject. • The rater should mentally select a living model for each trait. • A rater should not be called on to rate a man he does not know well. • It is not neglect to admit uncertainty on applying a trait. • The supervisor should acquaint command with system difficulties.

Rating Weaknesses. • Leniency is the most common deficiency in rating. • Too high an incidence of high markings is the sign of leniency. • The leniency of one rater will penalize a less lenient rater's men. • A cluster of scores around the mean indicates the error of central tendency. • "Halo" is avoided by looking at each subject as a dissected object. • There may be a heavy range of trait strengths in the same person. • Bias may improperly stem from long organizational memory. • The projection of preconceptions into rating can be avoided by effort.

Rating Policies. • An unenlightened administration may censure the rater who lists deficiency. • Management's policy must assure blamelessness in rating factually. • When a system is badly implemented the rated men are the pawns. • Revealing ratings to the subject will convey an image and permit appeal. • A member should have a clear view of what rating entails. • The rated subject should be aware of the rater's fairness and skill. • An appreciation of rating should be instilled by supervisor in the team. • If the men are to be convinced rating is worthwhile, the agency must make it so. • Chief and sergeant should join in making rating worthy of pursuit.

SECTION IV

CHAPTER 9

Promoting Police-Community Relations

A police-community relations program was virtually unknown before the 1960s. In most instances, it was probably popular pressure, rather than administrative imagination, that brought the notion into being. This stimulus came primarily from increasingly assertive ethnic minorities. Since then some police managers have tried hard to make the concept real in their departments. Perhaps more often the enthusiasm has taken the form of elaborate lip service, while realistic implementation was largely missing. Because the idea of community relations has been regarded an an individual program instead of a dimension of total police activity, the massive effort expended in its name may not have been matched by worthwhile results. The people to whom the program is primarily directed may often consider police-community relations to be nothing more than empty window dressing.

Weakness of implementation may have been due to an amateur approach to a sensitive problem. There may have been a failing in the reluctance to spell out community relations as being largely ethnic and subcultural group relations. In its early days, there was an almost pious insistence that police-community relations is something directed to all people, which it is. But as repeatedly made, the statement implied a careful effort not to identify lower class nonwhites and

Photograph courtesy of Newark, California, Police Department.

nonconformists of various kinds as the principal targets of the program. Thus there was an unwillingness to define the subject with accuracy, leaving a foundation on which a substantial edifice could hardly be constructed.

Similarly weak was the emphasis on the outgoing aspects of police-community relations. It was regularly directed to the community exclusively, and not inwardly to the police. Its objective is too often considered to be one of selling the police to a public which is not inclined to reject them. Thus police community relations has become identified with police public relations, the soft sell of a police department: You must understand us! You must help us do our job! You must support your police!

Supervising Police-Community Relations

A supervisor who feels it his basic duty to promote a real notion of police-community relations in his team may find the setting inadequate. The department's perspective may not be one of directing the idea to police attitudes and police practice as a necessary starting point. The supervisor must take the initiative in helping his men understand police-community relations as something more substantial than an obscure little box lately added to a department's organizational chart. He must convince them that it is not just a name for some vague effort performed by a few department specialists. He must dispel any misconception that it is some kind of tacit admission that police are abusive and oppressive to certain people of a different color, life style, or social level. He must insist that police-community relations is built-in and identified with every ordinary police activity which involves public contact.

Blocking the Trends of Hostility

It is the supervisor's task, regardless of the formal program in his department, to impress upon his men that they are living and working in a world where some hostility must be expected. He has to remind them that what matters about the perennial cries from the few that the police are brutal and racist and discriminatory is not whether the claims are valid. What does matter is that the cries are heard. He must guide the men to a realization that their own indignant hostility will be an improper and ineffective response to the assault. Hostility serves only to generate more hostility and a defeating chain reaction results. The first-line supervisor must convince his men that they must take the lead in breaking this spiral of escalating hostility between police and community segments.

Police-community relations is a structured effort to break down hatred and suspicion in the environment of the policeman's work. There must first be a lowering of hostility in his own outlook and work attitudes. To admit that the police hold negative feelings is not to acknowledge them as aggressors. Being the victim of assault in the form of threats, insults, and defiance, one may find reason for hostile feelings to have developed. But these have to be consciously reduced to the point where they will not influence the policeman's action or demeanor.

The supervisor must lead his men to appreciate that if hostility levels are going to be lowered in the community, it will not only be through the carefully worded speech of a community relations specialist. It will not be significantly accomplished by the communication of words at all. It will be a communication of experience that deescalates the hostile drive; nonverbal communication initiated by the street patrolman. The smile is communication. The friendly act is communication. The considerate gesture is communication.

The supervisor's guiding purpose is to insist that the patrolman entertains an awareness of community relations in every public contact—in taking a report, giving advice, or making an arrest. His ability to smile will be a far greater asset than the specialist's talent for giving fancy talks. The line officer's deliberate effort to be warm and kind to his clientele will contribute far more towards developing adequate relations with the community than will the specialized unit's sponsored meetings, dances, and athletic contests. But the supervisor must be aware that he can only teach the lesson of communicating by experience to his men through his own efforts to communicate by experience. If a patrolman is to be taught to smile, his teacher must know how to smile.

Conflict Between Specialists and Team

An inaccurate perspective of police-community relations may have been responsible for the limited success in its promotion. Too often the notion may have been identified with a department unit, rather than with total department attitudes. Police officers may be inclined to see police-community relations as the hodgepodge of vague social activities exercised by a few select members, who soon become identified with what the line officers see as hostile forces. The specialists may be looked on by the cynics as joining some kind of conspiracy against the police. A rift begins to develop. The men of the specialized unit are driven into a defensive group separated from the larger organization. As the chasm broadens there is an aggressive rejection of the unit. This in turn will cause the police-community relations officers to look upon themselves as the real department as far as the minorities are concerned; the larger body can be written off as hopeless. An intensified hostility directed by their associates is sensed, their own hostility towards the rest of the department is elevated, and a disruptive chain reaction of antagonism ensues.

Allowed to progress, the community-relations unit will develop a one-sided, close alliance with community sectors that are more inclined to see the police as the enemy. This will represent a kind of retreatism from their role as police representatives. The breach becomes wider as the men outside the unit respond to the specialist's antagonistic attitudes with more antagonism of their own. A complete distortion of the community relations notion is the tragic result.

Once this irrational and unwarranted split occurs, persuasion from the top will be ineffective in closing it. The line and special unit supervisors will be in the best position to combat the destructive trend. Their simple urging will not be a remedy, although dialogue can serve some healing purpose. The supervisors' obvious role will be to control the working relationships between unit and line. As the dialectic of experience is the communication more effective than words in getting through to hostile community segments, so will a friendly and cooperative attitude between special unit and larger department be the means of bringing to a halt this internecine warfare.

Understanding the Specialist's Role

Perhaps the biggest weakness in administering a police-community relations program is simply that no one knows what the unit is supposed to do. The fallacy which has been allowed to develop is that the police-community relations unit is identical with police-community relations as a concept. Another misconception coming from inadequate definition relates to whom the community relations officer really is. He may be seen by the regular officers as an artificially smiling, smooth-speaking member who has separated himself from the harsh realities of present day police contacts. His work is to explain, assuage, persuade, agree, sympathize, and backslap. He makes pretty speeches at service club luncheons, he sponsors dances for the kids in the low income neighborhoods, and tells a scowling community how nice policemen really are.

Management itself may hold an inadequate perspective of what the special unit should be doing. The real objective is overlooked. The primary purpose of a police-community relations unit should be to set the pace for the whole department in deescalating the mutually induced hostility between the police and some segments of the community.

The symbolic purpose served by the unit should also be realized. An objective already has been accomplished by the mere act of setting up a police-community relations office. Regardless of how ineffective the agency may be, the fact that one exists is what matters to many people. These are the ethnic and subcultural minorities who find their self-image enhanced by the creation of a unit directed to their interests.

Repairing the Split

The responsibility for communicating these considerations to the police officers is that of the supervisor. Limitations may be imposed on him by the shortsighted perspectives of higher administration. But he may still find himself able to assuage antagonism and promote cooperation regardless of the weakness above. He will accomplish his purpose by driving home the notion of what community relations means, and insisting on continuing community relations awareness in the team's total activity.

The line supervisor should seek out and define the actual antagonism that exists. He should separate simple personality clashes from what is a product of poor symbolism. He should take positive means to establish close working relationships between special unit and line. He should miss no opportunity to solicit the specific services of the specialists. Detailed problems of relationship arising from everyday patrol should be brought to them. Observations on given instances of public attitudes in a trouble area, which in turn elicit abrasiveness from patrol personnel, should be continuously conveyed to the police-community relations officers for analysis. The supervisor of the specialized unit should also offer the services of his men to the line.

The community relations officers should periodically ride the beats with patrol personnel, at least for brief spot duty tours. There may be a belief that this might hurt the image of the specialists among their clientele, but this cannot be considered well founded. To subscribe to this notion is an admission of the basic fallacy that community relations is something separate from department activities.

Whenever possible, the police-community relations personnel should attend headquarters briefings of the patrol force. Short informational oral reports to the line officers should be frequently made. The specialists should be present at public events policed by the patrol unit. It is the joint function of line and unit supervisors to set up this constructive mutual involvement.

Similarly, patrol team members should take turns attending sponsored community meetings of the specialists. Both before and after the sessions police representatives should confer, determining in turn what should be on the agenda and what has come out of these meetings. At all times, the patrol and special unit supervisors should schedule, control, and consult on this joint activity. This mutual activity will be a functional way of filling the gap between the parent organization and its unit offspring.

The line supervisor should personally be in communication with the specialists to receive a playback on attitudes from the neighborhoods. Rumors and folklore, as well as criticism of the department with likely substance, should be elicited. The expert suggestion of unit personnel on specific steps which patrol personnel might take should be sought. Where it appears that a solution to a problem calls for the combined contribution of line and specialists, necessary conferences can be arranged. The supervisor can serve as coordinator of the efforts aimed at difficulties encountered in the field. He simultaneously will be contributing to an environment of cooperation between his team and the specialists. A supervisor's individual effort to promote real police-community relations can be productive even though management is deficient in nurturing the indispensable idea.

Dealing with Prejudice in the Team

When we think of prejudice, the image conjured up is automatically that of race. The picture most likely to come to mind is a caricature of someone with heavy jowls, snarlingly proclaiming his dislike for the man whose skin color is different from his own. But the bias of thought which is frequently converted into action extends far beyond race. Religion, nationality, culture, social perspectives, and occupation all are the potential objects of prejudice. The policeman, frequently accused of bias in the exercise of his duties, is a perennial object of the same blind bigotry with which he is charged.

What is Prejudice?

Bias is a basic mechanism of thought. When it arises from experience and reason, it may be quite acceptable. No one can question the right of either the police officer or the victim to be biased against the gun-wielding holdup man. When hostility is unwarranted, when one closes his mind to demonstration which would disprove a belief, when bigotry is acted out—then the prejudice implied is unacceptable and perhaps harmful.

Freedom of thought is a basic right. But when someone is commissioned by society to perform a service, then society has a stake in whether his official act is influenced by negative thought processes. Thus the supervisor has a duty to identify a member's bigotry and to correct it if it touches upon his work performance in any way.

A policeman has a right to bristle at the never-ending charges of prejudice, discrimination, and racism that are hurled at him. He observes correctly that many of the persons who accuse him of an authoritarian personality are themselves reeking with bigotry. He probably believes with sincerity that his official acts are untouched by prejudice. He is convinced his actions are all objectively determined. He does not see himself as bigoted, or as featuring any irrational hostilities.

True prejudice is a process of unwarranted generalization. It is common to form a stereotype of Negro, Jew, Catholic—or policeman. Experience, culture, education, language, psychic mechanisms, social instincts, and thought habits form the complex tapestry of which a design of specific prejudice is woven. Persons differ greatly in their capacity to be bigoted. Studies on whether there are particular groups prone to prejudice, for example, a certain religion or socioeconomic class, have been inconclusive.°

The Development of Prejudice

The police supervisor does not have to be an expert on the psychological and social factors which underlie prejudice. His task is not one of grand inquisitor perpetually looking for biased thinking in his team. He does have a responsibility to determine whether there is a degree of blind bigotry in the ranks which inevitably must touch upon the interpersonal relationships that make up the policeman's work. Inasmuch as intensely felt attitudes are likely to be converted into strongly hostile actions, he has to find a way to neutralize them.°°

To illustrate the process by which prejudice grows, and the method by which it is acted out, consider a policeman who works in a black neighborhood. His social background may have been responsible for a long-time prejudice against Negroes. But he seldom or never has acted out this negativism. His police work has brought him into frequent contact with blacks who have committed a crime, or who were suspected of criminal propensities. Over his patrol car radio he has listened to an inordinate flow of "black male adult" descriptions applied to the perpetrators of armed robberies. Night after night the hostile mob in the black neighborhood gathers when he investigates an assault or makes an arrest. He is greeted with insult and invective by the street corner gang almost every time he drives into the neighborhood. His efforts to do a conscientious, objective job are rewarded by an unending chorus of charges that he is discriminating.

Then he listens to his peers, the working associates he admires and considers his closest friends. They continuously vent their feelings, and these serve to reinforce his developing thought patterns. Fellow officers repeatedly describe the crime and squalor and hostility they encounter daily. They give voice to generalizations and stereotypes about the people who live in the area. They criticize the political timidity and social dreaming which they believe contribute to conditions in the hostile environment. Mutual interplay of thoughts drives the men closer together as a besieged group. There is a virtual identification of all lower class blacks as the enemy. This gives rise to a common thought pattern that characterizes the team. His strong dedication to the peer group leads our subject to see it as the way a policeman should think.

Now there has evolved an acting out of the definite prejudice pattern. Response to the call for service in the lower class black area may be slower. Patrol of its streets may be less intensive. His personal demeanor while in the black neighborhood might now reflect his feelings of hostility. Field interrogations may be

°Gordon W. Allport, *The Nature of Prejudice* (Garden City: Doubleday Anchor Books, 1958), pp. 77, 78.

°°Allport, p. 14.

more abrasive and made with less cause. Prejudice has been converted into action and a supervisor cannot continue to ignore the phenomenon.

Confronting Prejudice in the Ranks

When the supervisor becomes aware of what has happened, he must design a course of action. First he has to identify the officers who are setting the pace for the team's outlook. Then he must analyze their significant verbal communication and expressions of attitude. Finally, he formulates a plan to handle the bigotry he has identified.

Exhortation and persuasion may have to be discarded as a remedy. To entreat and plead are worthless to combat the force of prejudice. The supervisor must select another method for dealing with the negative voices that are being heard. Recognizing that words and attitude are serving to reinforce the vicious circle of hostility, he must deal with them decisively and quickly.

If his patrolmen are able to set the tone for team attitudes, then he should be able to do so also. His own positive words may serve to counterbalance the negative expressions from his men. He does not have to be didactic or argumentative. That kind of communication may only reinforce what is already there. His strategy may be a simple one of getting the men to talk, rather than being spoken to.

In trying to change thought patterns, his approach should not be an "I'll tell you what to think" one. Were he to attempt this kind of intellectual strong-arming, those he wished to convince would simply not listen. More profitable will be the self-induced learning system of talking-through. This training may be conducted anywhere during the duty tour, a lone officer being the supervisor's partner to a quiet chat.

He should get his men to talk out their plight of working in, as they see it, enemy territory. He does not have to keep expounding the deep-seated causes of the hostility they face. He should not take the stance of trying to explain away the abuse poured out on the police. His plan should be to let his men talk as much as they like.

Along with listening, the supervisor will be playing back thought fragments in a way to allow a man to find out for himself their possible lack of substance. Through his own effort the man may soon be led to realize that he is dealing with generalizations and stereotypes which are contradictory and ridiculous. Pushed to the point of expressing it, the prejudiced one now will affirm that "all the people there aren't that way . . . everybody in that neighborhood doesn't hate cops." Thus the desirable conclusion will be his own, arrived at by himself. The new perception will continue to be valid for him because it is his own.

The Acting Out of Prejudice

When there is clear acting-out of the growing hostility in the team, the supervisor will have to supplement his talking-through with decisive head-on confrontation. If there is a slowdown in performing service, he will have to give a pointed order to resume normal activity. If there is growing abrasiveness in public contacts, his insistence on improved attitudes will have to be unqualified. If it appears that tactics of blind harassment are being invoked, the practice must be blocked. Lowering of work standards along either the mansion-bordered boulevard or slum-lined alley cannot be tolerated by any supervisor.

If the growing bigotry is being expressed in crude epithets, the supervisor may properly call for it to be stopped. Then his voiced disapproval may have to be supplemented by engaging in a positive practice of his own that will have a counterbalancing effect. Thus if there is a growing tendency to toss around the word "nigger," he should emphasize his own use of "Negro" or "black." If the patrolman is inclined to employ the inflammatory "boy" or "punk" in talking to the lower class youth, a supervisor should go out of his way to use "son" or "young man," within the hearing of the men. In this way he allows his own more efficient techniques of human relations to rub off on the officer he is trying to instruct.

The Experience of Contact

There is a remedy for gnawing prejudice which has proven effective. It is one that involves the experience of contact. A short, temporary confrontation by the object of one's prejudice is more likely to reinforce a negative attitude. A relationship within the team, where the two people are closer in status, may reduce prejudice.°

As an example, a person believes Negroes are dirty. Now he finds himself living next door to a family which is black. He finds that they keep their house clean too. The expectancy he had held is reduced. In wartime, it is quite probable that facing the enemy at the side of one of a different color and class was effective in tearing down stereotypes that the best logical persuasion would have left untouched.

The best way to lower the hostility levels of a police officer may be to set up a deeper relationship with one who represents the object of his hostility. If his prejudice is directed to a Black or Latin, then closer working contacts with the Negro or Latin police officer may have this neutralizing effect. The supervisor also should encourage friendly contacts with residents of the neighborhood. Here he is calling for the communication of experience to accomplish what the communication of words cannot touch.

Curbing Abrasive Public Contact

Police work involves contact where feelings might be hurt. This happens regardless of whether injury is intended. An arrest will be made; someone is frisked; an automobile or house is subjected to search; force or restraint are required; a service will have to be denied or curtailed; a roust will be made; firm words

---

°Allport, p. 454.

are spoken. A survey of ghetto attitudes revealed that up to 86 percent of the respondents believed these kinds of negative police activities occurred regularly in their areas without justification.° While the police officer will deny that he discriminates in doing his job, the thing which really matters is that the people in these neighborhoods believe he does.

Finding Out Why Hurt Occurs

Even the most considerate policeman should realize that the emotional pitch involved in contact with the public can cause his best actions to be looked upon as somewhat abrasive. The police officer who exerts an aggressiveness sometimes exceeding the demands of the moment must recognize that his demeanor reinforces the generalization that the police are brutal.

The first-line supervisor is immediately responsible for lowering the degree of abrasiveness involved in citizen contact. He has to impress on his men constantly that there is always a possibility of drawing hostile response from the client. Secondly, he must watch individual actions and attitudes for evidence of abrasiveness and discourtesy; finding these he should call attention to the deficiency. The team member ought to be constantly reminded that contact with the police is not a regular experience for most people. His own matter-of-fact callousness which comes from long-time job performance may make him unaware of the sensitivity of most people. Thus he may injure feelings where it was completely unintended. Perhaps this hurt could have been avoided if he had looked first at the situation through the eyes of the person whose feelings he injured. The emotional impact of the occasion may have brought out what looks like abrasiveness in the client. This in turn elicited harshness from the police officer. The supervisor should determine that each member of the team is always reflecting on the impact of his attitudinal response.

Emotional Brutality

Researchers for the President's Commission who studied police-community relations in the United States learned that the brutality regularly charged by minorities is not necessarily perceived by them as physical brutality.°° It was found that the respondents referred to the notion as unwarranted rudeness, violation of rights, harassment, and a refusal to render service. "These things happen because I am black," was an example of the continuing chorus. The white driver of an expensive sports car may also believe he is being singled out for the speeding citation simply because he is driving this kind of car.

Probably the most usual form of abrasiveness in public contact is that of real or fancied rudeness. When a policeman's rudeness is real, it has often been provoked by the overt rudeness of the client. One might be inclined to say, "Fine, he received

°*Task Force Report: The Police*, p. 147.
°°*Task Force Report: The Police*, p. 181.

what he had coming to him." But this aggressive response of an aggrieved policeman can be interpreted better as an unprofessional "fighting fire with fire." The sharp retort will serve no purpose other than to occasion hostility. The supervisor should remind the abrasive policeman that he is being paid to keep his cool, and he has given up the right to express himself in this negative way. He must adhere to the rules of the game when wearing the uniform, regardless of what might be considered a natural human reaction.

Arrests, stops, interrogations, searches, harassment; all potentially abrasive incidents, obviously have to be exercised in accordance with the law. Whether the team member likes or dislikes the statutes and cases which limit his exercise of duty makes no difference. The supervisor has to put himself in the position of umpire. He has to guarantee that the game will be played according to the rules. He must protect the citizen against having his basic rights violated. He also must guard the officer from charges or litigation which could arise from the incident.

But his surveillance should not be directed only to determining legality. Even where the stop and frisk are legally performed, even where the field interrogation is perfectly proper, there still can be fault in the way they are accomplished. These legal actions can cause injury to feelings, and they can inflame hostility. The supervisor's task is to insist on public contact being made in a calm, gentlemanly, and professional way. Any verbal communication accompanying the confrontation should be as warm as the situation dictates. If an explanation for an action is demanded by the person, adequate explanation should be given. This will be particularly necessary to assuage hurt if an action already accomplished is now found to have been unwarranted.

Communicating by Attitude

The routine traffic violation stop is an example of requiring communication to reduce the shock of the contact. Everyone has seen the helmet-and-leather encased motorcycle officer writing a citation. In the car, dwarfed to miniscule dimensions, is the unhappy law violator. He gestures futilely as he tries to explain away the driving maneuver which has attracted legal concern. In coldly ignoring the protest, the policeman fully believes he is acting properly. Correct, his supervisor too may agree. You say nothing, you just write. That way there will be no arguments.

But the cold, technically responding officer, in purporting not to communicate is doing just that: he is communicating. While not using words, he is communicating more pointedly by his attitude. The silent policeman, efficiently writing the citation, in fact may be considered brutal. What an attitude actually conveys is determined in the long run by the one to whom it is carried. Ignoring the defensive explanation of the person in trouble, no matter how invalid the protest may be, indicates contempt to the sufferer. It can contribute to a feeling that undeserved injury is being done. A supervisor might suggest that a few words in reply to an explanation or protest will not be unnecessarily argumentative. If spoken in a tone of quiet explanation they might even be convincing. For example, "I know you were only going one-way on a one-way street, Madam, but you were going in the wrong direction!"

If an officer assigned to a lower class neighborhood, where abrasiveness is more apt to be read into police contact, has a natural manner inclined to fan up hostility, a simple solution might be to transfer him. The primary determinant of assignment to duty in that kind of area should be whether the personality type is best suited to it. Some men are well-accepted in an area of lower social levels. Another's presence will be looked upon as glaring provocation. It is not conceding to enemy forces to move a man whose talents may be better appreciated elsewhere. While transfer ordinarily may not amount to a satisfying solution to personnel problems, in this case it may be. The supervisor has the responsibility of confirming the suitability of the man's assignment.

Police officers should be led to realize that attitudes can be used as a positive tool in setting up good relationships. Consider the man operating his squad car along the street where trouble is the norm. "Hey, pig!" yells the corner gang of youths. His most common response will be to proceed on his way without word or gesture. A more appropriate reply, and not necessarily a form of surrender, may be a wave, perhaps a smile, or even an unexpected "Hi, fellows" return greeting. Here he may be fighting fire with water, instead of with more fire. Perhaps next time he may not experience the same attack from enemy territory. The others on the team will not look upon this nicety as an expression of weakness, particularly if the supervisor has recommended it.

Controlling the Field Interrogation

The field interrogation has always been a vital and worthy part of police work. In recent years it has become more formalized. It may be used on a quota basis: recording the stop is now a usual part of the technique since the "f.i. check" is looked on as a strong indication of personnel performance. The Task Force on the Police of the President's Commission on Law Enforcement and the Administration of Justice found that it was a major source of abrasiveness in police-public contact. But, the report explains, it is not the f.i. check in itself, but in the way it is accomplished, that causes the ill feeling.[°]

Setting Standards for the F.I. Check

The police officer hearing criticism of this type of field duty is likely to bristle. He will say that the f.i. check is definitely an effective weapon when crime is running rampant. He will insist that it substitutes for the intimate street contact that used to be possible when policemen walked beats, when communities were smaller, and when there was considerably less criminal activity. He can site instances

[°] *Task Force Report: The Police*, pp. 183–186.

when a routine check solved a particular crime, or resulted in apprehending a wanted suspect.

The supervisor must keep in focus for his team an overriding principle: good relationships with the public make the job easier. If the f.i. check is looked on by any segment of the community as a source of grievance, then consideration should be given to modifying its form of use. The supervisor cannot ignore the possibility that the field interrogation stop may frequently be made poorly. What is needed is supervised control of the procedure and this should be one of his important duties.

The initial step in control is to interpret department policy on the field interrogation check. If there is none, then the supervisor may be free to define his own. His sound motions regarding the f.i. process are not likely to be rejected by higher administration.

First, he will have to be certain that his team understands the basic reasons for the check. Through its use the potential law violator is kept aware of police presence and diligence. Its most obvious objective is to turn up a known wanted person. The evasive comments of a subject may tie him into an accomplished or planned criminal act. A record of the contact is made and this may be used later in matching the person with a crime that becomes known. To make his field interrogation checks intelligently, the team member must know their purpose.

The patrolman must be instructed in the correct way to make a check. Known patterns of criminal activity in an area are the best indicators for making a stop. Resemblance to a known wanted person is the foremost reason for using the device. Loitering, cruising, "casing"—all may merit interrogation. When the stop has been made, the ownership of a car may be sought, as well as the significance of presence and activity in the neighborhood. Personal identification should be requested and simple questions to establish its validity should be asked. Inquiry by radio regarding a possible "want" should be made. Interrogation may have to be more detailed to satisfy a situational concern.

The demeanor of the interrogating policeman should be as warm and friendly as circumstances allow. The questions asked may be quite general, to acquire an overall background. Remembering the principle that it is virtually impossible to lie consistently, the detailed interrogation may be self-verifying if no hesitancy or contradiction is detected. Careful adherence to legal rights should be subscribed to if there is a possibility of later criminal court proceedings.

"Be sharp" is the perennial maxim that should guide the officer who makes the field interrogation stop. If there is a special reason for this check, it should be revealed to the subject. If the cause of a stop is demanded, it should be politely offered. If it turns out that the stop need not have been made, a friendly apology may be given along with any qualifying explanation. Mindful that the information derived from a check may be of value at a later time, all pertinent data should be carefully recorded for subsequent reference. It is the duty of the supervisor to impart these principles of correct technique to his men and to determine by observation that they are being invoked.

Along with positive instruction on how to make the f.i. check, the patrolman must be taught how not to make it. The supervisor must emphasize that there should be no random stopping of persons just because their appearance, dress, or way of life is disliked by the more conforming police officer. Unreasonable questioning of anyone merely because he is in a part of town where he obviously does not reside should be avoided. Any callousness of manner should be suppressed. Scowling and gruffness are not only unacceptable because of their negative impact; they will not elicit the useful cooperation of the subject. Epithets which may be considered insulting should never be used.

Acquiring Benefit from the Check

A major deficiency in doing police work is that the individual's efforts are not converted into benefit for the group. What one officer painstakingly learns is not communicated for the use of his associates. If a mistake is made, the other fellow rarely profits from the experience. If valuable knowledge is acquired, it is kept secret by the recipient. If supervision involves coordination and communication, the individual's accomplishment will become achievement for the team.

The inadequacy of communication applies equally to the f.i. check. It is questionable whether any other officer, much less the entire team, frequently benefits from the productive individual stop. While the member making it may discern nothing of value from the information gained, another might find an acquired name and address invaluable to his own purpose. The supervisor who has an overview of all the men's efforts is in the best position to determine another's informational needs in any given instance.

The records of stops should be examined daily by the team supervisor. He frequently should join his man when he learns by radio that a stop is being made. He should discuss field interrogation experiences and findings with the individual officer. He should pass on what is worthwhile to the team. He should match the total of information acquired with the total of information required. His role should be that of controller and coordinator of the field interrogation process.

The supervisor must hold himself accountable for the proper performance of the function. His attention should be directed to the worthiness of each stop. He must guarantee the polite and professional approach in performing the duty. He must minimize the possibility that this effective device may be converted into an instrument that fosters public hostility.

Handling the Case of
the Target Policeman

Something unprecedented in running a police department is becoming increasingly common in this age of conflict. It is the occasional demand from an area of particular ethnic or subcultural minority concentration that it have a voice in assigning and removing the policeman assigned to the locale. The ultimate example of neighborhood control is found in the call for an all black police force in a black neighborhood. Sometimes this principle is invoked in the modified form of a demand for screening privileges of personnel assignments in the community.

Singling Out the "Target"

It is hardly possible that these proposals for local control of the police will ever be realized. But there is a growing incidence of attack upon particular police officers by demanding their removal, and this can be expected to continue. For example, it has become quite common to single out a policeman as being brutal, and to raise a widespread cry for his transfer. The specific charges in a given case may be nebulous, and it is not likely that substantiation is attempted. Regardless of the merit involved, the man has become a target for the community's hostility. He is seen as a living symbol of the oppressor in occupied territory.

Now a dilemma is presented to command and supervision. The accused may be considered efficient, zealous, and highly capable and highly respected and well liked by his working associates. It is likely that his having become a "bad guy" was a product of the folklore of the neighborhood. The symbolism is obvious. If it is not possible to hate in the abstract, the object of hostility will have to be something concrete. A kind of scapegoat may have to be invented. But his attackers sincerely believe in the validity of their claim. He has to go!

The campaign for his removal becomes concrete. His name has become a household word in the neighborhood. Community meetings feature a stereotyped chorus charging his brutality. The street youth shout their derision when they see him. When he makes an arrest, both suspect and bystanders become threatening. Perhaps a delegation of young persons will appear at headquarters calling for his ouster.

The Administrative Dilemma

The administration's easy way out is to resort to transfer. But this shortcut solution will have a negative impact on the team. His associates will look upon the move as conciliatory and punitive. They will see it as cowardly surrender. Because of his recognized efficiency and zeal, which presumably contributed to his being attacked, his fellow officers will vociferously claim that "you can't even do a job anymore with the bosses running scared!" No one will stand behind his man! It is brazen and unjust appeasement! Internal furor will have replaced external furor.

To ignore this community clamor may not be in the best interests of all concerned. There is the possibility that despite his well-approved work performance, a real weakness might be found in the way he relates to people. Perhaps an untempered aggressiveness has contributed to his adverse image. His caustic manner may have been particularly unsuited to his contacts in the lower class neighborhoods. Regardless of how little his reputation is merited, his usefulness is impaired by it. Even his personal safety may be in jeopardy.

Command may be responsible for ultimate solution of the dilemma. But supervision will be necessarily instrumental in arriving at a decision. At the first indication that a particular member is attracting the "bad guy" label, the first-line supervisor must be on the alert for impending trouble. The problem will not fade away with time. The immediate superior must set out to discover what really is involved in the assault on his team member.

Getting the Whole Picture

The supervisor should talk to the neighborhood accusers. He may find little factual data to support the vague allegations being voiced. This does not mean he can disregard the matter. If he does, the problem will not disappear. Nor should he be hasty in denying the merit of the charge. He must remember that the validity of the attack is not the only consideration. Symbolism is not always based fully on justified cause, and in this case the assault may be largely symbolic.

The supervisor should use intensive observation to find out what is happening. He should look closely at the man's general mannerisms and habits, to detect any element of cause. In making his evaluation of performance, he particularly should watch how the subject confronts street-corner youths. The way young people in a low income area are handled is generally indicative of the policeman's overall skill in human relations.

His technique of making arrests should be studied. Whether he patrols with a customary smile or officious scowl may be highly significant. How he confronts complainants when on assigned calls should be observed. How he talks to people must be analyzed. His own hostile feelings should be evaluated by engaging him in as much casual conversation as possible.

The opinion of the community relations specialists may be of value in learning what underlies the labeling. Talking to the other team members may help to complete the picture. The charges and their impact should be freely discussed with the subject himself. It should be made clear to him that just because there is supervisorial concern does not mean there is a prejudgement of the validity of the charges against him. He must be guided into an understanding of the dilemma involved. He should be led to understand that guilt versus innocence is not the objective of inquiry. He must be made to appreciate fully that his continued effectiveness and even personal well-being are at stake.

Solving the Dilemma

The analysis may reveal that he has strongly contributed to his victimization. He is largely insensitive to the sensitivity of his role in the neighborhood. His personal perspectives or personality factors make it clear his selection for duty in this kind of neighborhood has been a poor one. This being determined, the supervisor should not be hesitant to request his transfer.

But the conclusion may be reached that the need for a scapegoat largely underlies the assault. Applying traditional standards, the supervisor may then decide to reject the attack as unfounded. A hard, defiant administrative stance is the only one to be taken. But the uproar has grown to critical proportions. Will this hard-nosed decision serve a completely worthwhile purpose?

As an alternative, the target officer can be offered an opportunity to agree to a new assignment. If he is unwilling to do so, the supervisor may have to decide whether removal will be best suited to the good of the officer, the department, and the community. If transfer is the decision, the semblance of surrender can be avoided by making the new assignment important and attractive. Thus that practical administrative mechanism of "kicking upstairs" is in a sense invoked. Further blunting the charges of appeasement from the ranks can be accomplished by identifying the move as temporary.

The assumption that graceful transfer is the wisest remedy rests on the premises that the attack was unwarranted, the crisis has to be rapidly resolved, and a determination to stand firm can result in more harm than good. If the supervisor has time on his side, he may set out to salvage the victim's usefulness. If it appears his abrasiveness has encouraged the attack, the subject might be guided into improving his duty relationships. If he scowls too much, perhaps smiling a little more will revamp his image. If his demeanor has been cold, injecting warmth into his street contacts may be found to be pleasantly effective.

The first-line supervisor in a lower class district should convey an understanding to his men that a concrete enemy may have to be created to serve as a focus for an abstract emnity. The team members must be alert to the possibility they too may become scapegoats in the undeclared war being waged.

The command or supervisory officer is not likely to become this scapegoat. It is invariably the patrolman who is chosen: he is the reality for the people in the streets. While in a position of immunity, the supervisor must remain close enough to his men to detect the vulnerabilities that may arise from the way they do their jobs.

SUMMARY

Police-community Relations. • It is a dimension rather than part of police work. • Its objective is to lower hostilities outside and inside the organization. • Adoption of the idea is not implying the police are abusive or oppressive. • What matters is that hostility is directed to the police.

Breaking Down Hostility. • A hostile response to hostility engenders more hostility • The police must take the lead in combatting the hostile trend. • The communication that blunts hostility must be of experience rather than words. • The smile can be a disarming weapon. • If a policeman is to be taught to smile his supervisor must smile.

Working with the Specialists. • The specialized unit's role should be clarified for the men. • Instances of friction between specialists and team should be sought out. • Reasons for the antagonism should be analyzed. • Specialists should be called on to work actively with line officers. • Playback from the community should be gotten from the specialists. • Line officers should receive rotated assignments to community meetings.
• Conferences between specialists and line team should be held.

Police and Bigotry. ● The policeman is a victim of the bigotry with which he is charged. ● Bias may be acceptable when it arises wholly from experience and reason. ● A policeman has no right to a bigotry which affects official acts.

Developing Prejudice. ● True prejudice embodies unwarranted generalization. ● Peer attitudes will stimulate individual prejudice. ● Intensely felt attitudes may be converted into hostile actions.

Acting against Prejudice. ● The men on the team who are influencing attitudes should be identified. ● Entreating is ineffective in eliminating prejudice. ● A supervisor should get men to talk out their prejudices to him. ● A man should be led into seeing for himself the irrationality of his prejudices. ● A supervisor will have to be decisive in confronting the acting out of hostility. ● A supervisor should halt the use of crude epithets by the team. ● A supervisor emphatically should use acceptable terms to cancel out crude usage.

Effect of Contact on Prejudice. ● Prejudice may be reduced by the experience of contact. ● Contact with those against whom a man is prejudiced should be encouraged.

Hurt in Police Contact. ● Always remember that feelings are subject to hurt. ● The ordinary person is inexperienced with police contact. ● Intention is not always the main factor in causing hurt.

Emotional Brutality ● The charge of abrasiveness is what matters, not what underlies it. ● Research has shown brutality more often refers to the emotional variety. ● Explanation should always be given if explanation is asked. ● There is always room for attitudinal warmth in doing the job. ● Hostility may be elicited unconsciously by the police officer.

Meeting Abrasiveness ● A policeman should never return rudeness with rudeness. ● A particular personality may be more suited to another beat. ● Friendliness exchanged for hostility can be disarming.

Teaching the F.I. Technique. ● The men should understand the reasons for the f.i. check. ● The men should be reminded of the potential abrasiveness of the check. ● They should be instructed in the correct way to make the stops. ● It should be cautioned that stops prompted only by personal bias should be avoided.

Supervisor's Participation. ● A supervisor should try to be with his men frequently when they make f.i. checks. ● He should learn their experience and results in making the checks. ● The informational needs of the men and their caseloads should be known. ● Records of daily f.i. checks should be studied. ● What is learned fron one's check should be matched with the other's needs. ● F.i. check data should be made available to the entire team. ● A supervisor should hold himself responsible for the proper making of checks.

Dynamics of the Attack. ● The role of area folklore in directing the attack must be recognized. ● The men must be kept alert to their proneness to becoming targets.

Confronting the Attack. ● A supervisor should look for earliest signs a man is becoming a victim. ● He should learn as much as possible about the stigma being placed on a man. ● Work habits and demeanor of the target should be carefully studied. ● The attack should be discussed in detail with its object. ● A supervisor should confer with community relations and team members on the matter. ● He should learn whether deficiencies can be corrected and usefulness salvaged.

Acting on the Attack. • If transfer is merited the supervisor should be decisive in demanding it. • The value of taking an unbending administrative stance should be weighed. • If transfer is advisable, the man should be led to concur in it. • If transfer is decided upon, it should be accomplished gracefully.

CHAPTER 10

Processing the Citizen's Complaint

In an analysis of the emotion-packed subject of the citizen's complaint against a policeman, there are three roles to consider. First is that of the police officer. He acutely senses a vulnerability in his repeated public contacts. His clientele represents the entire spectrum of sensitivity, hostility, and aberration that is a potential source of a complaint. When the grievance is voiced, he automatically will be defensive. An inquisitorial procedure where he must prove himself innocent will follow. He will have no available appeal to any immunity, or to a right to remain silent. If the complainant has political support or social prestige, his self-administered defense will have to be all the stronger. Perhaps a fearful and naive superior will listen to an outlandishly concocted tale of wrongdoing, and, in his timidity, hardly question the allegation. Thus the policeman will be surrendered as an appeasing sacrifice.

Next is the role of the citizen who is complaining against the action or attitude of a policeman. It is likely this person fears the power vested in the police. He sees the officer garbed in a cloak of immunity against redress from the outside. He perceives himself as being at the absolute mercy of this man in uniform. If power is abused and he seeks a hearing, it will be word against word, and he fears that neither the court nor the police agency will question what the policeman has to say. The moment a civilian goes to a police superior with his story he imagines he will be the one who is put on trial. Thus the abuse he has already received will be compounded, and intensified. His self-image is one of the lone citizen who lies helpless in the omnipotent hands of a despotic police bureaucracy.

The third man in the cast is the police superior, probably of supervisory grade.

He has the formidable task of investigating and adjudicating the complaint. His self-conceived role is that of the middleman in an ugly situation. He is at one with the patrolman in sensing vulnerability to forces from the outside. There is such a thing as the "cop hater," and the world is full of them today. He has never lost touch with the men in the lower rank. There has to be strong bonds between policemen. If they don't stick together for protection, where else will they find it? The complaint probably is phoney anyway. After all, nine out of ten of them are. Whatever happens, a police boss cannot let himself be looked on by his subordinates as a sellout. The reputation would follow him forever. He has to be known as one who backs his men.

Not all potentially victimized patrolmen, aggrieved citizens, or investigating superiors will fit these examples exactly. However, the attitudes illustrated may be considered fairly typical. These perspectives of the citizen complaint are glaringly negative from all sides. But the complaint should be seen as a perfectly good, positively conceived supervisory tool. A fresh and penetrating look at the citizen complaint against police personnel may reveal a positive and constructive dimension to a traditionally negatively conceived subject.

Understanding the Concept of the Citizen's Complaint

In 1966, a task force of the President's Commission on Law Enforcement and Administration of Justice made a detailed study of police citizen-complaint processing. The published findings imply that the police hitherto may have been directing insufficient attention to citizen grievances. The statistical data outlined in the report reveal that at the time, only one-half of the sampled agencies had specialized units assigned to the function.° One study was cited indicating that seven out of ten departments has no formal hearings for even serious complaints, and half of the authorized hearings were held in secret.†

More significant was the suggested prevailing tendency to discourage complainants from making an allegation against an officer. For example, a practice designed to deter a person from pursuing his complaint of police misconduct may involve harassing calls to home or work. The case of one city is narrated where 40 percent of the persons who complained against police personnel were charged with making a false report; interestingly enough, only a small fraction of one percent of all types of complainants there were charged for falsely making criminal charges against other citizens.°° Of course, there is always the possibility that added charges can be placed when a complainant against a policeman has already been arrested.

The surveys made for the President's Commission implied that too few forces had complaint processing systems that were at all close to being adequate. They pointed out that a mistrusted citizen's grievance procedure is detrimental to the

°*Task Force Report: The Police,* p. 195.
†*Ibid.,* p. 196.
°°*Task Force Report: The Police,* p. 195.

cause of police-community relations.† Most glaring was the cited inconsistency of the various agencies in determining the merit of processed complaints. The report illustrates the differential graphically:

> Of the 63 departments reporting, 5 percent found that 40 to 50 percent of the complaints they received had some merit and were sustained. In contrast, 50 percent of the departments found that less than 10 percent of the complaints they received were valid . . . A more detailed examination of excessive force complaints in five cities, based in part on confidential department records, also indicates a wide variation in the number of complaints sustained.°

Any working familiarity with police administration prior to the tumultuous Sixties was sufficient to demonstrate the prevalence of inadequate citizen complaint processing. Granted, there may have been fewer complaints before that decade which featured an assertion of individual rights and privileges. But what matters is not the historical perspective involved. What is relevant is how the police look on the personnel complaint in this age of complicated relationships. Regardless of whether a department has a specialized unit for complaint processing, every supervisor should have a clear understanding of the nature, handling, and particularly the significance of the citizen complaint against the policeman.

The Value of the Complaint

Nothing in police personnel administration carries so negative a stigma as the citizen's complaint against a department member. A supervisor may shy away from the possibility of encountering the accusatory civilian. The academy instructor will purposely omit the subject from his class material. The patrolman will be emotionally taut while waiting to be victimized by a complaint. Obviously, few superiors will assert that the citizen grievance holds anything from which benefit may be derived.

Let the first-line supervisor see himself as a hotel manager. He places little suggestion cards on the dresser for the guests to fill out and leave behind when they check out. One is left that makes a flattering comment on the establishment's excellence. How will he receive it?

The natural reaction will be to read it, smile—and then quietly deposit it in the wastebasket. But what about the card that carries a curt message that a bellboy has been discourteous? The executive will read the account, and perhaps read it again. One thing is certain: He will not discard this item. Without prejudging the merits, he will detect in the patron's complaint an important tool for fashioning the successful commercial enterprise.

The police supervisor may not be as prone to welcome the client's grievance. Running a police department is not a matter of dollars and cents profit. Here there is a particular question of solidarity and morale which has to be kept in mind. Somebody has to stand up for the men. Somebody has to watch out for

†*Ibid.*, p. 194.
°*Ibid.*, p. 196.

the department's interest. Reassuring himself in this comforting way, a misguided superior will take a defensive stance, tighten up, and prepare to pit his wits against the onslaught of some badly motivated, hostile, vicious complainant!

What the police representative may fail to realize is that the citizen complaint is a natural and appropriate part of personnel administration. Its foremost value is to provide evidence of a weakness, which if left uncovered and unheeded, will become a massive problem for the organization. For example, if a patrolman is inclined to pocket an occasional bill from the drunk's wallet at the booking counter and remains unchallenged in his continued enterprise, there is a great probability that he will begin to exploit more lucrative fields. Thus the organization may ultimately have a grand theft or burglary personnel-case on its hands. Or if a policeman's proneness to deal out physical abuse is left unnoticed, a major assault charge may be his fate.

It is not only the department that will gain from the citizen grievance. The man complained about may be the one to reap the greatest benefit from the disclosure. The inconvenience of being investigated is certainly preferable to a later felony charge destined to arise from a more serious case. The errant one will be the individual who really profits from having his unwise ways nipped in the bud. That citizen who was responsible for making the charge in the first place may turn out to be the greatest benefactor he has ever encountered.

Using the Complaint to Advantage

A weakness in citizen complaint processing is the legalistic perspective that holds guilt or innocence to be the only dispositions available. There is much to learn, regardless of the merits of the physical elements of the complaint. Few cases that are investigated are found to be without at least some evidence of inadequately defined policy, poor judgement, sloppy procedure, personality fault, questionable supervision, or early warning of bad habits. The deficiencies that are disclosed may relate to the individual, or be directed at the department. But even where they are focused on the man, the remedial steps undertaken will invariably involve the organization.

The big question that has to be answered by the investigating supervisor, and similarly by the chief of police who receives the findings, is, "What went wrong that the complaint had to be made in the first place?" In seeking an answer, the first look should be directed at the accused; then the man's supervision should be subjected to scrutiny; finally, the organization itself must be examined. Just as the report of industrial injury may include a final entry that asks, "How could this accident have been avoided?" so should the investigation's closing paragraph respond to the query, "How could this complaint have been averted?"

Because a lesson can be learned from almost every citizen complaint, regardless of the findings or disposition, the entire department should share in the benefits of what has been taught. An ideal method for imparting information on the completed case studies is for the agency's administrator to conduct seminar sessions for managerial personnel at regular intervals. At these times there should be informal discussion and analysis of recently conducted investigations. The commanding officers in turn would convey selected information to line supervisors. If the case indicates a need for adjustment in policy or procedure, suggestions for change could be made. Then the supervisors might select case factors from which the men could profit. Without necessarily making identifications, these could be given to them for their consideration.

This dissemination of complaint data can serve yet another purpose. The review of concrete cases can neutralize the strongly negative connotation the personnel complaint conveys. Laying the facts of processed complaints on the table for consideration will indicate three things for department personnel: first, that the policeman sometimes can be wrong; second, that a fair investigation is customarily made; and, finally, that trouble can be avoided.

Warding Off Outside Pressures

Sharing the emotional impact of the citizen complaint is the allied question of the police practice review board, a citizen's group organized to receive, process, and refer complaints made against the police officer. Despite its demise through court and electoral action, the notion of an outside check on improper police action is by no means defunct. The demands for review boards may be increasing. Proponents postulate its need on the failure of police administration to take action in cases of well-founded complaints made by citizens against individual officers.

There is little question that in some places unexpressed policies still may result in complainants being treated unfairly. Even where an administration may be honestly dedicated to the comprehensive processing of citizen complaints, there may be certain supervisors prone to discourage, play down, or disregard the grievance presented to them by outsiders. These incidents which infringe on the rights of citizens to seek redress have contributed to the ever growing call for the review board. Awareness that management is keeping its house in order partly through adequate complaint handling can do much to neutralize the arguments for independent boards.

The police supervisor has the responsibility to remind his subordinates that unless their department handles the reported personnel breach efficiently, the complaining citizens will seek the processing of their grievances without the agency's administrative aid. The best defense against the feared and threatening police review board can be found in eliminating any justification for its establishment.

How to Receive the Citizen's Complaint

There is an obvious sequence of steps in processing a citizen's complaint against a police officer. Hearing the allegation, assigning it to a superior, investigating the charge, and judging the merits make up the basic procedure for handling a person's grievance. The most important step often is that which involves simple listening to the complainant's account. As most complaints are of a relatively minor nature, this first phase will frequently produce both satisfaction for the maker and constructive disposition.

It makes little difference whether the supervisor's organization has a specialized unit for handling a complaint. Every first-line supervisor should be prepared to receive the citizen's grievance on the spot. Thus he should be familiar with the kinds of complainants he is likely to encounter. He should know how to communicate with them. His adept initiation of processing when the complaint is first presented may well determine the adequacy of its ultimate disposition.

The Threatened Patrolman

Although the superior officer himself may occasionally become the target of a citizen's accusation, the usual object of the complaint is the patrolman. While ordinarily the object of the civilian's grievance, a police officer will only rarely receive a complaint about another policeman. Consequently, his mental image of the typical complainant may not correspond with reality. A policeman's own strong feelings about the injustice involved will shape his less than valid concept, which is reinforced by the customary defensive attitudes of his working associates. Consequently, his image of the kind of person likely to complain about a police officer may take a misleading grotesque shape.

He probably will envision the typical complainant as a person who hates police and resents authority. That individual is seen as imbued with a desire to revenge some experience he has had with a police officer. Practically every citizen's complaint is unfounded, the patrolman tells himself angrily. What is more, the complaint represents a malicious attack aimed at doing injury to the dedicated police officer.

While not every police officer subscribes to this kind of exaggerated thinking, there appears to be a dominant group attitude which supports it. Neither patrolman nor superior is prone to challenge this unsupported perception. When a poorly managed and poorly supervised department is its setting, the basic personal dissatisfactions that are the products of weak administration may take the form of imagined victimization in the face of the complaint. Thus the frustrated officer substitutes this more tangible feeling for the sensed inadequacy permeating his badly run organization. He fails to recognize that the complainant is not of one type, but of many. He does not see that each comes forth with his allegation prompted by a different kind of motivation.

The Malicious and the Defensive Complainants

A complaint can be the product of pure hostility, but experience has shown this to be rare. Where malice and hatred are found to be the unmistakable ingredients of specific complaint, there is strong reason to suspect a psychotic bent in the complainant. Paranoidal imagining may be at the root of the allegation, and, at least temporarily, can deceive the interviewer. Particularly indicative of this kind of abnormality will be a sudden transfer of attack to the superior who is listening to the grievance. Where sickness is suspected, the supervisor should look for an obvious distortion in the facts recited.

Revenge conceivably might be the motivating force which prompts the malicious complaint, although this is not probable. Perhaps at one time an arrest occurred, although it was made by another officer in an unrelated incident. Maybe real or fancied undue force had been used, or some kind of harassment exacted. Thus something in the irrelevant past may have set in motion a current of deeply rooted hostilities that are now largely, or at least partially, responsible for the newly registered complaint. Careful questioning may bring these to the surface. Scrutiny of records may shed light on an aspect of the complainant's background which could lead to a false complaint.

However, the mere presence of a complainant's arrest record is not necessarily significant in identifying his motive. The mark of a felon, which once suggested his want of truthfulness on the witness stand, is not always relevant. A supervisor receiving a complaint may be inclined to look on an arrest sheet as a trump card that will discredit the man making a charge. While listening to the allegation he should avoid the error of positing malice and falsehood simply because of an item on the record.

The defensive complainant is far more common than the malicious one. Rationalization is one of the most usual defense mechanisms. This means that a self-convincing justification or excuse takes the place of realizing blame. One seldom holds himself completely at fault in a vehicular accident; the recipient of a citation for a moving traffic violation is not likely to find himself grossly in the wrong. The natural tendency to invoke self-justification is all the more common when an arrested person is threatened by a jail term. When the general absence of criminal propensities has left him unfamiliar with the processes of justice, a genuine fear of the unknown may produce a sincere belief that unfairness and abuse have been his lot.

It is possible that crude legal thinking will suggest a defense in accusing his accuser. Perhaps he believes compromise is more likely if he can put his adversary on the defensive through a countercomplaint. It is possible that strong egotism makes it difficult for him to accept blame, with the consequent belief that he has been done an injustice.

The strong position of the prosecution in having definite and substantiated facts usually invalidates the allegations of the defensive complainant. In most of these cases, court conviction terminates the investigation.

The Mistaken and the Aggrieved Complainant

It should not be overlooked that a complainant can be honestly mistaken in reporting a police officer's wrongdoing. In his own matter of fact familiarity with police procedure, the officer complained against may fail to take into account the citizen's ignorance of what he considers to be well known by everyone. It should also be recognized that the tension of the occasion may lead a layman to misinterpret something said or done by the policeman.

For example, the quotation of a bail figure may be erroneously seen as a solicitation of a bribe. The routine search for contraband in a change of clothing brought to the jail by the prisoner's wife was looked upon as contempt directed at her. The groundless charges that sometimes arise from misunderstood actions and misinterpreted words of a police officer may proceed from misconceived meanings found in ordinary police practice. In this kind of case there should be little difficulty uncovering the distortion of fact that underlies the grievance.

Perhaps the most common example of the mistaken complainant is the otherwise well-meaning person who champions the cause of the stranger being placed under arrest. His instinct to rally to the underdog's defense may blind him to the reality of the situation. Perhaps he only has seen the display of force needed to effect the arrest, and not the suspect's prior aggression that has made it necessary. Inexperienced in observing criminal acts and disorder, the witness is sincere in his conviction that gross injustice has been wrought by the police officer. Thus it is not uncommon for the bystander to complain of physical abuse when the arrested person himself makes no claim of unnecessary force. It is obvious that unless the defendant is prompted to file his own complaint on the strength of his champion's protestation, a most unlikely event, this type of third-party charge is disposed of as easily as that of the mistaken complainant.

As to the aggrieved complainant, most complaints are made by persons who have been hurt in their relations with police officers. One's sense of dignity is most vulnerable to official rebuff. An analogy may be found in our economic life. Almost everyone has experienced the reaction of becoming indignant at the note erroneously advising us that a bill has not been paid. The realization that the form letter had its origin in a completely automatic process, the recipient being no more than a punch card in the company credit files, does little to relieve the sting.

Police contact is unique for most persons. Brusqueness and official coldness to one's sensed importance are likely to be traumatic events. If the emotional impact of the encounter is compounded by a policeman's actual physical affront, inadequate response to a request for assistance, or the indignity of real or imagined verbal abuse, the citizen will be particularly sensitive to the occurrence. A feeling that he is a victim of officialdom's disregard and rejection will provoke counteraggression in the form of seeking redress. It is not uncommon for the matter to be referred to the district attorney, with a demand for the arrest of the offending officer.

In processing this form of complaint, the supervisor must place himself in the position of the injured person. He should remove himself from his role of the bureaucracy's representative. It is necessary that he see the technicalities of right and wrong to be inadequate reference points in determining the merits of the complaint.

The Related and the Objective Complainant

In referring to the "related" complainant, membership in the family sphere is not specifically intended. The entire constellation of wives and ex-wives, girl friends and ex-girl friends, creditors, neighbors, and landlords, serves as a reservoir of potential complaints. All of the "related" persons recognize that police department membership implies the threat of negative sanctions against the errant employee. They frequently turn to the district attorney for relief, but he refers the incidents to the law enforcement unit as disciplinary matters.

Where the case involves a noncriminal dispute which will require litigation to be clarified, it is entirely proper for police management to suspend investigation pending civil adjudication. However, if even a borderline criminal factor is implied, the department must proceed as fast as it can to make its own findings. This class of complaint obviously involves the greatest technical difficulties in processing.

To the category of objective complainants are assigned those persons with well-founded grievances against police officers, extending from simple discourtesy to criminal assault. There is no hidden motivation or mistake of fact. He has been wronged, and seeks official redress.

In an age when the citizen is strongly aware of his role and responsibility in government, it is not uncommon to report dissatisfaction with the action of a public servant, even though there has been no individual involvement. Most complaints are relatively minor—the officer reading in the patrol car, his taking a drink at a bar, his extended stay in a neighborhood theater. Criminal acts may also be uncovered by the observant citizen.

Receiving the Complaint

The meeting of the complaint-making citizen and the complaint-receiving supervisor is invariably marked by mutual doubt, if not outright suspicion. The complainant expects resistance, that his grievance will not be received, that the officer's word will be taken over his. The supervisor feels defensive, suspicious of the motivation of the complainant, and anxious to find fault. This mutual distrust will be a barrier to the communication required for the efficient processing of the complaint.

So it is necessary for the supervisor to establish rapport. The display of a human attitude will have a magical effect in tempering the pugnacity and distrust of the reporting citizen. Rising from the chair, smiling pleasantly, offering a firm handshake, will contribute much towards dispelling hostility. The courtesy of taking a hat, indicating a chair, asking what service can be extended, all will be acknowledged by an attitude of ease, which will make it more possible to reason with the complainant. This will be particularly true if a misunderstanding was the basic factor which brought him to the office.

Other physical acts can help to thaw the atmosphere. Taking his name and other identifying information and recording it on a large pad will imply the promise that there will be a thorough processing of the complaint. A parenthetical comment or question, such as inquiring as to the nationality of a name, can add to the spirit of friendliness that will ease communication. Only after these preliminaries have been accomplished should the interrogation begin.

The citizen should be permitted to offer the account in his own way, as in all cases of questioning. Then, as in ordinary procedure, detailed interrogation will follow. First a decision must be made on whether a stenographic statement should be taken. Careful transcription of complainants' accounts may not always be worth the work entailed. It has been found more worthwhile to use a tape recorder in complaints of little gravity. Where the grievance carries criminal or serious regulatory implications, particularly where the complainant is suspected of lying or exaggeration, the statement should be taken down by a shorthand reporter. In minor cases which require little formality to process, notes on the conversation are adequate.

Communicating with the Complainant

Complaint reception embodies what may be the most vital phase of processing—the first response to the complainant. The resistant, argumentative receipt of a grievance will have the effect of promoting hostility and additional hurt. Perhaps it will drive the citizen to higher authority, not infrequently the district attorney. No prejudgement of his accusation ought to be made, but he should be convinced that all the facts will be subjected to honest analysis.

This kind of sincerity from a supervisor frequently will be met with the assurance that "I am not trying to make trouble for anybody; all I want is for you to know about it." A comment that a department is anxious to have this sort of grievance brought to its attention for appraisal will have the effect of reinforcing the complainant's conciliatory attitude. In less serious incidents, it might virtually close the case as far as the complainant is concerned.

It must not be forgotten that the complaining citizen has suffered either a real or imaginary wrong. The familiar method of simply letting him get it off his chest can be employed without his knowing the significance. Where he would not be heard, now he is heard; where he has met what was interpreted as enmity, he is now confronted by a friend. The kind word and open ear have served as palliatives and he emerges from the office into a friendlier world.

However, when investigation must be pursued, he should be given some idea of its steps: the record check, the interrogation of the accused, the interview of witnesses. He should then be told when he will again be contacted. If there is obviously no merit to the complaint he should be told so, and the reasoning behind this determination made clear. The explanation might well include an expression of regret that a misunderstanding had occurred and embarrassment was experienced. Any attitude of triumph should obviously be avoided.

If there is no reason to doubt the details of the complainant's account, but there is cause to question the significance of the matter, the fact that the accused is a member with a good record should be emphasized. This new picture that has been conveyed, coupled with a fresh police image created by an understanding supervisor, might effectively replace the unfavorable one that arose from the incident. If the complaint is unworthy of intensive consideration, rapid disposal may be made possible through the supervisor's tact.

How to Investigate the Citizen's Complaint

The range of complaints made against police personnel extends from the claim of an unwarranted traffic tag to the criminal charge of felonious assault. The first consideration in determining how much effort should go into processing the citizen's complaint obviously will be the flagrancy of the alleged act. Other factors prominent in deciding how deeply the matter will be probed are what can be accomplished by the investigation, and the economy of time and resources.

Consequently, some complaints may be settled soon after they have been received and the complainant advised. Others may require prolonged and intensive inquiry and involve the prosecutor or outside enforcement agencies. While there should be a broad rule that citizen complaint investigations must be completed in the shortest time possible, experience has shown it to be impractical to impose inflexible time limitations on the investigator.

Recognizing the wide spectrum of complaint types and degrees of seriousness that come to the attention of a police supervisor, it is impossible to establish a universal format for processing. Each case will call for a kind of investigation based on particular need. Thus it is not possible to establish a rigid formula which will apply to every kind of grievance that comes to a superior's attention. When a supervisor is assigned the citizen's charge, and the interview of the complainant has been completed, he must first plan the steps of his investigation. While actual processing may have to be adjusted to fit circumstances as they unfold, there are well-founded guidelines to govern his activity. Keeping these in focus, the supervisor is ready to uncover the facts relating to whether the act complained of did happen, why it happened, and—most important—how to keep it from happening again.

Interviewing the Officer

Except in cases of criminal import where evidence should be procured before confrontation, it is essential to call the officer to respond to the complaint early. Summoning him to the office is the proper way of notifying him of the accusation. Rarely should he be visited at home in initiating the investigation, as this may carry unnecessary emotional impact to his family. If at the time of the telephone call he asks the reason for being summoned, in most cases the supervisor should suggest that it can be discussed better in the office.

The direct approach involving a minimum of concealment should be used in the interview. With the exception of a few cases where prosecution is anticipated, and the investigation would be hindered by the revelation of facts, details should not be held back in describing the complaint. The accused should be allowed to present his version of the case freely, and without challenge. Interrogation on the specific points of the allegation can follow.

The attitude of the investigating supervisor is as important in interviewing the officer as it is in interrogating the complainant. The experience of being brought in for investigation is highly traumatic. If there turns out to be little merit in the complaint, an indiscreet accusatory attitude on the part of the superior might turn out to be a remembered experience of morale shattering impact. However, a demeanor of apology should not be assumed, as this may encourage a purely defensive, if not completely false, explanation of the occurrence. While the hearing is in a sense inquisitorial, and may be followed by a criminal or disciplinary trial, it must take on the semblance of a neutral and necessary administrative process. Its purpose must be kept in conspicuous focus: to uncover factual data and to propose constructive remedy.

The Officer's Statement

Along with sensing the somewhat inquisitorial nature of his interview, in more serious matters the officer will be thinking of potential legal jeopardy in making a statement, inasmuch as a formal trial may follow. Similarly, the investigating superior will have to decide whether the possibility of criminal prosecution suggests legal demands which supersede administrative requirements. Thus it may be necessary to advise the accused that he need not answer the questions asked. Since many personnel complaints involve some possible criminal violation, someone may suggest that a policeman never should be forced to make statements that could be used against him. However, this would make it impossible for a supervisor to pry into alleged rule violations. Accordingly, except in cases which promise to be referred for criminal prosecution, there should be no hesitancy in interrogating the officer.

In all but relatively small matters, there must be some kind of record of the policeman's account. But experience has shown there is strong feeling against the written report in answer to a complaint, because it is seen to indicate a presumption of guilt. So if he asks for it, the supervisor should clearly state that there has been no predetermination of the matter in question. In view of the need to blunt the inquisitorial character of the interview, it is suggested that the use of a stenographic reporter be reserved for only major cases.

If an interrogatory statement is taken, evidentiary rules should be observed when questions are formulated. The protection of the rights of the defendant is implied by the law of evidence. So asking legally admissible questions is in keeping with the possibility there may be a judicial or administrative hearing at a later time.

The accused will seldom demand to confront his accuser. Personal identification of the officer may be required, although this can usually be accomplished by displaying photographs. Up-to-date pictures of individual employees should be on file for ready reference in every police personnel bureau. However, photos are adequate only for preliminary screening, and in serious cases may have to be supplemented by live identification. In general, with the exception of the major case, personal confrontation should be avoided as serving no useful purpose. The implication of a complainant's intimidation is always present in the face-to-face encounter.

Investigation of Allegations

There is little to differentiate the comprehensive investigation of the personnel complaint from that of the criminal charge. In cases where there should be substantiation before the officer learns of the complaint, it may be necessary to exercise surveillance, perhaps of an undercover variety. Where intensive investigation of a serious case is required, a door-to-door search for witnesses may have to be begun at once.

There may be difficulty finding witnesses who will testify against a policeman. Contrary to general belief, there is not a horde of people who through plain hostility are ready to join in the attack on a police officer. Except in cases where he has displayed gross criminal misconduct, there is usually little inclination to take sides with one who complains against a policeman. Witnesses who can be produced by a complainant ordinarily will be those of his personal circle, or who have shared the experience which is the basis of the complaint.

Particular difficulty can be expected in obtaining witnesses from among the accused's working associates. While the reluctance of a fellow patrolman to get involved might be understandable, any tendency of a supervisor to shirk his responsibilities should be considered neglect of duty of the first order.

Records are a valuable tool in conducting police personnel investigations. They provide a virtually indisputable chronology of on-duty activity to explain or contradict the allegations made against the officer. The search of records to locate the relevant material should be extensive and complete.

Surveillance may be used to advantage before confronting the accused with the complaint. "Putting the tail" on a member may sound reprehensible from the standpoint of professional standards and fellowship. However, it must be remembered that the scandalous action of any given member has jeopardized the status of the group, and fraternalism cannot be the sole consideration in meeting this attack on organizational integrity.

If an investigation is necessary prior to confrontation, it may have to be conducted with the greatest secrecy. One anonymous phone call of warning to the suspected member will be enough to make a successful investigation impossible. While the member issuing the warning will believe he has contributed to fraternal interests, the wrongdoer is permitted to cover his tracks and continue preying on the reputation of the organization and his co-workers.

Anonymous Complaints

The idea of an unnamed informant carries emotional impact for the police officer. He senses defenseless vulnerability at the hands of the faceless complainant. A bare allegation which cannot be readily disproved obviously puts the accused at an insurmountable disadvantage. However, the anonymous complaint is in most cases about a continuing violation, in the interest of the department and not that of the informing citizen.

If there is a disciplinary breach and it is continuing, it should make no difference how the complaint originated. It is not a matter of being convicted by the testimony of an unknown accuser, against whom the accused has no redress. The anonymous letter may be the first step in a process that might correct a chronic violation; correction which will be to a department's advantage.

What His Associates Think

Except where an incompletely developed allegation makes a high degree of secrecy imperative, the working associates of the accused are usually well aware of the complaint being investigated. In some cases the officer complained about has made every effort to spread the word that the accusation has been made, particularly if it has come from an individual or group representing a perspective seemingly at odds with police interests. It is not uncommon to find the accused identifying the complainant with an unpopular organization or movement, even though there is no evidence for his counterattack.

Sometimes sympathetic fellows who are convinced that malice underlies the charge consider the investigating supervisor veritably duped. Then he may find himself being approached by the accused's associates who ask whether he is aware the complainant has a police record or questionable connections. Once this defensive undercurrent becomes manifest, the supervisor may have to take positive steps to spread word that the countercharges are false or irrelevant. This may be necessary to combat the undercutting of confidence in the intelligent and fair investigation being made.

Reaching the Findings

It appears that the most usual department policy on processing complaints against police personnel calls for decisive determination of either guilt or innocence, with impasse considered innocence. Formal trial by the administrator or board will only follow a decision recommending this when there is a strong presumption of guilt. Thus the disciplinary hearing will be kept for confirming the findings of an investigator who has already ruled guilt in a particular case.

The obvious weakness in this procedure is that the investigation has constituted an inquisitorial process without the benefit of sworn testimony, personal confrontation, and other evidentiary guarantees either for the accused or the accuser. Also, placing responsibility for virtual adjudication on one or more supervisors may be used to save the administrative echelons the embarrassment of having to "stand and be counted" by public or police personnel. The wrath of the membership may fall on the supervisor who prefers charges, while the more highly placed person or structure will be seen as forced to act because of the decision of an examining supervisor.

A superior officer who has been assigned a personnel complaint should be considered a fact-finder only. His investigation should be so complete that the administrative unit at the top level should have to but study the ordered facts for determination of the last step. A decision to close the case, to take informal action in disposition, or to initiate a formal hearing now should be made. Ultimate decision must be a responsibility of top command. The de facto determination of guilt at a lower level will leave the impression on the membership that the decision has been made without complete processing, and a courageous and fair lesser official might become a scapegoat.

Adjudicating the Matter

It is an unfortunate standard for handling a police personnel complaint that a flat conclusion of right or wrong alone can close the investigation. While the administration of criminal justice may demand this inflexible disposition, the primarily remedial character of police discipline implies a broad scope of potential determinations. In most cases the evidence will be word against word, with no witnesses or physical evidence available to the supervisor. The experienced investigator has found that both the accused and the accuser have made some contribution to the commission or omission which is at the basis of the grievance. Often it is a singular incident of poor judgement among the many decisions an officer has had to make that has resulted in the complaint.

In the majority of cases, strict determination of right and wrong will be impossible. While the agency chief must take final action, it will be most proper for the investigator to couple his fact-finding with a constructive recommendation as to how the incident could have been avoided, and how a recurrence might be avoided.

If a formal hearing is ordered, a supervisor may have to conduct an advanced form of investigation. This may involve a more intensive pretrial interrogation of witnesses, seeking out the services of experts, or consultation with the district attorney. The stage of supervisorial investigation proper has been replaced by a more legalistic one.

Telling the Accused the Findings

The officer against whom a complaint has been made will be spending sleepless nights. He will be waiting for word of a verdict with the suspense of the prisoner living under the uncertainty of an undetermined execution date. This anxiety might not be apparent to the investigating supervisor. The officer seldom will come to him requesting information on the status of the case. This will be because of a belief that curiosity will reflect his concern, and that it will build up the implications of his involvement. However, the best indication of innocence might be found in the officer's interest in the progress of the investigation.

Except in the most special cases, the accused should be told of the findings as soon as they are formulated. If disposition implies trial or disciplinary action, he should be advised of the conclusions with a formal notification of hearing, or an issuance of a reprimand.

If aware of the complaint, his working associates sometimes will suffer with the accused through its processing. Ideally the results of the investigation should be communicated to all. This communication is not the proper subject of a departmental bulletin, but information can be made verbally through regular channels.

Telling the Complainant the Findings

Notifying the complainant of the investigation's outcome may be the most difficult step in handling a complaint. Where the complaint is unfounded, final confrontation of the malicious or mistaken complainant will be easy. In the case of findings that indicate an impasse, or the strongly suspected but unproved guilt of the accused, the investigating supervisor will have to employ tact in making the notification. Otherwise he may convey an impression that he believes the complainant has been judged wrong. This would appear as a cover-up and might result in a threat to carry the grievance to a higher authority or the courts, or, at least, a blow to the agency's prestige.

The supervisor who received the complaint should be the one who tells the citizen the findings. The revelation of the facts uncovered by the investigation should be frank. However, he may omit details which could be used to the unwarranted disadvantage of the organization or the accused. Evidentiary considerations should be explained. Unsupported allegation and bare denial should be pointed to in the context of the stalemate they present for the investigator. The possibilities of several types of ultimate action should be given, along with the probable outcome of each. It is most important for him to describe the process that was employed in arriving at a determination.

Where a stalemate has been encountered, the supervisor should remind the complainant that constructive remedy is the most desirable of potential dispositions. It may dispel the implications of whitewash to discuss the general significance of the citizen's complaint against an officer. Mindful that the complainant might want some punishment of the offender, the person having an apparently valid grievance should be told that the making of a complaint itself has a significant punitive aspect. The accused was punished by having to face the investigation. The reports will become part of his personnel file. A definite determination of guilt or innocence is really not the important thing. If propensities towards violation were in a man, the trauma of investigation may have corrected them.

Furthermore, the complainant may be told, if there is a repetition, the record of this occurrence will stand out and lend support of a new accusation. The complaint as filed, regardless of disposition, will follow the officer through his career for future reference. If the complainant is seeking retribution, this was conferred automatically the moment he made the complaint. This analysis, factual and unexaggerated, will satisfy the most irate of aggrieved citizens.

Finally, where the complaint has been found valid, it will be easy to convey this information to the complainant. Here he should be fully apprised of the probable action to be taken by the agency. After disciplinary hearing, or when the case has been closed in any other way, he should be told of the ultimate disposition.

That Matter of the Press

The foremost source of a police officer's grievance against the press, real or fancied, seems to be found in the publicity given serious personnel complaints. Over and over we hear the protestation that "anything a policeman does is news," and that coverage of his misfortune is anything but fair. A police officer's less salutary acts do constitute news. The policeman reading the morning news will be the first to turn to the story of his errant associate. No one "makes news" in the strict sense. Because it is news, it is printed as news. No one ever will change this basic principle of journalistic endeavor.

The policeman may loudly object to the department offering the press the story of a police officer's wrongdoing. A policy to release this kind of story usually goes with a practice of making information on police matters available to the reporters. He must remember that a tightening of news sources could be met by harsher journalistic treatment of the accused. The policeman should face the reality that he can hardly demand more from the press than any other citizen.

The question is frequently asked whether an official photograph of the officer in the personnel files should be turned over to the press. The question becomes academic when it is realized that the news photographer can get a fresh picture at will if he wants one. The spontaneous, unposed photograph is usually less dignified and flattering than the one taken from the personnel folder. What has been said about harsher treatment when news is withheld applies equally well to withholding photographs.

SUMMARY

Attitude to the Complaint. • The man sees himself helpless in the face of the potential complaint. • The aggrieved citizen feels helpless before the police bureaucracy. • The complaint should be regarded as an efficient supervisory tool. • Traditionally the police may have handled citizen complaints poorly. • There is a tendency for the police to discourage citizen complaints. • Too few departments were found to have good processing systems. • A mistrusted grievance system underlies much police-community tension. • Departments differ from each other in determining complaint merit. • A supervisor should understand the nature, handling, and significance of the complaint. • The matter of the citizen complaint carries a strongly negative flavor. • Customarily the supervisor takes a defensive stance in the face of a complaint.

Positive View of the Complaint. • The complaint is a natural and appropriate part of personnel administration. • A purpose of complaint processing is to uncover a weakness. • The individual will be helped through disclosure by a complaint.

Effects of Complaint Processing. • The big weakness in complaint processing is the quest solely for guilt or nonguilt. • Few complaints are completely without some indication of personnel deficiency. • Defects uncovered by a complaint may be those of a person or the department. • The big question posed by a complaint is, "What went wrong that made it necessary?" • In processing a complaint, the man, supervision, and agency should be scrutinized. • Always to be asked is, "How could this complaint have been avoided?"

Learning from the Complaint. • The entire department should learn something from the complaint. • Complaint data should be communicated in command seminars and then downwards. • It may be learned from complaint processing that personnel can sometimes be wrong.

The Review Board. • The complaint reveals the way trouble can be avoided. • The demand for police-practice review boards is not defunct. • By keeping their houses in order, the police may discourage review boards from being established.

Image of the Complainant. • A patrolman may have a distorted view of the typical complainant. • Attitudes of associates may reinforce this false perception. • The typical complainant may be seen as imbued with malice. • Policemen may believe virtually all complaints are unfounded. • Distorted views of the complainant may predominate where agency weakness prevails.

Types of Complainants. • Complainants are of many types, each with his own motivation. • The purely malicious complainant is a rarity. • Obvious malice may be indicative of a psychotic bent. • Distortion of facts should be sought out where mental illness is suspected. • The sudden transfer of attack to the superior may reveal abnormality. • Revenge for some policeman's past act may motivate a complainant. • Scrutiny of records may suggest a malicious motivation. • An arrest record in itself does not signify a lying complainant. • Self-justifying rationalization may underlie a complaint. • Self-justification may arise where the complainant fears jail. • Ignorance of the processes of justice may lead to sensed victimization. • In putting a policeman on the defensive, compromise may be sought. • Pronounced egotism may make it difficult to accept blame. • The defensive complainant should be revealed by the prosecution's strength. • A complaint is likely to come from a mistake of fact. • Familiarity with a process may lead an officer to overlook the citizen's misinterpretations. • Tension of the occasion may lead to misconstruing word or deed. • A bystander may complain through knowing only limited facts. • Most complaints come from persons who sincerely feel hurt. • Inexperience with police contact may sensitize one to brusqueness. • Denial of service, perceived affront or indignity will give rise to hurt.

Confronting the Complainant. • In hearing the aggrieved complainant, one should adopt his role. • A mere right-wrong perspective should be avoided in listening to the aggrieved complainant. • A policeman's "related" ones provide a reservoir of complainants. • The "related" may see police membership as a whip over personnel. • A complaint may arise even where there is no personal involvement. • Doubt and suspicion may stand between complainant and listener. • The complainant often expects official resistance to a complaint. • The complaint taking superior may clumsily put up his guard. • Mutual distrust is a barrier to communicating with a complainant. • The supervisor taking the complaint should lead the way in establishing rapport. • A supervisor's human attitude will allay pugnacity and distrust. • Taking a hat, shaking hands, offering a chair will facilitate reasoning.

Hearing the Complaint. • Prominently recording complaint data will inspire confidence. • A complainant first should tell his story in his own way. • Detailed questioning should follow the complainant's narration. • Transcription of the complainant's story is not always worthwhile. • It is better to use the tape recorder in less serious cases. • A reporter should be used in the more serious cases, or where a complainant is suspect. • In small incidents notes on the conversation will suffice.

Responding to the Complaint. • Response to the complainant may be the key factor in reception. • Argumentative receipt of a complaint will breed hostility. • A complainant should be convinced allegations will be analyzed. • Expressing a desire to hear worthwhile complaints will inspire confidence. • There may be resolution in merely "getting it off one's chest." • Having been heard, a complainant emerges into a friendlier world. • The steps in investigation should be made clear to a complainant. • The complainant should be advised when he will be contacted again. • Where there is no merit, full explanation should be given. • Sometimes rapid disposal may accompany the complaint's receipt.

Investigation Guidelines. • The flagrancy of the act sets the investigation emphasis. • Inflexible time limitations on investigation are impractical. • There is no universal format for processing a complaint. • There are well-founded guidelines to govern investigation.

Confronting the Accused. • Most often there should be an early call for the officer's reply. • The best way to present a complaint is to call him to the office. • Details should not be withheld when describing the complaint.

Getting a Response. • He first should be permitted to present his story freely. • This interview should take the form of a neutral process. • The purpose of investigation should be to uncover data and propose remedy. • There may be legal jeopardy in the accused's making a statement. • Legal rights should be considered where criminal action is likely. • In all but small matters, a record should be made of his reply. • He should be told calling for report is not to judge merit. • The stenographic transcript should be reserved for major cases. • In taking a formal statement, evidentiary rules should be observed.

Identification of the Accused. • The accused will not often demand to confront his accuser. • Identification of the accused can usually be made from photos. • Live identification may be needed in serious cases. • Confrontation between accuser and accused at the start is of no value.

Getting Witnesses. • Little differentiates the complaint investigation from the criminal. • It may be difficult to find witnesses against the officer. • A complainant's witnesses usually will be those of his personal circle. • It will be hard to find witnesses among the working associates. • Records are of value in getting a chronology of on-duty activity.

Secrecy in Complaints. • Surveillance and secrecy may be necessary before confronting the man with a complaint. • The anonymous complaint usually involves a communication about a continuing breach. • It should make no difference how the complaint originates if it is of agency interest. • The working associates are usually well aware of the investigation. • It is not uncommon for the accused to spread word of the complaint.

The Investigator's Role. • Sympathetic associates may see the investigator as being duped. • Usual policy calls for decisive determination of guilt or innocence. • A superior assigned to a complaint should be a fact finder only. ● Ultimate findings should be the responsibility of top command.

Nature of Findings. ● A weak standard is that there may only be a right-wrong determination. ● The remedial character of discipline calls for broad determinations. ● In most cases evidence will be purely of word-against-word quality. ● Both accuser and accused often are found to have contributed to the act. ● In the majority of cases, determination of right and wrong will be impossible. ● It should be recommended how the complaint could have been avoided. ● Advanced form of investigation may be needed prior to formal hearing.

Advising the Accused. ● The accused should be advised of the findings when they are made. ● Communication of findings should also be made to the team.

Advising the Complainant. ● The complainant should be advised by the supervisor who received his complaint. ● Advice to the complainant may be difficult in face of a stalemate. ● The revelation of facts to the complainant should be frank. ● Evidentiary considerations should be explained to the complainant. ● He should be presented the various possibilities of disposition. ● The process that led to determination should be presented to him. ● He should be advised constructive remedy is most desirable. ● In stalemate he should be told ruling guilt or innocence is not the most important thing. ● He should be told if there is repetition the record will stand out. ● A factual analysis will satisfy the most irate of complainants. ● The complainant should be advised of the final disposition.

Complaints and the Press. ● The police criticize the press for its handling of the internal breach. ● Keeping news stories from the press may result in harsher treatment. ● A personnel photo provided the press may be better than the one it will take.

CHAPTER 11

Police and Press

There are traditional enemies in all natural and social habitats. One that figures in the police environment is what is seen as a demon press. While the age-old split is seldom documented, except by the quiet grumblings from both sides, the Kerner Commission's report of the 1967 riots made a flat statement on how the breach looked then:

> A recurrent problem in the coverage of last summer's disorders was friction and lack of cooperation between police officers and working reporters. Many experienced and capable journalists complained that policemen and their commanding officers were at best apathetic and at worst overtly hostile toward reporters attempting to cover a disturbance. Policemen, on the other hand, charged that many reporters seemed to forget the task of the police is to restore order.°

The Relationship of Press to Police

The split between the police and the press has not been without cause. Simple everyday factors, along with more complex political, historical, and psychological forces have created it. However, both vocations have had to live side-by-side for a long time. And inasmuch as it is unlikely that a kind of national *Pravda* and state-sponsored radio and television will replace the media, it appears that police and press will have to continue sharing the same environment.

A vital, though neglected, part of police education is to learn how to deal

°*Report on Civil Disorders*, p. 208

Photograph courtesy of Alameda County, California, Sheriff's Office.

with the reporter. The policeman should be taught the basic philosophy of the journalist, and the fundamentals of how that journalist operates. He must be familiarized with the needs of the press, how he can help satisfy those needs, and how the press can respond to his own needs. The climate for mutual learning has to start somewhere, and a chain reaction of exchange learning will follow the initiating effort of law enforcement.

The supervisor is in the best position to provide this very practical and essential indoctrination for the patrolman. The purpose he serves is dual. While he is teaching the team member how to relate to the press, he simultaneously is learning to play the particular important role of news disseminator. When an occurrence is newsworthy, it is probable that the superior officer at the scene will be a sergeant, or his equivalent. Consequently, it will be he who provides the "who, what, how, when, and where" for the newshawk. So in teaching his patrolman press relations, the supervisor will have ample opportunity to practice and profit as well.

The Right to Report

The First Amendment of the Constitution—or rather, 11 words included in the First Amendment, summarize the basic privilege of the press: "Congress shall make no law . . . abridging the freedom . . . of the press." Consequently, the initial lesson on press relations for chief of police and patrolmen alike is a very simple one: there is a right to read; and there is a right to write what is read. Neither the top echelons of executive, legislative, or judicial levels of government, nor the patrolman near the bottom of the ladder of authority, has the right to interfere with these basic rights.

Of course, this does not mean the press has the option to print or otherwise utter falsehoods. In fact, the threat of libel is a healthy restraint tempering the doctrine of complete freedom. Yet, many people complain that the press does not present enough "good" news. But news is a matter of demand and supply; the press recounts what people want to know about. The person who most loudly deplores the damage to lives and character a news story might entail will most probably be the first to turn on his radio to hear the noonday news, or buy the morning paper to read all about it. So what the policeman should remember as he berates the press for taking his department to task or disclosing his fellow patrolman's breach is that he too will be looking for the latest edition to read all about it. It is this desire for news that the press aims to satisfy.

Accordingly, while by no means implying that the patrolman must seek out the reporter with every scandalous tale that comes to his attention, his supervisor must tell him he cannot prevent the press from investigating what is worthy of a story. It is neither for the man at the top, nor for the one on the lowest level of the agency, to play the role of news censor.

Affairs of War and Love Between Police and Press

If relationships between reporter and policeman have traditionally been strained, the animosity may have a very tangible basis. Perhaps the policeman laudibly made the big arrest and subdued the miscreant handily, but in the process suffered minor injury. "COP BEATEN" summarizes the careless headline, to the embarrassment of the heroic officer.

On the other side of the ledger, perhaps the reporter felt the wrath of his editor when he failed to uncover a big story. But it was a policeman who conveniently concealed the facts from him while the rival paper got the pickings. In either case, there has always been this kind of byplay between policemen and newsmen.

Perhaps of greater significance are the more subtle, yet deeply embedded, reasons for the hostility. There is the psychological factor. The police operate from a position of strength. Actual restraints on the way they administer justice have been minimal. The decision-making in the field is largely invisible, and not really subject to official review. The other branches of the administration of justice—the courts, probation, even the prosecution—have more legal checks than the police.

However, the press places a check on police action, but in a more free-floating way, since there is no legal formula with which it must comply. Thus the media may ignore the "good" case, and build up the one which brings less credit, or perhaps discredit, to the police agency. A newspaper may place its own interpretation on given facts not in keeping with the policeman's perspective. It may criticize policy. It may belabor police violations or weakness. The policeman is acutely aware of his limitation by the press, and he believes no one has a right to impose restraints on the way he exercises his craft. But the press senses a kind of unjustifiable limitation placed upon its function by the police as well. It is aware of having to go after its own story in almost every instance. It knows stories are customarily withheld and buried, and that partial facts may be offered begrudgingly in place of a complete account. Yet the press is at the same time conscious of its power and privilege to expose or withhold, to elaborate or to minimize. Consequently, it is a matter of power versus power, and of strength versus strength. The irresistible force clashes with the immovable object, sparks fly, and animosity is the natural end-product.

There are also political roots to differences. The press takes sides in choosing parties and candidates in all kinds of elections. Thus when it comes to attacking the powers in office, what is a better way of making the assault comprehensible than through an attack on the police? The police are a natural symbol, and where can a better scapegoat be found?

Of course, every attack on the police is not politically inspired. Inefficiency and ineptitude may have become focal points of attention in an age when a municipality's bills are getting harder to pay. Consequently, the press may publicize reports of inferior police response and operation. Or a feature reporter may simply come up with his account of how bad things are in a department. Although the individual patrolman may benefit from exposure of deficiencies in the organization, the officer's response is likely to be an all-out defense against an attack which he sees as personal. This is not to say, of course, that inaccuracy and unfairness are never found in investigative reporting.

Most emphasis has been placed on how badly the police and the press get along, ignoring the frequent instances of compatibility. Both city hall and police headquarters have commonly played up to the press, almost to the point of servility. There are chiefs-of-police who owe their office to earlier friendships with the media. Privilege and immunities always have been awarded by the press to the high and low in police ranks. The price paid was their friendship and cooperation.

Nor should this form of structured compatibility be looked upon as a breach of faith. Policemen have always been politically minded, and they have seldom strayed from the good graces of those who wield power. Leaving aside these considerations of ulterior motives, there is no reason why strong personal friendships of policemen with editors and reporters cannot be expected to spring up, as they do elsewhere in the social sphere.

There is actually no genuine reason for a vendetta between the two groups. The press can be of great help to the individual policeman and to the police department. Similarly, the police can be of great help to the newsman and to the news media. Consequently, the superior should impress upon his squad that when an atmosphere of friendly cooperation between the two factions has developed it is better to have it that way.

Developing a News Nose

It is not often that a man of the press quits and goes into police work. Accordingly, it cannot be expected that a policeman is likely to be a newspaper reporter in his own right. Nor is there any reason why he should have to be a skilled newsman. But it would certainly improve police-press relations if he were. There is nothing contradictory in a policeman having a sensitive nose for what is news. In fact, there will be times when a police supervisor on the line of the mass disturbance will be a victim of a de facto news blackout when it comes to getting full information from the battle area. These are the occasions when he will yearn for a departmental nose for news that just is not there.

Determining what is news may not always be easy for the layman. Thus the police novice may be disappointed to find what he considers his big story not only fails to make the front page, it does not even provide filler material! For example, when the proud officer arrests the man who has just burglarized a dozen houses, this masterpiece of police endeavor is ignored. But where an insignificant housebreaking of the lowest order occurs, and "Killer" the watchdog is locked in a closet by the burglar, the news borders on the sensational!

Again, what the patrolman can learn from the sergeant, who is more experienced in the mysterious ways of the press, is that news is what the public wants to be told. Sometimes even the city editor differs with his reporter in deciding what is newsworthy. But the policeman-newsman can set up his own workable formula for making the determination, and this can be quite valid. If it contains the unusual, the dramatic, the humorous, or the human—then it may be news. But even if all of these qualities are missing, then the people involved, the place where it happens, and the particular significance it has to the public may make it news. Thus there will be cases where the murder is not news, but a punch in the nose will make the headlines, providing it was a newsworthy nose that was punched. And the near fatal auto crash will go unheeded, while cutting oneself on a marsh-mallow will be a story of accident proneness that can be converted into a fantastic item!

If one feels there is merit in winning the productive favor of a newsman, there will be no better way of doing it than to feed him the tidbits that can be transformed into human-interest features. Even if the story is not what the paper wants, there is no harm in making the gesture of offering it. Newspapermen may be seen as hardboiled and unfeeling in the abstract, but they can be genuinely appreciative in practice. They have a job to get the news, and no news is *not* good news for the city editor. Reporters do not have the job security of the police officer. Policemen rarely are fired for unproductivity, but newsmen are. Consequently, the sincere gratitude of the reporter for a germ of a story when nothing else is happening is readily understandable.

Unless department policy dictates otherwise, the supervisor should help his men get rid of the empty notion that talking to the press is tantamount to negotiating with the hostile camp. The team leader himself can look at all the incidents and cases coming to his attention with the objective of detecting news value. When he sees the seeds of a story, and its revelation is otherwise proper, he may take it upon himself to convey the item to the press. The overriding rule for him to follow is that if there is credit due to a policeman, he is the one who should get the credit.

A news nose is a worthy appendage for the policeman doing his job. But for both reporter and police officer, a nose for news is not something with which one is born. It has to be developed. The supervisor as teacher is the best one to impart this form of practical learning.

How News Is Reported

Whether the policeman volunteers a story, or whether he reveals it only after it has been dug out by the newsman, there is a right way and a wrong way of telling it. As an astute newspaper reporter noted, "The trouble with daily journalism is that you get so involved with 'Who hit John?' that you never really know why John had his chin out in the first place."°

Regardless of any journalistic deficiencies, the reporting officer should get into his account for the reporting newsman all about what preceded the assault on John. The policeman should guide the reporter into perceiving the story in all its dimensions. Most important, if there are aspects of the occurrence that may appeal to the human interest of the reader, these should be blended into the officer's narration.

The legalistic orientation of the policeman may prompt him to impart only what he considers relevant and material from the perspective of judicial processing. Similarly, he may present only what has been definitely established concerning the occurrence. While fact should be clearly labelled as fact, and opinion as opinion, the total story in all its ramifications should be narrated. Otherwise the account can be laborious, hesitating, and clumsy, and the full import and significance will be lacking. A word of caution though. When criminal processing is anticipated, the legal restrictions on official comment imposed by current court decisions *must* be observed.

There is the obvious fear of being misquoted. While the possibility of putting unspoken words into the policeman's mouth exists, police veterans of contact with the press know this rarely occurs. Where the overall story is made clear, where fact is called fact and opinion is dubbed opinion, the danger is not a real one. It is obvious that the policeman who timidly, hesitatingly, and vaguely presents the facts to a newsman is making himself more liable to error in interpretation than the one who does so with decisiveness and ease.

In providing his informal course of instruction on how to deal with the press, the supervisor should familiarize his student with what the reporter will do with the story. Usually, he will pass on the account by telephone to a rewrite man. At that time he will present a brief summary, the name of the principal, a chronological account, the names of others involved, and finally comment on the significance of the item. The story will be filled in by the rewrite man asking questions, and by the reporter answering them.

°Charles McCabe, column in the *San Francisco Chronicle*, August 23, 1971, p. 33.

Consequently, the policeman who is presenting the story in the first place might employ the same format as the reporter. The summary will be a kind of headline, that tells the story in a few words. Next comes the important matter of names. The main personality should be identified, his name carefully and accurately spelled. Invariably information is needed on age and occupation. This should be available, regardless of how irrelevant the policeman may think the data.

Then the story should be told simply and chronologically: this happened, then this, afterwards this, etc. Next the other party or parties should be identified, again names being spelled out, and relationships to the principal and incident being carefully described. Finally, all overtones, significances, human interest, and stories within the story should be presented. This will provide the reporter with the total view needed for a good story. For the narrating police officer, there will be gratitude for his skillful effort and perhaps a new friend in the grateful reporter. As a bonus for the policeman, there may be a flattering word, a quote, or just being named in the finished news article.

There will be times when the reporting policeman will want to protect someone involved in an incident from publicity. In almost every case, the try will be futile. Even if there is a temporary concealment of a particular identification, almost inevitably the information will leak out. The explosive impact of suddenly involving one who was hitherto protected can only amount to harsher treatment. It probably would have been better to have made the otherwise proper disclosure while specifically suggesting or requesting that there be concealment of identification. Of course, if there is the slightest uncertainty as to a person's involvement, this in itself may be a deterrent to publication, inasmuch as there is an omnipresent journalistic fear of libel action.

On the other hand, there are times when news must be withheld in the course of duty performance. The most important example, of course, is when it relates to a forthcoming prosecution. In fact, there may even be a court order prohibiting comment. If there is not, the supervisor may have to make a decision on the propriety of revealing evidentiary information. When there is a question as to the effects on judicial mechanics, the supervisor will be on firm ground if he issues a "no comment." If there is any doubt on the propriety of disclosure, the supervisor should issue a positive order to his men to make no statement. In this case he must assume full responsibility for nondisclosure.

The other occasion that will call for concealment of facts is when their release will jeopardize the necessary follow-up investigation. The classic example will be a kidnapping where ransom has been demanded. Perhaps more common is the arrest of one person before a potential codefendant has been located. Even if the press gets hold of the information, its cooperation can be solicited. Experience has shown that newsmen may be expected to cooperate. In the first place, the press more often than not displays a sense of ethical responsibility. Secondly, the failure to work with the police can affect future cooperation on which the press is dependent. Finally, and perhaps most practical from a here-and-now perspective, an editor would rather have the story on the big case, and the big one might not develop if the lesser one were publicized prematurely.

Here again it will be the supervisor who plays the key role in the decision-making on concealment. He may have to order his men specifically not to divulge the information at hand. He may have to set up a plan to keep data on an occurrence from falling into the hands of reporters. He may have to call on the press to withhold facts it has learned. Perhaps he should set a policy that when the curtailment of news in any way becomes necessary, responsibility for it should be placed on his supervisorial shoulders.

Learning to Live with the Media

While an all-out, ongoing love affair between press and police perhaps will always be short of reality, it will at least benefit both occupations to live in a state of truce. In the final instance, the way in which the individual policeman relates to the media will have to be determined by the specific policy of his agency. However, police administrators are apt to shy away from spelling out a clear-cut formula of relationship. There is too much danger in setting up restrictive guidelines that may draw down the wrath of the press on police management.

There is usually no exact policy on news release. This being the case, the supervisor should be relatively free to develop his own principles of proper press relations for his team. But along with setting up guidelines on what stories should be released, on how much should be included, and on what initiative should be taken to get the story to the media, the principal lesson for the supervisor to impart is that it is quite possible to live amicably and profitably with the press. He can teach his men that it is acceptable to suggest that the newspapers, radio, and television can and do help law enforcement. That the papers in particular need the cooperation of the police can be shown from the worrisome statistic that in some cities all but one or two of the journals that were on the streets a few years ago have ceased operations. Consequently, no editor will go out of his way to erect barriers to get the news he needs for publication. In fact, some newspapers of uncertain future have gone out of their way to cooperate with the police in order to set up a relationship condusive to good news flow.

Conversely, law enforcement needs all the support it can get from the media. Administrators are becoming more and more aware that police agencies are unable to put the brakes on crime by themselves. Police officials know that big cases have been cracked as a result of the citizen's telephone call made after reading about a key clue in the evening edition. Crime prevention implies public education that can be better achieved through the graphic news story than by the slick official brochure.

Press Relations on the Battle-Line

Critics of the press, both police and laymen, often point to the lack of objectivity and the inflammatory tone in reporting mass disturbances. It is quite fashionable to condemn the press for fomenting strife by its sensational coverage. Contrariwise, the Kerner Report in its analysis of the 1967 disturbances does not really support this popular attack on the media. While the press is not held entirely blameless, the following quotes from the conclusions of the study are significant:

> In contrast to what some of its critics have charged, television sometimes may have leaned over too far backward in seeking balance and restraint. By stressing interviews, many with whites in predominantly Negro neighborhoods, and by emphasizing control scenes rather than riotous action, television news broadcasts may have given a distorted picture of what the disorders were all about.°

> Like television coverage, newspaper coverage of civil disturbances in the summer of 1967 was more calm, factual, and restrained than outwardly emotional or inflammatory.†

> Of 955 television sequences of riot and racial news examined . . . a small proportion of all scenes analyzed showed actual mob action, people looting, sniping, setting fires, or being injured, or killed. Moderate Negro leaders were shown more frequently than militant leaders on television news broadcasts.°°

> Of 3779 newspaper articles analyzed, more focused on legislation which should be sought and planning which should be done to control ongoing riots and prevent future riots than on any other topic.††

While the Kerner Commission did cite scattered unsupported scare headlines and empty rumors, along with the riot events actually staged by some less responsible newsmen, officialdom itself is accused as having contributed to circulated distortions:

> . . . the press obtained much factual information about the scale of disorders—property damage, personal injury, and deaths—from local officials, who often were inexperienced in dealing with civil disorders and not always able to sort out fact from rumor in the confusion.°°°

Although the police are not identified specifically with what the report refers to as "local officials," one might validly conjecture that there were instances of law enforcement agencies involved. This is another way of saying there must be coordination between police and press to present a true picture of what is happening in a mass disorder. Coordination can only stem from an atmosphere of cooperation—a mutual, reciprocal and complementary effort to gather the news, organize the news, and report the news. Before this can be accomplished, there must be an end to the sterile negativism which nurtures the empty antipathy between police and press. Someone has to change the mistrustful attitude policemen demonstrate when a reporter is present. That someone who is charged with the duty of promoting healthy police-press attitudes is the superior officer closest to the men—the squad sergeant. With the sergeant recognized as the educator, the Kerner Report summation on the poor conditions of police-press relationships in the riot

°*Report on Civil Disorders*, p. 206.

†*Ibid.*, p. 205.

°°*Ibid.*, p. 202.

††*Ibid.*

°°°*Report on Civil Disorders*, p. 202.

cities, along with its more important proposal for solution, can be looked to in formulating the task of education the supervisor should assume:

> After considering available evidence on the subject, the Commission is convinced that these conditions reflect an absence of advanced communication and planning among the people involved. We do not suggest that familiarity with the other's problems will beget total amity and cooperation. The interests of the media and the police are sometimes necessarily at variance. But we do believe that communication is a vital step toward removing the obstacles produced by ignorance, confusion, and misunderstanding of what each group is actually trying to do.°

SUMMARY

Rift between Police and Press. • There is little documentation of the split between press and police. • The Kerner Report said the police were hostile to reporters in the riots. • There are complex political, historical, and psychological factors involved. • It is a vital part of police education to learn to deal with the press. • The policeman must learn the needs of the press and how he needs the press. • The supervisor is the more likely contact of the press in everyday practice.

Freedom of Speech. • The First Amendment guards against abridging the freedom of the press. • A healthy restraint against press irresponsibility is the fear of libel. • The norm of what is to be printed is what the public wants to read. • The supervisor should impress on the men that they may not block newsgathering.

Hostility and Friendship. • Experience may have given rise to animosity for both sides. • Contributing to the split is the press' checking of police action. • The police have a built-in control of press newsgathering. • The police may symbolize city hall in providing a tangible target. • The press may attack the police for inefficiency and ineptitude. • City government and the police traditionally have sought press favor. • Privilege and immunity have been exchanged by the press for police cooperation. • It is natural for friendships to exist between police and press personnel. • The supervisor should teach the men it is better to have friendly cooperation.

Sensing What is News. • The police should develop a sensitive nose for what is news. • In times of disorder, police supervisors feel the absence of news. • Determining what is news may not be easy for the layman. • It may be news if it contains the unusual, dramatic, humorous, or human. • A particular place, person, or significance may turn something into news. • One may win the favor of the newsman by feeding him tidbits of news. • In practice, newsmen may be found to be quite appreciative of favors. • In reality, most officers would like to get along better with the press. • A supervisor should look at all incidents he encounters for news value. • The ability to scent out what is news is a learned capability.

Telling the Story. • A story should be presented to the reporter in its full dimensions. • Human interest facts should be included in the narration to the press. • The

°*Report on Civil Disorders*, p. 208.

total story in all its ramifications should be told to the reporter. • The supervisor observed relating to the press can set an example for his team. • The danger of being misquoted is not too great. • Timidly, hesitatingly, and vaguely giving the news may cause misinterpretation. • The supervisor should acquaint the men with how a story is processed. • Usually the reporter will telephone the story to the rewrite man. • The initial summary presented by officer and reporter will be a headline. • Invariably the press will want information on age and occupation. • The reporter will appreciate the officer's skillful narration. • The attempt to conceal an identity will almost inevitably be futile. • It may be better to request the press to keep a name out of the story. • It is virtually impossible to keep a story in all details from the press. • Forthcoming prosecution or follow-up may be valid reasons for concealment. • If disclosure is blocked for cause the supervisor should accept the responsibility. • News of an arrest may have to be concealed if a codefendant is still at large.

Getting Along with the Press. • Specific policy is ultimately the best way to control police-press relations. • The supervisor should make the decision when a question arises on policy. • A supervisor should stress that good police-press relations are possible. • The supervisor should impress on his men that the media help the police. • An editor will avoid creating barriers to getting the news. • Law enforcement needs all the help it can get from the media. • The graphic news story may be a better crime preventive than the brochure. • The Kerner Report is complimentary to the press for its 1967 riot coverage. • In the riots, officialdom itself contributed to distorted news dissemination. • The police and press must cooperate to produce valid mass-disorder news. • A supervisor should rid his men of their distrustful attitude before the press. • Communication is needed to remove misunderstanding between police and press.

CHAPTER 12

Promoting Professionalism

What's in a name? A lot, if it refers to an occupation. Too much, in fact, for it leaves a great amount to be determined as to what the job in question really is. For example, the sergeant who boasted that his uncle was a diamond cutter failed to explain he was hired to cut the lawn at the local baseball park. Similarly, "following the medical profession" actually may mean one practices the worthy art of the undertaker. Also, "painter" equally refers to Rembrandt and the fellow down the street who includes house decorating in the scope of his handyman services.

The qualifying term "profession" is also bandied about somewhat freely in attaching affluence to a particular vocation. Thus it is customary to speak of the "professional this" and the "professional that," diluting the more prestigious meaning of the word. The police occupation has long been involved in a debate on whether the field deserves the classification of profession. And while the controversy goes on, there is a continued demand for professionalism in the police service. As elsewhere in the area of administration, here the supervisor is the key man to promote attitudes and self-image that constitute the professional touch. In view of this role, he should know what is meant by professionalism, how it may become identified with police work, and what he can do to improve the quality of both the vocation and its practitioners.

Thus the supervisor has to develop some sound notions on the subject of professionalism. He should know what the traditional earmarks of a profession have been and be able to apply these to the area of police endeavor. He must be able to identify those that are missing in police work. He should determine how professionalism can be promoted even though police practice may not be a true profession. Finally, he should know how to contribute to the growth of a professional attitude among his men.

The Notion of Professionalism

There have traditionally been three great professions: law, medicine, and theology. If one is a slave to history, he may be inclined to limit the term to these three honored vocations. But if they have identifying qualities characteristic of other occupations as well, then the term might have to be broadened to list more vocations.

Much effort has been devoted to isolating the qualities which characterize the professions. Some of this has been accomplished from within individual fields themselves, when it became recognized that it would be good to affix the tag of profession to a career. Thus the International Association of Chiefs of Police, even before World War II, set up its Committee on Professions. This group listed five requisites for attaining professional status. These were a fund of knowledge, training facilities, admission standards, an organization of practitioners, and an ethical code. From the many studies on the question of professionalism, it is possible to compile a working list of qualifications that will make a vocation worthy of the professional tag.

First there is that reservoir of knowledge that the professional has at his disposal. The finest example may be found in the practice of medicine. From the days before Hippocrates to the age of the organ transplant, there has been the gradual accretion of findings and techniques. The skill of the professional is the ability to apply this tested knowledge to the case at hand. His knowledge is not conferred through birth. It must be acquired through arduous, painstaking effort during a long period of preparation. It must be extended through years of applying one's art. There is no shortcut to the knowledge with which the professional exercises his art.

Then there is that specialized expertness that characterizes the professional. The client must have full confidence in his knowledge of what is to be done, and how it should be done. Thus we accept the physician's diagnosis and remedy that follow the examination. But one does not seek advice from him on a lawsuit, which is the province of the professional lawyer; or on one's spiritual problem, the area of concern for the professional theologian. The professional is expert in a particular field only.

Next is the professional avoidance of identifying emotionally with the person who is being helped. No close attachment to the patient or client is permitted. The case must be handled impersonally; not necessarily with cold detachment, but without feelings which will influence the dynamics of relationship or judgement. Sympathy and scorn, love and hatred have no place in what goes on between the professional and his client.

After this there is the professional's separation from self-interest in handling a case. The surgeon may not push a patient into an unneeded operation, no matter how much he needs the money. The professional, unlike the tradesman, must carefully identify what is of advantage to the client, and this may be the sole determinant of what is to be prescribed or advised.

High in the order of importance as to what determines professional identity is a code of ethics. This sets the standards that will govern the practice of the profession. The formulation is not merely a public-relations nicety which a profession is free to adopt or disregard. It is not just a set of moralistic principles that spring up from some idealistic point of origin. The code embodies a set of very practical rules to which the occupation will have to comply if it is to function with efficiency and prestige. An ethical code is an essential tool for the group's survival and prosperity.

Allied to this notion is the voluntary organization of practitioners. This is not to be thought of as a backslapping, self-congratulating marching-and-chowder-society of peers. It is not to be considered a kind of union in the quest of the greatest financial rewards and the finest conditions of labor. The professional organization is first of all a self-policing agency, one that insists on adherence to ethical standards. It is a group made up of practitioners, for exercising self-control over practitioners. It even may call for the suspension of practice by one who violates the tenets of the profession. Medical societies and bar associations are obviously models of discipline-wielding professional organizations.

These are the characteristics of a profession for a police team leader to consider when he sets out on his promotion of professionalism. These are the marks that separate the profession from the mere occupation, the professional man from the nonprofessional careerist. The supervisor must see these characteristics as determinants which may give police work the status of profession, give his own role the mark of professional, and give the men whom he supervises the identity of professionals.

Is Police Work a Profession?

While the strictly traditional concept of profession has applied to that great trio of honored vocations of law, medicine, and theology, many other occupations have appropriated the qualifying label of prestige. Some of these are clearly deserving of the title they have earned, teaching, nursing, and engineering being prominent examples. But others may have assumed the designation without really having paid the price which would justify the taking. It is prominent in the police academy valedictory to refer to a police profession. But is the vocation deserving of the title? Can the policeman justifiably be called a professional? The question might be realistically answered by subjecting the components of police endeavor to the standards of professionalism.

First, relating to a fund of knowledge. There is a mass of learning that underlies efficient police practice. Police education is liberally interspersed with the social and physical sciences. Complex skills have been developed to constitute the policeman's craft. There is a repository of techniques available to the police officer to supplement the application of knowledge.

Given the reservoir of knowledge and skills, this does not mean all practitioners possess them. There are no licensing provisions that determine the qualifications of anyone to engage in the occupation. Educational requirements for entry extend from none, all the way to a four-year college degree. Nevertheless, the organized body of knowledge does exist, and has been given full academic recognition. Thus police work may include the fulfillment of one requirement for professional identification.

Then there is the question of whether police work also involves the specific expertness that would qualify it as a profession. One frequently fails to recognize his own special abilities and talent for a job. The patrolman may not be aware of his own skill as a craftsman in even the commonplace pursuits of settling the family argument, finding the lost child, and caring for the mentally disturbed subject. But the outside observer riding in the patrol car with an officer is acutely perceptive of the officer's craftsmanship as he performs both simple and dramatic duties. So while the policeman from his vantage point of the overfamiliar may not see himself as the artist at work, the objective spectator may perceive his special ability.

Next is the principle that the professional must be free of emotional involvement with the client or his problem. The police officer will protest his neutrality vehemently. He will insist that the law is enforced and service rendered without consideration of the person or circumstance involved. But differential treatment in fact may creep into the individual officer's practice. Consideration of the client and what relates to him may often validly enter into decision-making. But when it becomes the object of an emotional drive, a basic dislike, or some irrational sympathy, then this special focus negates an otherwise professional relationship. Thus the degree of affective involvement differs among different officers. Some display a remarkable degree of professionalism in the emotional restraint they exercise when they deal with persons. Others do resort to an involvement of feelings that marks a departure from professionalism. As a qualification for attaining professional status, the potential for personal detachment is built into police endeavor and often is the standard of the present-day practitioner.

Then for the supervisor's consideration is whether police work entails a rejection of self-interest in its exercise, a prominent mark of professionalism. Anyone who has observed the coolness of the uniformed man at the mass confrontation, who has watched the patrol car officer close in guardedly on the armed maniac, or who has seen the detective pick up the trail of the rape-murderer and persistently seek him out, will have recognized that selfless dedication is built into the role of the policeman. Whether the officer consciously perceives it or not, the nature of the policeman's duty is based on a selfless devotion to society's well-being. It is this identifying mark that might be considered the key step towards professionalization.

Thus we find that the police do exhibit some of the qualities that are prerequisites to their work being called a profession. But are there others in which they may be wanting? The supervisor charged with the promotion of professionalism should know of these. First, there is an absence of the voluntary organization of practitioners required of the true profession. But, it will be protested, there is the International Association of Chiefs of Police, state peace officer associations, and all kinds of other mutual benefit groups filling this organizational demand. If the supervisor examines the existing associations closely, he may feel that these formal peer groups that have sprung up among the practitioners do not quite fill the needed bill. Regardless of how much they are devoted to the general improvement of administration, performance, and skills, they do not contribute to the self-policing of the vocation. While the American Medical Association and American Bar Association fill the role of watchdogs on standards, unhesitatingly calling for the censure of those who depart from accepted norms of conduct, this is virtually unheard of in the police field. It is questionable whether the malfeasance of a particular agency that has become public is ever mentioned in police organizational meetings, much less seen as a cause for reprimand or censure.

Nor may there be fulfillment of the prerequisite calling for loyalty to profession that overrides the loyalty directed to a specific agency. The orientation of police officials and personnel has always been built around the employing entity as the controlling force. This is practically made necessary under the traditional system. But this sense of full devotion to the whims or policies of an organization continues regardless of how wanting in standards the agency may be. If for no other reason, this uncompromising notion of loyalty to an agency exists because a police officer does not always have the opportunity of changing his employment to another organization when his dissatisfaction mounts. If he is young enough, a man may take a test for admission to another department. Recruitment of outside chiefs-of-police is becoming more common, and occasionally a promotional examination is open to members of another organization. But regardless of these tokens of professional mobility, there is little semblance of lateral entry and transfer in the American police service. Thus a policeman identifies with a particular agency, spends his career there, and ultimately retires.

The supervisor should also recognize that there is little contact of policemen of one agency with members of another, except near political boundaries, in common investigations, and in associational regional activities. Without disparaging the need for loyalty to the organization that employs one, there appears to be no concept of an overriding loyalty to a profession that characterizes the attitude of doctors or lawyers. Here we find another area of professionalism that is not well identified with the police work we know.

Finally, perhaps the most important question for the consideration of the first-line supervisor: Is there a sufficiently comprehensive police code of ethics? Will it be preferable for him to develop his own code for use in instilling professional notions in the attitudes of his team members? An analysis of the idea of an ethical code, and an application of the findings to the realm of police endeavor, may afford the answers.

The Notion of an Ethical Code

If the supervisor is to promote professionalism by conveying a sense of ethical standards to his personnel, he first may have to help them understand what is meant by the word "ethics." For his own usage, if he is going to transmit the concept of ethics to the team, he first must understand the difference between the ideas of what is "legal," "moral," and "ethical."

The law, of which a policeman has the most acute working awareness, is objective. It deals with measurable social conduct and sets corresponding penalties for violation. Morals may be considered a field broader than law. It includes a scope of human activity which is too socially intangible to provide the possibility of legal control. The sanctions occasioned by moral breach involve censure which is short of penalty, and which may not lend themselves to ready application.

While the province of ethics may include what is embraced by both law and morality, it is actually more restricted. Ethics refers to the actions of members of a particular group, while law and morality apply to the larger society. While quite closely akin to, although not identified with, the area of morals, there is a prominent way in which ethics is different. Rules governing morality are founded primarily on an idealistic foundation. A code of ethics is an essential tool for the group's survival and prosperity, and this is the ultimate reason for its being.

There are many models of ethical codes that have been formulated by the professions and businesses. As far back as 1924, Heermance published a unique work which compiled 198 different codes which were in existence at that time.° While the reader certainly would expect to find the well known *Canons of Legal Ethics* and *Principles of Medical Ethics* contained, a surprising array of other codes are found. There are those of the "Peanut Butter Manufacturers," the "Subscription Book Publishers," the "Piano Merchants," and the "Ice Cream and Paper Box Manufacturers." The codes ranged in quality from the purely professional to what might be classified as mere trade and labor agreements. No law enforcement contribution was found.

There are many codes of ethics and not all confined to the establishment of standards for the recognized professions. Those of the legal and medical practitioners probably provide the most prominent examples of detailing specific norms of professional conduct. Witness the specificity of Canon 28 of the legal code: It is unprofessional for a lawyer to volunteer advice to bring a lawsuit, except in rare cases where ties of blood, relationship or trust make it his duty to do so.°°

Note the attempt to spell out a doctor's obligation in the American Medical Association's Code of Ethics: A physician should not dispose of his services under terms or conditions which tend to interfere with or impair the free and complete

°Edgar L. Heermance, *Codes of Ethics: A Handbook* (Burlington, Vt.: Free Press 1924).

°°*California State Bar Act and Rules of Professional Conduct—Canons of Professional Ethics of the American Bar Association* (San Francisco: State Bar of California, 1963). Canon 28 in *Black's Law Dictionary*, Revised 4th ed. (St. Paul, Minn.: West Publishing Co., 1962), p. xvi.

exercise of his medical judgement and skill or tend to cause a deterioration of the quality of medical care.°

A code of ethics should ideally present practical principles in such clarity that they are readily applicable to the typical cases encountered in practicing an occupation. They should define conduct in a way that the public, before whose criticism the vocation is vulnerable, may clearly perceive and understand the provisions that are made for maintaining the highest standards of practitioners. It is a definite, comprehensive, working instrument for governing the conduct of those who represent a particular calling.

If the supervisor is to promote professionalism in the ranks, he must do so through continuing to insist on a subscription to the principles of a code of ethics. Any other endeavor to raise police work to the levels of a profession must come from forces that are outside any given law enforcement organization. The supervisor's promotion of professionalism is independent of whether he is working within a profession. Granted that there may be no true police profession in the United States. There still can be "professionals" in police work—in any given agency, any given command, any given platoon or squad. The stamp of the professional will be independent of rank. It is entirely possible that there may be many professional patrolmen and a few unprofessional captains in the same agency. The supervisor who is a professional will be the one who creates these professional patrolmen—all through evoking principles contained in a living ethical code.

Granting the need of a code of ethics, is there one at his ready disposal? If there is, it should define standards comprehensively, and with specific phraseology. The canons should be as all embracing and as definite as those that specify the conduct of the lawyer and the physician. They should cover all areas of potential conduct which will be detrimental to the best interest of the men who make up the police vocation.

Does the rule book provide a substitute for a code of ethics? While police rules in a limited way reflect the underlying thinking on what is acceptable and unacceptable in behavior and practice, they are not synonymous with a code of ethics. Most agency-formulated rules and regulations are peculiar to the specific procedures and arbitrary disciplinary standards in that organization. There often is considerable generalization. There are catchall regulations as the one defining "unofficerlike conduct," really remaining undefined in their wording. The rules are negative in their essence. They do not reflect a spirit of positive obligation, which has the purpose of safeguarding group prestige and efficiency. Thus, unlike the ethical codes, principles contained are not universal in their scope. They are not applicable to the exercise of police duty in itself, but to the way it is exercised within the confines of a particular agency.

Thus an examination of the rules and procedures of the many police departments shows they are wanting in the basic ideas of inherent obligation which are the

°Section 6, *Principles of Medical Ethics,* in *Opinions and Reports of the Judicial Council* (Chicago: American Medical Association, 1971), p. vi.

building blocks of an ethical code. It is the spirit of these indigenous notions of duty that thread through the great ethical codes. This is what should influence the design of the proposed model canons of police ethics.

So it may be desirable for the first-line supervisor to create his own personalized code of ethics as a tool of supervision, if he deems those available to him wanting. He may wish to set up his own working model of principles which he will communicate to his men. Perhaps the *Canons of Professional Ethics of the American Bar Association* provide the best model of what is specific and concise. The tone of the improvised formulation should be sincere and realistic. What is aimed at should not be a mere demand for compliance under threat of sanction, as called for by the rules manual. The objective must be the promotion of a living codification of thought on what constitutes good police practice. The purpose of a code should be to develop a dynamic attitude towards good police practice.

A Police Supervisor's Code of Ethics

A police supervisor may easily design his own working code of ethics. Largely using the *Canons of Professional Ethics of the American Bar Association* as a prototype, the form of the provisions, and the subject matter of their content may resemble this model:

1. *Necessity to act.* The police officer's oath of office implies an obligation to enforce the law, and to protect life and property. As a paid employee, his duty to act may extend only to the span of determined working hours; as a professional practitioner, in emergencies he may have to act outside these periods of time. It thus will be unethical at all times for a police officer to fail to identify himself and to act within the interest of anyone when such neglect would endanger life, permit the accomplishment of a serious crime, cause personal injury or undue anguish to any person, or create a great hazard to property. An officer may not fail to offer assistance to anyone at any time when the average person who is outside the police vocation, with no official duty to act, nevertheless would be moved to render help to a subject in need of aid.

2. *Use of authority.* The right to impose the will of the police officer on any person in the form of order, restraint or arrest should always be exercised in response to objective circumstances alone, and in complete independence of subjective feelings. It may never be predicated on emotions founded on a desire for reprisal or to inflict punishment. While all necessary firmness may be employed, a police officer, in making contact with any person, may not resort to verbal abuse or discourtesy. An impersonal relationship with the subject must always predominate the police officer's performance.

3. *Imparting full effort.* Because it does not represent a measurable productive enterprise, the exercise of police duty offers the opportunity of devoting less than full effort to a case or assignment. Accordingly, the police officer has an ethical obligation to direct full effort to all work he is called upon to perform.

4. *Ascertaining innocence and guilt.* While it is reasonable for the officer in practice to consider himself an agent for the prosecution, in which capacity he instinctively labors to establish evidence of a person's guilt, he is still bound by an ethical duty to explore all paths that might determine the subject's innocence. From this it follows that it will be unethical to act as if guilt were a moral certainty before sufficient evidence has been gathered to support the hypothesis.

5. *Sincerity with the public.* A police officer should be frank and open in his communication with the citizen. Deceit or exaggeration should not be practiced except when needed to make a valid arrest, or as a necessary part of the investigative process.

6. *Respect for confidentiality.* A barrier to the ready flow of needed information to the police is the citizen's fear of disclosure. With the exception of fulfilling judicial and departmental needs of reporting, the strictest confidence must be promised by him and maintained.

7. *Prejudice and bias.* A police officer must avoid comment and activity that would typify him as subscribing to a prejudice or bias that will influence his official action. Thus it will be unethical for him to join or take part in the activities of any organization which has as its expressed or implied purpose the condemnation of any group, party or class.

8. *Immunity and favor.* The nature of law enforcement gives the police officer extensive latitude in the recognition or disregard of violation, the granting or withholding of privilege, and the rendition of expanded or restricted service. It is natural that familial relationship, personal acquaintance, organizational membership, physical and personal attractiveness, social pressures, human sympathy, and friendly intercession are all factors that may influence his necessary decisions. It is imperative that the police officer condition himself to remain emotionally neutral to these extraneous impulses that may affect his otherwise proper decision-making. Similarly, a police officer should never use his relationship with another person to urge a special official favor or immunity to be bestowed on himself or another.

9. *Rendering assistance to a fellow officer.* It will be unethical for a police officer to fail to assist a fellow officer when there is apparent need for assistance, regardless of whether he has been recognized or help has been requested, and notwithstanding his being off duty.

10. *Case interference.* Whenever it is known to a police officer that a case investigation or prosecution has been initiated, except where effort is normally required, he must not pursue any independent action related to it without making his involvement known to the assigned officer, and without receiving approval of his involvement.

11. *Withholding information.* When another officer of his own or different jurisdiction has been assigned to an investigation, and when he has knowledge which would be of value to the other, a police officer is obliged to forward this information through proper authority for the benefit of the investigator.

12. *Jeopardization of colleagues.* A police officer should never endanger an associate through indiscretion, recklessness, or incompetency; either by subjecting him to physical harm, placing him in jeopardy of civil suit, or making him liable to public ridicule.

13. *Publicity theft.* A police officer should never deprive another officer, or any other person, of due credit arising from praiseworthy action or heroism. Unless secrecy is demanded by circumstances, reports submitted to superiors and statements made to the press should not be designed to mislead anyone into misdirecting the credit due any individual.

14. *Abuse of influence in self-seeking.* While it is proper to have factual data concerning one's qualifications presented to competent authority in order to be considered for any form of advancement or betterment of position, it will be unethical to solicit the influence of another to achieve this end.

15. *Solicitation or acceptance of gifts and favors.* The police officer has no right to request openly or through inference, or to accept, any gift, favor, reward, or privilege from anyone with whom he has become acquainted through duty performance, or in return for any official service rendered.

16. *Improper referral.* A request received in the course of duty performance for referral to any kind of professional or commercial service should be met by providing several names of persons or agencies from which the person requesting may make his own choice. Where complete lists are available, these should be placed at the person's disposal, in order that he may make his own selection.

17. *Criticism and derogation.* While there is no obligation for a member to defend the action or policies of a police department or fellow officer, it will be unethical for a police officer to criticize the official stance or activities of his own or another agency, or the official action of another officer, to anyone outside the police occupation, except in the course of legal or regulatory process.

18. *Public utterance.* While departmental policy usually permits comment on an incident or case to the press, it will be unethical for a police officer to express personal judgement on any policy, group of persons, or individual philosophy related to the facts he is reporting.

19. *Criticism of related agencies.* It will be considered unethical for a police officer to criticize in public, either directly or indirectly, official actions of another public agency involved in the administration of justice.

20. *Acceptable moral standards.* The professions and public offices traditionally are identified with the persons who occupy them. Thus the moral unfitness of a professional practitioner or public officer is tantamount to a breach of dignity owed his profession of office. While a police officer deserves the basic right to live his own private life in the way he selects, any manifest and pronounced departure from accepted moral standards brings on the vocation a discredit which will be destructive of its dignity and honor, and should be avoided.

21. *Social intercourse.* A police officer may find it to his occupational advantage

to become personally acquainted with those who are prone to becoming engaged in suspected criminal activities. Nevertheless, it is obvious that there is a need for the highest discretion in exercising actual friendships with persons who come into conflict with the law. To negate the possibility of actual and suspected compromise, social relationships with these persons should be avoided.

22. *Outside employment.* While the right of a police officer to work for compensation outside his regular occupation is recognized, it is of moment to consider whether the secondary employment engaged in is a proper one. Accordingly, it will be deemed unethical to become involved in tasks which potentially might conflict directly or indirectly with the enforcement of law, which are potentially dependent on the influence of his office in their accomplishment, or which are of reputedly low prestige.

The Supervisor's Personalized Drive for Professionalism

If police work is to become a true profession, effort will have to be directed to this end from others besides the first-line supervisor. The needed code of ethics may have to be more universally recognized than a private creation of the individual superior. An organization of peers may be required that polices its own membership, insists on adherence to ethical standards, and calls for sanctions when there is a violation. There ultimately may have to be an accepted system of lateral entry and transfer, perhaps based on a licensing principle of the kind that characterizes the historical professions.

Meanwhile, there is no disparagement of the vocation if a supervisor acknowledges to his men that policing as now constituted may not fully qualify for the designation of profession. It will not be contradictory for him to insist that professionalism is possible and necessary in an occupation which may not be a true profession. It will not be an empty gesture for him to predict that law enforcement will continue on its path towards professional status.

The promise of universal professionalism in the police field is not just a pious hope. There are thousands of police officers in the United States who are fully deserving of the professional label. Many are the product of the growing occupational prestige that is attracting better personnel. There are mushrooming collegiate programs that provide a reservoir of educated, rather than merely trained, recruits. There is the expanding realization by police management that talent in the ranks is necessary, this implying promise for the young man of ability that a place for his talent may be found in police work.

The man of quality being drawn into police service knows he is entering an occupation in flux. He envisions a police career that is not just a form of livelihood, but is a life in itself. He is led to perceive himself as the raw material from which a profession is rapidly being forged. The police supervisor can be the modern Pygmalion: fashioning the new professional taking his place in the new profession.

SUMMARY

Meaning of "Profession". • The term "profession" is applied loosely to many occupations. • There is an ongoing debate as to whether police work is a profession. • The supervisor is the key man in creating professional attitudes and image. • The supervisor should understand the essence of true professionalism. • The three great professions have been law, medicine, and theology.

Elements of Professionalism. • Much study has been made on isolating the qualities of the profession. • A fund of knowledge is one of the characteristics of a profession. • The expertness of the practitioner characterizes the professional. • The professional must detach himself from self-interest in processing a case. • A professional directs loyalty to the profession, not only to an employer. • A code of ethics is high on the list of determinants of professional identity. • There is a voluntary organization of professional peers that is self-policing.

Police as Professionals. • Police work may have the fund of knowledge and expertness for professionalism. • Police work entails detachment from emotional involvement and self-interest. • There is an absence of a professional organization of peers in the police field. • There is no superseding loyalty to profession over organization among the police.

"Legal," "Moral," "Ethical." • The supervisor should know the difference between "legal," "moral," and "ethical." • The law deals with personal conduct it can measure. • Morals refers to activity too intangible for legal controls. • Ethics refers to the actions of members of a particular group. • There are many models of ethical codes, some of which are mere trade pacts. • The ethical codes for lawyers and physicians provide foremost models. • The better codes spell out specific norms of professional conduct. • The principles of an ethical code should be readily applicable to specific acts. • An ethical code is a definite, comprehensive, working instrument of control.

Police Ethics. • The supervisor may promote professionalism even though there is no profession status. • Professionalism is a mark independent of police rank. • The supervisor fashions professionalism by evoking principles of an ethical code. • A code of police ethics should be as definite as those of law and medicine. • A book of rules and regulations is not a substitute for a code of ethics. • A supervisor may wish to formulate his personalized code of ethics. • The principles of a code should be clear and realistic. • The objective of a code should be to suggest what makes good police practice.

Police Professionalism. • The promise of professionalism in police service is not a mere pious hope. • Forces are at play attracting professional quality men to police service. • The supervisor fills the role of fashioning the new professional.

INDEX